A HISTORY OF CHIDDINGSTONE

A History of Chiddingstone

Publication history:
Originally published, 1939
Re-issued, 1988
This edition, 2013

Published by Stuart Notholt Communications Ltd
Stumps Cottage, Chiddingstone Causeway, Kent TN11 8JL, United Kingdom
www.notholt.net

Overleaf: Cover from the 1988 edition.

Front cover: Chiddingstone High Street, c1975. From a watercolour by Dennis Keenan.

Proceeds from the sale of this book are donated to the Church funds of St. Mary the Virgin, Chiddingstone.

ISBN 978-0-9554657-8-9

CONTENTS

FOREWORD TO THE 2013 EDITION

Chiddingstone in Kent has a history spanning well over a thousand years, and it is hardly surprising that many books and papers have been written about the village and its people. As time passes, these documents themselves become part of the historical record, as is the case with this collection of research, notes, and commentary.

The majority of the contents was originally prepared by Dr. Gordon Ward in the late 1930s, with Dr. Ward himself drawing upon even earlier references and information. When this book was first published in its current form in 1939, this material was supplemented by the then new lecture and foreword by Commander F.N. Stagg. Nearly fifty years later, the book was re-issued, this time with additional notes and a 'looking back' retrospective by E.D. Hardcastle.

When the idea of reprinting *A History of Chiddingstone* was first mooted, we did think about comprehensively updating the text or of re-typesetting the 1988 manuscript in our possession. This was in part because it must be noted that the text does contain a number of typographic errors and, in at least one place, a repetition of a couple of paragraphs. On balance, however, we decided that in order to retain as much of the feel of the original we should reprint the manuscript 'as is', hopefully leaving it to today's researchers to augment and update the living story of our village.

In addition to acknowledging our debt to earlier contributors, and to the Streatfeild family who helped with the provision of much of the early source material, I would like to thank our contemporary team of workers, especially Bob Golds for his diligent work on the book's material, and to Stuart Notholt for his help with its publication.

So it is that I welcome the reappearance of *A History of Chiddingstone*, making this unique and fascinating collection of material available to a new generation.

Rev. Martin Beaumont

The Rectory
Chiddingstone, Kent

September 2013

CHIDDINGSTONE HISTORY - NOTES

Foreword

This collection of Local History Notes is an attempt to assemble (within one binding cover) as many references to the History of Chiddingstone as possible.

Although a number of printed sources have provided much of this material - yet by far the larger number of notes have been taken from the MSS books of Dr. Gordon Ward - whose investigations among the Streatfeild Papers have yielded such a wealth of knowledge of the past of Chiddingstone.

The Sevenoaks Library is the repository of ancient parchments connected with this parish - and, should anyone wish to go further into the details of the past than these NOTES provide - they would do well to begin their enquiries at the Sevenoaks Library.

F.N.S.

9th February, 1939.

A LECTURE given at the Village Hall, Chiddingstone on 9th February 1939 on:

The HISTORY of the PARISH of CHIDDINGSTONE

In telling the history of Chiddingstone it should suffice to commence at the time of Christ - and we can leave Stoneage man and the very remote past for others to speculate upon.

What was there in Chiddingstone when the Romans came to Britain shortly after the time of Christ? - endless oak forests with a few unimportant clearings - most of which were doubtless near the banks of the Eden and Kent Water, where the land was richest. But although the Romans were in England for 400 years, and only left these shores a mere 1,500 years ago - yet the only tangible remains of their presence in the immediate vicinity was a **burial urn** which was found close to Chested House. They also left us a relic of their land-measurement in the **Yokes** of Chested and Vexour - for the **Yoke** was the Roman measure of a quarter of a Suling - and since the latter was generally about 200 acres, a **Yoke** must have averaged about 50 acres.

Trouble nearer Rome forced the withdrawal of the Roman Legions from these islands - and England became a prey to hordes of pagan barbarians from the shores of Denmark and the Baltic coast. Actually, there ensued a period of 150 years after the departure of the Romans during which we know virtually **nothing** as to what happened in our England.

It seems that Kent was the first district to be **settled** by the invaders - and that we here were so fortunate as to be conquered by a tribe called **Jutes**, who came from the west coast of Jutland - now in Denmark. It is believed they did not come directly from their original home, but stepped off awhile at the mouth of the Rhine, where they came in contact with the outposts of the Roman Empire and possibly learnt to appreciate some of the institutions which they found in what are now called Holland and Flanders. At all events they left the Roman methods of cultivation and certain Roman measurements as the **Yoke**, untouched in their kingdom of Kent, in contra-distinction to the Saxons and Angles who removed all trace of Roman civilisation from the other parts of England where they settled. They were great big fellows, these **Jutes**, and their blood runs through the veins of the Kentish Yeoman to this very day - making of him the fine fellow he is.

We do not know whether the Christian Romans erected an **Altar** in Chiddingstone - but if they did, the Jutes effectively destroyed it - for when St. Augustine came to Kent in the year 597, he had to begin all over again to convert this country to Christianity. And it is with his coming that a little historical light is once more shed upon this land of ours. Kent has always been the most civilised part of England - not perhaps solely owing to its proximity to the higher civilisation of the Continent - but also because we were blessed in having Jutish Danes as our conquerors. It is probable that we can attribute to them the division of Kent into **Lathes** - that is, military divisions for the defence organisation of the country, - and a name which is practically confined to Kent, even as is the land-measurement of the **Yoke** which the Jutes inherited from the Romans. Chiddingstone comes within the **Lathe** of Sutton-at-Hone, and it was certainly in that town that the Military Commander of this district lived, and took his orders from the King of Kent at Canterbury. The actual word **Lathe** points to the Danish origin of our invaders - why this very day when a Danish Recruiting Officer goes out recruiting he goes "on **Leding**" (Pron. Lathe-ing).

But for long after the coming of St. Augustine there were **seven** kingdoms in England - first one King acquired the suzerainty and then another - and Christianity had a hard fight to make way - encountering many a serious set-back.

Just before the year 800, King Offa of **Mercia** (Mercia was what we now call "the shires") defeated the King of Kent at a great battle at Otford, and **COENWULF**, the successor of Offa, made a grant of land to the Archbishop of Canterbury - in the year 814 - on a piece of parchment, the contents of which have been preserved to this day. This Charter of King Coenwulf in 814 A.D. contains the very first mention in any script of any portion of the present parish of Chiddingstone. Actually it is the gift of a "**den**" - that is a **pig-pasture** - and the land given is easily recognisable as being the major portion of the present parish of Hever.

Where **our** interest lies in it, is in the **eastern-boundary** of the gift, which is called **SPACHRYCG**. Now **RYCG**, in old-English, meant a **bank** or **ridge** - but what "spach" meant is unknown. In deeds of the 14th, 15th & 16th century we find that Spachrycg has become **SPOKEREG** and **SPOKEREGGE**, whilst the Tithe Map of 1841 calls it **POKERAGE**, and defines Pokerage Field, Old Pokerage Mead, and Old Pokerage Hopgarden. The ancient farm house of Pokerage has ceased to exist, and its foundations as well as Pokerage Mead now lie under Hever Lake - but Pokerage Field and Hopgarden lie at the south-east end of the lake between Woodland and water - but inside Chiddingstone Parish.

After this burst of knowledge in 814, darkness descends on Chiddingstone for 250 years - but we can perhaps make shrewd guesses as to certain factors in life here 1,000 or more years ago. The centres of population at that time were in River valleys where the soil was rich, and - there being no roads - communications by water were essential. But the meat diet that these populated districts required could only be supplied from where the oak forest lay - where acorns provided food for herds of swine. In those days, of course, such feeding staffs as "middlings" were used for human consumption - since arable agriculture was extremely primitive and there was no import whatsoever of what we consider the "necessities of life". During early days, these vast oak forests of the Weald belonged to the King in person - and we find the various Saxon Kings presenting "dens", or pig-pastures to populous centres and to the Church - whence pork could be supplied to those dwelling in towns and religious institutions. What is now the Parish of Chiddingstone thus became divided up into "**dens**" - where the butchers of Archbishop's **Sundridge** and King's **Dartford** drew their pigs from.

At some date unknown, these "dens" were collected together to form the Parish of Chiddingstone - and some Saxon Thane of - probably - Sundridge, with religious zeal, built the first Church at Chiddingstone long before the Norman Conquest, for the benefit of those swineherds who reared the pigs in the pastures of Frienden, Oakenden (or Alkinden as it was originally called) Somerden and Bore Place. When the ecclesiastical parish was formed it was necessary to include within it some of the **"eight large and three small dens"** which the King had granted to his own Royal borough of Dartford - since these latter were in some cases intermingled with those dens which some King had granted the Archbishop for the benefit of the latter's people at Sundridge. Where were these royal "eight large and three small dens" which belonged to the King and Dartford? - and which were united for purposes of taxation and administration into the "Borough of CRANSTED"! Well! the very name "**Cransted**" tells us where the principal large one was - for you all know Cransted Mead, even if you have never heard of Cransted House, Cransted Mill, Cransted Bridge, or of that "Lord Roger of Cransted" who controlled these "eight large and three small dens in the year **1290**. If you walk down Cransted Lane (which can be reached from Bough Beech by going past Gravelpits), you will find before you reach Cransted Mead and the River, a broken piece of rough land hedged in, and lying right up against the boundary of Hever Park. This is the site of **Cransted House,** and was probably the home of "Lord Roger of Cransted" who, on behalf of the King and Royal Dartford, held sway over Bough Beech, Pokerage, and the land up to and including that Mill which to-day is called **Chiddingstone Mill** - but which was known through nigh upon a thousand years as **Cransted Mill.**

When we try to locate the other Dartford "dens" which were embraced in what is now the parish of Chiddingstone, we are up against some difficulties - but Stonelake (which we now call Chiddingstone Causeway) and Charcott close by, seem certainly to have been two of them, whilst the district round **Watstock** and **Scotland Reed** and possibly even **Gillridge** seem to have found a fourth, and **Bore Place** is also a doubtful starter, amongst the "dens of Dartford".

But since, when the Parish of Chiddingstone was formed, the Yokes of **Chested and Vexour** came neither within the Archbishop's Sundridge dens or those of Dartford's Cransted group, we must assume that they belonged to some other authority, and hence is to be explained the strange configuration of the Eastern boundary of Chiddingstone, where it would seem some Penshurst giant has bitten a huge mouthful out of the side of Chiddingstone and kept Chested and Vexour in Penshurst.

But we must now go back again to a period 1,100 years ago - to the time when the first Danish Viking invasion had driven Alfred the Great into the cottage where he burnt the cakes - the fugitive King of all the Anglo-saxons, in a land which was overrun by Danish Vikings. When Alfred had once again restored Anglo-Saxon rule in the west and south, and had established a frontier with Danish England along Roman **Watling Street** from London to Chester - he had to organise his part of the country more efficiently than before, and hence to establish the **"Hundred"** system on a more thorough basis. And so it may have been in the 9th century that the **Hundred of Somerden** was formed out of what are now the parishes of Chiddingstone, Hever, Cowden, Penshurst, Leigh, and Speldhurst, with small bits of Chevening and Edenbridge. And so for many hundred years, the headmen of the "dens" and clearings in those six parishes used to meet by the **Green** at **Somerden** to levy and pay taxes, and to settle all questions concerned with law and order, and the public peace of their district. The word **"Somerden"** means simply "Summer pasture".

And then, 270 years after King Coenwulf's gift to the Archbishop, we find an entry in "The Domesday Book of the Monks" (not to be confused with the Domesday Book of the King) - compiled in about 1086, which tells us that Sundridge (and therefore most of Chiddingstone as well) "was held unjustly by Earl Godwin at the time of Edward the Confessor, but that Archbishop Lanfranc recovered it rightfully by leave of the King". Although there is no mention of a church at Chiddingstone in Domesday Book,it is certain that a Saxon one was standing here at the Norman Conquest - it may even have been built by the Archbishop himself at some time after he received the gift of the "dens" of Sundridge around here. Certain it is that after Lanfranc's recovery of the Archbishop's rights here, it has been Canterbury's privilege to appoint rectors to the "living" - although we have their names for only 700 years.

It would not appear that the Norman Conquest made much difference to life or ownership at Chiddingstone - seeing that the King himself retained Cransted and the other 10 dens, whilst the Archbishop recovered possession of the remainder of the parish at the "Shire-Mote" held at Benenden Heath, Maidstone in 1076, and passed the control of it over to his Lord of Sundridge. Chiddingstone went on quietly producing pork for the dwellers in Dartford and Sundridge, whilst at the same time slowly developing a village life more or less self-contained.

In the year 1200 we get the earliest deed of conveyance of property which has survived - and so sidelights on local life begin to peep through. There were then no less than 6 **manors** having their original centres in Chiddingstone. Now a **manor** was the medieval unit of country life - and in the surviving manor-houses one can see how the Lord of the Manor or Yeoman farmer built their dwellings in 3 sections. In the centre was a big Hall, open to the roof, at one end of this was the "**solar**" where the owner lived with his family, and at the other end was the "service" portion. All who worked on the farm used to feed in the Great Hall, the owner and family on a dias at the "Solar end - the labourers and their families in the body of the Hall. The labourers went to bed as the sun went down in their poor huts made of timber smeared with clay.

It would seem that the oldest manor in this parish was that of **Rendsley** which later however came confined to an area round **The Hoath** - correct name of which is **Rendsley Hoath** and **NOT** Chiddingstone Hoath. Owners of manors often left more than one heir to inherit and so the manors got divided up - with the result that **Tyehurst, Alkinden** (or Oakenden) and **Smithstreet** (by the Blacksmith's Arms) became manors on their own - whilst **SOMERDEN**, otherwise called **MILLBROOKS** - has been a manor containing 560 acres from a very remote past, which was uninterruptedly the property of the owners of Bore Place.

But out of either Rendsley Manor - or possibly an actual **Manor of Chiddingstone** - there were carved a little more than 600 years ago, the two manors of **Chiddingstone Burghersh** and **Chiddingstone Cobham,** which became the most important sub-divisions of the Parish for as long as the system of manors played any part in the life of the village.

Old "Peter de Chiddingstone" died sometime before the year 1300, leaving two daughters to divide the manor between them. Legend says that they married the two Lords who gave their names to the respective manors - but it seems more likely that they sold their rights to the Lords in question. The Lord Burghersh, it is said, settled in Chiddingstone, and built a stately mansion surrounded by a moat - by the stream close to **Weller's Town.** Then came the **"Black Death"** which caused a frightful mortality, and the French Wars of King Edward III - and so we cannot be surprised that decay set in, and we read in a deed of **1383** that a yeoman named Richard Chapman was leasing "the site of the manor with the forlese". Or again when we read a note written in 1591 (i.e. 200 years later) - "The house of the manor of Chedyngeston Burghersh is clean fallen down, but the great motes remain as a token of the stately building". There are to be seen to-day faint traces of the two great moats - an old inhabitant tells me that when he was a gamekeeper 30 years ago they called them **"Baggim Moats"**. A ploughman told me last autumn that whenever he ploughs up the lower part of what is now **"Slips Field"** he turns up tiles - and that he had often thought there must have been a house there long ago. The lower part of Slips Field was once called "The Forelese"- an old name commonly denoting land before the gate of a mansion.

These **Burghersh's** came out of Burwash in Sussex - their name being altered to Borowashe and later to Burghersh. It was the elder Lord Burghersh who rebuilt the Church, and much of his building is standing to-day. He took the cowl and entered a monastery on one occasion, but King Edward III so badly needed his military skill in France, that he obtained a dispensation from the Pope releasing him from his vows. Both he and his son took an active part in the battles of Crecy & Poitiers - the latter being a companion of the Black Prince. The younger Lord Burghersh died in 1369, leaving an only daughter, Elizabeth, who disposed of the Manor and left the parish.

The portion of the second daughter of old Peter de Chiddingstone, came to the family of **COBHAM**, a younger branch of the great family near Rochester. They had 3 stars in their coat of arms - so when the first Lord built a castle for himself near Lingfield, 'he called it **STERBOROUGH** Castle - the ruins of which are most picturesque. It is called **STARBOROUGH** to-day - in medieval English such words as "star" and "far" were pronounced and spelt "ster" and "fer" - but about the time of Queen Elizabeth this spelling changed - though we still have "further off" as well as "farther off" in modern english. The 1st Lord Sterborough was responsible for counting the bodies of the slain after the battle of Crecy - and it is his record which gives us the list of grandiloquent slaughter in that famous battle.

The two Lords surely took many a parishioner with them to the French wars-trained archers who had practised drawing their bows in the two **TARGATE FIELDS**, which lay between Gilwyns and the Rectory grounds.

But, like the Burghersh's the family of Cobham ended in a girl, Anne. She, however, clung to her Manor of Chiddingstone Cobham. Her lst husband was **Lord Mountjoy,** and it seems certain that the house called "Mountjoy", up Breeches Lane, (which the present owner was designated **"Collingwood Kennels"** was was named after him. Her 2nd husband has Edward **BURGH**, and it was their grandson who became the lst husband of **Katharine Parr** - the first of her 4 husbands, King Henry VIII being the third. Had Sir Edward Burgh not died young, one wonders who Henry VIII would have married as his sixth wife - and whether she would have been as clever as was Katharine Parr in keeping her head on her shoulders.

So here in Chiddingstone - somewhere in the early 1530's - we can picture the future Queen of England riding throughout the forests and clearings of her father-in-law's manor of **Chiddingstone Cobham** - enjoying the excitements of the "chase". And here in this parish which has recently become so peculiarly a "game preserve" - it may not come amiss to describe what the "chase" meant in those days.

Among the Streatfeild papers was found a much mutilated original, as follows:-

> Thomas Felton and William Chiffinch
> Masters Marchalls and Surveyors of his
> Majesties **Hawks**
>
> To all **Gamekeepers** and others whom this may concern Whereas His Majesty has given us full power and Authority for the preservation of **Hawking** - either by ourselves or deputies to take away all guns, nets, tramills, tunnils, setting-dogs and all other engines as destroy the game of Hare, Pheasant and Partridge, and other wildfowl contrary to the Laws and Statutes of this Realm. And we do hereby appoint John Tichborne our lawful deputy to take away all guns etc.:................dated 1677.

This notice was issued 150 years after Katherine Parr's life at Chiddingstone, and after the Great Civil War had brought other ideas as to rights of property and use of firearms. In her days the hawk and falcon were the killing agents in "sport" - and if she herself did not loose her favourite falcon from her wrist, it is certain her husband Edward Burgh did from his.

So Penshurst can claim its Queen Elizabeth, and Hever its Queen Anne Boleyn - but Chiddingstone can feel equally proud in its possession of a definite link with Queen Katherine Parr.

Away in the extreme north-east of the parish lies that ancient seat of **BORE PLACE**. Many people believe it got its name from "boar" - otherwise "pig" - but a great placename expert thinks it was derived from the old english word meaning **BOWER** i.e. cottage. A family calling themselves "atte-Bore" lived there in very early times - but 500 years ago, a man named **ALPHEG** or **ALPHEW** acquired it. Once again in Chiddingstone History the male line dies out - and a daughter carried the property with her when she married Sir Robert Rede, who became Lord Chief Justice of England, and Executor of the Will of King Henry VII. This Robert Rede was a wealthy and powerful man - it was he who built the chapel on the north side of the chancel so long known as "Bore Place Chapel", and in Chiddingstone Church he buried his only son Edmund in 1501. And so once again baby boys would not thrive in Chiddingstone and the Lord Chief Justice's daughter inherited. She married Sir Thomas Willoughby, who became a judge of the King's bench, and was buried in this Church in 1545, having founded a family which inhabited Bore Place for 100 years. In maps of the 16th century it frequently happens that **BORE PLACE** is the only name inscribed for many miles around.

And then at the end of Elizabeth's reign about the year 1600, we find all over England that the nobles who had owned the land and manors became impoverished as a result of the Queen's demands on their purses - and that they had to sell their estates and make way for a new landed gentry. This happened very definitely in Chiddingstone - not merely do we find that the Lord Burgh of Chiddingstone Cobham Manor had to raise money by parting with his estates here to the first of the Streatfeilds, but the formerly wealthy Willoughby's are raising mortgages on their lands - though Sir Percival Willoughby was so fortunate as to marry an heiress of Nottingham, and with her to found the family now represented by Lord Middleton. The day of the **IRONMASTERS** in Chiddingstone had come - and these corners of Kent and Sussex became the **BLACK COUNTRY**, where the embryonic chicks of modern industrialism began to peck at their shells.

For many centuries **IRON** had been smelted in these parts by most primitive methods - but the progress made by French smelters at last reached our country - and the demand for cannon during the wars of Queen Elizabeth caused a sort of "re-armament" programme which brought much wealth to smelters in this neighbourhood, and to those who provided the timber for fuel. Richard **STREATFEILD** of Cransted & Chested, and Thomas **BROWNE**, who may have been his partner, and who, at first, probably lived at **BOUGH BEECH** - are the two names which have come down to us in this connection.

As for Richard **STREATFEILD** - we know that at his death he had iron at **PILBEAMS** and **CHIDDINGSTONE** worth more than £15,000 in to-day's money (in 1939) - whilst Thomas Browne, only two years after the Armada, was lending money to the Willoughby's of Bore Place.

You all know there is a **Furnace Farm** and a Furnace Wood just a few hundred yards north-west of **BOUGH BEECH** - but the stream flowing from that Furnace Farm passes through the eastern edge of what is now Hever Park, a little before it joins the Eden - and it is just inside the boundary fence and close to the site of Richard Streatfeild's Cransted House that one finds one of two gigantic **dams or bays** - which would seem to point to the existence of a furnace close to Cransted House. The old names of the fields there, (before the face of nature was so altered in Hever Park 30 years ago) likewise point to the same conclusion - namely, "Great pond field", Third Pond Field - show that dams were constructed to hold up the flowing stream in order to provide water power to blow the bellows which heated the charcoal, whilst after it had been drawn from the charcoal furnace, the iron could be washed in the ponds. Thomas Browne is described in deeds as "of Chiddingstone, Ironmaster", and was almost certainly Richard Streatfeild's technician, who had acquired a mastery of the latest French methods. He moved to Ashurst soon after 1600, where he and his son cast cannon for many years - and provided a main source of ordnance supply to the contending parties in the **Great Civil War**.

Let us look back for one moment to the **REFORMATION** in the 1530's. Up till that event the Poor Law Relief had been administered by the Priesthood; who, out of their vast estates, had found the wherewithal to assist those in want or distress through no fault of their own. With the Reformation and the dissolution of the Monasteries, all this charitable work ceased, and there has probably never been a time when the homeless and aged poor suffered so terribly as immediately after that great upheaval in our National Life. And so it came about that Queen Elizabeth enacted that the Parishes should take on a secular side to their activities, and that the Churchwardens and Overseers of the Poor should control all parish relief. A Parish thus became a self-contained unit to an extent that is quite new - and thus things remained until about just over 100 years ago. And so 400 years ago the poor of Chiddingstone became the care of the entire parish, evidently it seemed to the parish authorities in 1601 that it would be cheaper to build a workhouse where the old and helpless could all be housed and looked after together - and thus there was erected the **POOR HOUSE** on **SOMERDEN GREEN**. Many parishioners gave bricks and timber, and others voluntary contributions in cash, but despite all these gifts in "kind" a sum of £3.13.0 had to be found through a general assessment of the whole parish - the final cost being £16.6.1. - which, even when multiplied by ten to get something like to-day's values, (in 1939) seems little enough, especially when one considers that it was so well built that much of it is standing to-day after 380 year of weathering and use.

And then, over 300 years ago, began that major National Tragedy, the **GREAT CIVIL WAR**. The Rector was no "Vicar of Bray" and remained a staunch Royalist - he was deprived of his living and the Rev. Thomas **SEYLIARD** was instituted - he to allow the discharged vicar one fifth of his income. But the majority of the parishioners were also ardent royalists, and refused to pay tithe - with the result that the Rev. Thomas Seyliard was reduced to dire straits. The wealthy family of **HYDE** who had bought Bore Place from the Willoughbys in 1609, were ardent parliamentarians, and raised large sums in Chiddingstone for the cause of Parliament. The **WOODGATES** of Stonewall were certainly royalists, whilst the Streatfeilds of High Street House appear to have sat on the fence. Chiddingstone was mulcted successively in tax, fine, voluntary contribution, ticket, excise and sequestration - whilst in addition there is a list of those **"plundered"** in 1643, when England went through the experiences of unhappy Spain a few centuries latter.

And now the time has come to talk of the old houses of the parish, and it will be best to begin with the "Street" or "Towne" as it is so frequently called.

The **CASTLE** as we see it to-day was built by the Streatfeilds of 1760 - and before he undertook the work he got authority to deviate the **STREET** which at that time ran in a straight line from Churchyard to Castle. He built the wall by the Castle Inn to block up for ever access to the old road, and the new road was given its twist over the bridge to Gilwyns - the lake being constructed at the same time. The Castle replaced a house known as "High Street House" which had been built in 1679, and which in its turn had replaced a very old house of the same name in which the Streatfeilds began their period of prosperity, and their 400 years as squires, patrons and benefactors of the village of Chiddingstone.

Between the Castle and the Castle Inn was another large house, which seems to have also been pulled down in 1760 when the Castle was built. It was known as **WARE HOUSE**, after the family of Ware - an offshoot of that which gave the name to **DELAWARE** in Brasted. The John **WARE** who sold it to Henry Streatfeild in 1573 is described as "one of the officers of the pantry to our Lady the Queen's Majesty". The grounds extended to 10 acres and included "Sandfield Mead" - they were bounded by the Castle Inn on the east and a lane called **SPRATMAN'S LANE** on the west. This Spratman's Lane ran from where the head of the present lake is up to a point 400 yards on the east side of Hill Hoath House, where it joined the road from the Lodges in the SLIPS. The **WARE**'s at one time farmed "Somerden Green Farm", and have left their name in two fields there. Thomas Streatfeild lived here in 1724.

The CASTLE INN before becoming an Inn about 1730 was called "The Rock House" - and still earlier seems to have been known as **"WATERSLIP HOUSE"**. It was called "The Five Bells" for a short period about a century ago. Wakelyn, a butcher, lived there in the 17th century, but Thomas Weller, a tailor, bought it to live in, in 1712 and it appears that he and his brother George founded the "Castle Inn" a little before 1732. George Weller had owned the "Three Horseshoes" at Tyehaw - which seems to have been the Village Inn until its transference to the Castle Inn in 1730.

The next house eastwards is the **"MANOR HOUSE OF CHIDDINGSTONE COBHAM"** - over the porch of which one reads in the pargetting "A.1695.W" - and it was in that year that Anne Woodgate, widow, bought it from Benjamin Wakelyn, the butcher, for £150. It was in this house - (which is probably far older than 1695) - and in its predecessor, that the Manor Courts of Chiddingstone Cobham were held for many centuries. It came into Streatfeild ownership in 1739 - exactly 200 years ago.

The next house east was known for a couple of centuries as **CHIDDINGSTONE SHOP.** It seems to have been built in the middle of the 16th century - to have had no predecessor - and to have come into the possession of the **BEECHER** family in 1595. Over the fireplace on the Italian panelling are carved the initials G.J.B. - meaning George and Jane Beecher. The **Beechers**, who were "mercers", sold it in 1699 to Henry Streatfeild for £306. They farmed the 20 acres around the new churchyard, between the path to Somerden and the parish boundary - and on one old map these 20 acres are called **"Shoplands"**

The next house eastward of "Chiddingstone Shop" is now the **"POST OFFICE"** - and the Chiddingstone Shop of to-day - which until comparatively recently was not connected with the Chiddingstone Shop we have just described. The earliest record of the "Post Office" is in a deed of 1453, in which Anne **CHALONER** grants **"Longhouse"** to William **Hunt**. The **"Chaloners** were an ancient family who owned a farm between Larkins and Wellers Town which was first called "Challoners", later "Chaundelers" and now **Chandlers**. This present Post Office keeps changing its name through the centuries from HUNTS to LONGHOUSE and back again, and must have stretched across where the brick cottages of a far later date have been erected. It became the **'MANOR HOUSE OF CHIDDINGSTONE BURGHERSH"** (presumably after the decay of the moated mansion near Wellers Town) and was frequently called **Burgherst Court.** It came to the **SEYLIARDS** when they bought it from the Hamonds in 1537, who appear to have acquired it from Anne Boleyn's father at Hever Castle, who had himself bought it from the old family of **HUNTS** in 1517. Sir John Seyliard Bart was living in it in 1662. The Seyliards sold it to Henry **STREATFEILD** in 1700, and William Streatfeild died there in 1727, though the house was then once again divided into two parts, which were known as **HUNTS** and **BURGHERSH COURT**. There is little doubt that **HUNTS** was pulled down to make way for the brick cottages 100 or more years ago - whilst **BURGHERSH COURT** still stands as **"The Post Office".**

And now we come to a house quite as old as the Post Office, that at the end of "the Street", which may be called the **"atte-Wood House"**. A man called Roger lived there in the very long ago - and since there were other "rogers" in the village and this one lived or worked near a wood, he was called "atte-Wood" - a name which one meets frequently still - even as Atwell etc. We know this **Roger-atte-wood** - was farming Catsfield in 1453, but except for this one deed we know nothing about the occupants of this house until, in 1724, there were two tenants - William Pope and Thomas Egleton - the latter a name still met with in these parts.

And now we must leave "The Street" and wander east just out of the parish into that piece which the Penshurst Ogre bit out of the side of Chiddingstone, to the farm of **'LARKINS"**. IN 1250. Theobald and Bartholomew **LUVEKYN** paid rents for it - but the farm had passed out of their possession before 1392, when it belonged to John Dorkynghole of Leigh, from whose family the **DURTNALLS** of to-day descend. The **WARES** of Ware House owned it in 1517, and a witness to the delivery is Richard Everest of the "Street of Chiddingstone", butcher, whose descendants are with us today. The **ASHDOWNES** bought it in 1557, and Henry Ashdowne is described as a "butterman" i.e. "dairyman". It remained with the Ashdowne's till 1700, when Henry Streatfeild bought it under the name of **LORKINS** -but it was not till 1752 that the modern name of **LARKINS** is found.

As for **WELLERS TOWN** - there were two Wellers flourishing about the year 1700 - one, George, a blacksmith and keeper of the Inn at Tyehaw called "The Three Horseshoes". He worked at the Tyhaw Smithy which has only recently been demolished. The other Weller - Thomas - was a tailor who lived in "The Street" before he moved into what is now the Castle Inn in 1712. These two Wellers no doubt made a modest fortune out of tailoring, blacksmithing and innkeeping, which they invested in bricks and mortar at "Wellers Town".

And now we arrive at **Stonewall** - the home of the Woodgates who first came to this parish 500 years ago, and resided at Stonewall nearly 400 years. Not the present Stonewall, but originally in a house called Woodgates, which was pulled down in about 1570 - when a house called Stonewall was built on its site which stretched across the main road running from The Hoath, (Rendsley Hoath by the way) to the Blacksmith's Arms. When it in its turn came to be pulled down in about 1810 this main road was run across its old foundations, the kitchen premises were left and now form the main Lodge to the new Georgian house of Stonewall which was built in 1810.

The **WOODGATES** spread all over the parish and country. Truggers was a seat of one of the branches for many years whilst **WATSTOCK** (called "The Stooke"), **SKIPREED**, and **GILLRIDGE** all houses Woodgates at one time or another. Indeed the Woodgates played as big a part in the life of Chiddingstone as did the Streatfeilds, with whom they intermarried countless numbers of times. In early years they used **FRIENDEN** to lodge the eldest son or widow. When the Tonbridge Bank crashed in 1818, the Woodgates of Stonewall were heavily involved and compelled to sell their ancestral home. It was acquired by the Meade's who came from Devon, and later assumed the name of Waldo. The name of Waldo has romantic associations - the first of that name to land in England being a refugee from religious persecution. In the Waldensian Valleys of the Italian Alps these people were persecuted by the Pope, and by the Duke of Savoy for their heretical beliefs which were a form of Protestantism. When the poet Milton was Cromwell's Foreign Secretary, the tragedy of the Waldensians caused him to write one of his finest poems, to send the British fleet to Genoa, and to organise an enormous list for the persecuted compatriots of that Waldo whose descendants live in the mansion of Stonewall to-day.

PILBEAMS was the "Forge-House" belonging to Richard Streatfeild, where he or Thomas Browne smelted iron. It was afterwards farmed by the Medhursts - a family which I understand has by no means died out in these parts. **PRINKHAM** belonged to the Bassetts - an old Cowden & Chiddingstone family whose name remains in Bassetts Farm and Bassetts Mill.

HOBBS HILL - called Hobbyshellys in 1482 - probably was originally called "Hobgoblins Hill" - it belonged to the Saxby family for 200 years and then came to the Everest in 1700.

HOATH HOUSE was known as Batts in 1420, and retained that name till quite recently. It belonged (probably long before 1420) to the Ashdowne's - perhaps the oldest of all the Chiddingstone families. They intermarried on more than one occasion with the Streatfeilds, so that Colonel Streatfeild now lives in the house where his ancestors did more than 500 years ago. There is evidence that the Ashdownes descended from Henry Ashdowne of Chiddingstone and Agnes, his wife, - who was the daughter of Peter Manning of Chiddingstone - a lady with 12 quarterings in her coat of arms. And it may well be that Peter Manning was that Peter de Chiddingstone of the Moated Mansion near Wellers Town.

LOCKSKINNERS was farmed by the Everests for several generations, but some 250 years ago came into the care of the Saxbys.

GILWYNS was given its name in a remote past - for we read in 1363 that John de Chiddingstone sold a house formerly called **GYLEYEYNS** to William Partridge. In 1422 it became the property of **RICHARD WHYSLER**, a tailor, and passed through the hands of the Seyliards before it became the property of the **STREATFEILDS** in 1718.

The proper name for **CHIDDINGSTONE MILL** should be **CRANSTED MILL** as has already been explained - and under that name was almost certainly grinding corn 1,000 & more years ago.

BOUGH BEECH was a centre of some importance long ago, when the Courts of the "Borough of Cransted" (afterwards called "Kingsborough") were held there. These lands of Cransted came into the hands of Sir John de **CLINTON** in the 15th century and were then known as "**CLINTON LANDS**'. The high road from Bough Beech to Seyliards and to that queer detached portion of Chiddingstone Parish called **KNOWLANDS**, is called "**CLINTON LANE**" on the Ordnance Map. Since we know that Thomas Browne's **FURNACE FARM** smelting works were quite close to Bough Beech in the 16th century, and that there was probably a second furnace by Cransted House, it would seem probable that the workmen at the two furnaces made a respectable sized hamlet of Bough Beech.

WATERLAKE is a very old name - there was a "water pit" there 600 years ago. **HILDERS** was known as **SALMONS** and occupied by an Everest 200 years ago - whilst **LITTLE HILDERS** was called "**DANES**'. **IVY HOUSE** went under that name 200 years ago when Edward Cronk lived there.

COLES was the old home of the **HOLLAMBY** family and the house **BAYLEAF** was called **BAILEYS** and occupied by a Speed.

HICKENS has been called **HAMERHAWE** and **ALLENS** whilst **SHARP'S PLACE** was called **FOWKS** 300 years ago and was farmed by the BOAKES family all through the 18th Century - Boakes being a name very frequently found in Chiddingstone records - and they are still here.

STONELAKE - which we now call Chiddingstone Causeway - was owned 200 yrs. ago by one of the old name of **HAYWARD** - the same name as the occupier of ancient **POKERAGE** in the 14th century.

Stepping out of the parish, for one last moment, into the **YOKE of CHESTED** one comes upon **WEST CHESTED MEAD**, which, until about 100 years ago, was divided into 20 long strips each with a narrow frontage to the River Eden at their short bases. All the major farms in this parish had 1, 2 or 3 strips, and had a regular rotation in an annual change-over. Here, no doubt they bought their stock down in dry seasons - and the system of Perpetual change over shows how careful the wise old men of Chiddingstone were in days long since gone by, not to allow jealousy to creep into the lives of the farmers because one had a better strip than another.

And here I stop this evening - with an expression of admiration for the wonderful work which Dr. Gordon Ward of Sevenoaks has done in elucidating the past of Chiddingstone - and with my thanks to him for permitting me to dive into the extracts he has made from countless parchments of bygone years.

NOTES ON THE HISTORY OF CHIDDINGSTONE

Reprinted - Summer 1988

1. A lecture given at the Village Hall, Chiddingstone on 9th February 1939 by Commander F.N. Staff R.N.retired.

2. General historical notes from various sources

3. Officials of Chiddingstone Parish down the ages

4. The Manors of the Parish of Chiddingstone and their families

5. Some year by year details of certain property and sketches of some of the mead lands

6. The Parish divided into Zones - according to 1841 Tithe Map with field and place names

****

We are grateful to Mrs J.E. Streatfeild of Hoath House for allowing these notes to be reproduced from the original book in her possession. We thank all those who have assisted in the preparation of this edition in aid of St Mary's Parish Church Restoration Fund Chiddingstone.

****

CHIDDINGSTONE FARMS

		Zone
1.	Cooper's Corner alias ? Grove alias Woods Grove 1724	11
2.	Hilders (Little Hilders, Hilders Cottages) 1724 Salmons	7
3.	Harborough	7
4.	Slater's Farm	not shown
5.	Bough Beech (Smithy)	7
6.	Clout's Farm	7
7.	Pickett's	11
8.	High House	11
9.	Ivy House 1724	7
10.	Bailey's Farm - Bayleaf. 1724 Baylys	7
11.	Chiddinghurst. The Woodman in 1870	8
12.	Waterlake	7
13.	Somerden - Millbrook (Manor House of Millbrook)	6
14.	Bore Place 1724	8
15.	Blue Boar - 1745 & Smithy	8
16.	Polebrook Farm 1724	8
17.	Hicken's Farm alias Hamerhawe - Allens. 1724	8 (530)
18.	Coles Farm 1724 Coals	8
19.	Sharp's Place 1724	First field map
20.	Little Sidcup	8 (290)
21.	Great Hale - 1463. Hail House 1724	9
22.	Little Hale	9
23.	Mountjoy - 1639 - (Anne Cobham's lst husband circa 1480)	9
24.	Brownings - Great & Little 1724	9
25.	Charcott (part)	9
26.	Camp Hill 1724	10
27.	Gravel Pits	5
28.	Chequers P.H. 1724	5
29.	Cransted 1724	5
30.	Sorrelfield	Not shown
31.	Chiddingstone Mill (house) 1724	5
32.	Somerden Green - house 1724	6
33.	Pokerage (now mostly under Hever Castle Lake)	-
34.	Gilwyns 1724	6
35.	Rectory	6
36.	Burghersh Farm (second manor of Chidd:	-
37.	Chiddingstone Castle (High Street House 1724)	3
38.	Chiddingstone Cobham Manor (Manor House of Chidd. Cobham)	-
39.	Tyehurst (Manor of Tyhurst)	-
40.	The Moats (Manor of Chidd. Burghersh)	3
41.	Hill Hoath. - Withers 1724 - Hill Hoath House: Heldhouse 1724: House at Hill Hoath	3

42.	Highfield - Highfield House 1724	3
43.	Lock Skinners - 1724	2
44.	Geers - 1724 - Gears	-
45.	Slider's Bridge - 1724	3
46.	Lew Cross - 1724	3
47.	Battle Oak	3
48.	Watstock - 1724	4
49.	Gillridge - 1724	4
50.	Stonelake - 1724	10
51.	Baldocks	10
52.	Newtye - 1724	-
53.	Truggers 1724	2
54.	Walnut Tree Cross	2
55.	Hoath Corner	3
56.	Skipreed 1724	3
57.	Oakenden - Manor House of Alkinden - 1724	3
58.	The Hoath - Manor House of Rensley - 1724 Renleighs Manor Hse	1
59.	Brookers Farm	1
60.	Hoath House - 1724 Batts	1
61.	Stonewall 1724	1
62.	Woodgates - (a house near Stonewall 1724)	1
63.	Blacksmith's Arms	1
64.	Smith Street - Manor House of Smith Street	-
65.	Finch Green - a house near Finch Green 1724	-
66.	Frienden - Frienden 1724	1
67.	Bassetts Mill (house) 1724	1
68.	Prinkham - 1724 Frankham	1
69.	Hobb's Hill - 1724 Hobshill House	1
70.	Pilbeams - 1724 Pilbeams	1

****

PLACE NAMES from Wallenberg's Kentish Place Names

SOMERDEN Hundred

> Summerdene - Sumerden - Sum'denn' - Sum'denne - Somerdene - Sum - dene - Sumerdne -. Old English - **sumer** "summer" plus **denn** "pasture".

The Hundred Meeting-Place was at Somerden Green in Chiddingstone.

Chiddingstone

Cidingstane circa	1100 (Textus Roffensis)
Chidinggestan	1218 FF (Feet of Fines of Kent)
Chydingeston	1240 ASS (Assize Rolls for Kent)
Chidingstane	1254 ASS
de Chiddingestan	" "
Chidingestone	1254 FF
Chidingstane	1258 FF
Chidingstane	1261/2ASS
Schedingestane	"
Chetingeston	1262 FF
Chidingstan	1263 Ch (Calendar of Charter Rolls)
Chi (n) dinghestone	1264 PAT (Patent Rolls of Reign of Henry I)
Chidingston	" " Henry III)
Chithyngstone	1270 ASS
Chythynstane	" "
Chydingstone	1278 "
de Chityngston	" "
Chidingestane	1280 Ch
Chuddingestone	1284 Peck (Reg.epist.fratri J. Peckham
Chidingston (e)	1288 " Archbishop Canterbury)
Chydenstan	1292 ASS
Schydyngstan	" "
Chydynstan	" "
Chydyngton	" "
de Chithyngstone	" "

The great majority of - **d** - spellings in early and later forms is in favour of assuming an original base (Old English) **Cid-**. This fact makes it likely that the name should be interpreted together with the place-names **CHIDLOW** (Cheshire) and Chidgley (Somerset), which names derive from old English **Cidda, Cidd**, personal names. Mawer points out that an old-english **Cidda,** personal name, not given in Searle's "onomasticon", is found in the Calendar of St. Willibrod. Compare also **CHIDDINGFOLD**, the early forms of which strongly resemble those of Chiddingstone. Chiddingstone may accordingly be a compound of old-english **Cidda**, personal name, plus - **ing** (a) plus **stan** "Stone". A personal name old-english Cidding is the first element, or it is the genitive plural of ol(english **Cidding** is the first element, or it is the genitive plural of old-english **Cid**(d)**ing**ɛ "the contending, quarrelling, men", or the like, a nickname of the early settlers, derive perhaps from the same stem as old-english **gecid** "strife", "altercation", cidan "to conten quarrel". Old-english **Cidda** may perhaps originally be a nickname from this base.

It is perhaps most probable that the first element of the names discussed is a designation f(human beings (singular or plural). But a topographical interpretation may also be possibl Chiddingstone is situated at the source of a small tributary of the Eden; it must have a rap course. A stream-name may perhaps have been formed from the same stem as old-englis **cidan**. The Oxford Dictionary interprets this word as "to contend with loud and ang altercation"; to brawl, wrangle". In modern-english the word is also used about a brawlir stream.

A name meaning "the brawler", or the like, seems quite suitable for a rapid stream. Tł other places mentioned are also on or near streams.

The origin of old-english **cidan** is not known. The guess may be ventured that the ster may be a German-**dh**- extension of the Indo-Germanic base **gi**- "to cleave". The secon element is old-english **stan** stone.

BASSETTS MILL

Joh. Basset q in chydyngston' 1377. FF. Manorial

BATFOLD WOOD

perhaps **de Berkefaud'**	1240 ASS
" **de Bercfold**	1254 ASS
" **de Berkefolde**	1301 SUBS (Subsidy Rolls Kent)

all above under Somerden Hundred. Old-english **Beorc** "birch" plus **fal**(o)**d** "fold"

BORE PLACE

atte Bore	1313 ASS
John **Bore** of Chydyngston	1406 PAT
the **Bore**	1518 Arch. Cant. ex V., 12
Bore Place, **Boreplace**	1661, 1669 Arch Cant XXII 112, 115.
Boreplace	1690 (Index Villaris)

It is probably no mere coincidence that there is a Boar Hill less than 2 miles away. N early forms are found. The early material is not much to go upon. The name may be a cas of old-english **bur**, "bower, cottage". The evidence of early forms, no (**o**)**u** spellinę being found, does not, however, corroborate this interpretation.

According to Hasted, Bore Place was from the time of Hen.III the estate of a family whic took its surname from here and was called BORE, and assumed a **boar** for its arms. Tł earliest form (**atte Bore**) as well as the absence of genitival forms makes it unlikely that this is a manorial name, named after a man nicknamed "the boar" (old-english **bar**)

The early material does not take us much further. Until more early forms have been brought forward I prefer to interpret this name as an early corruption of old-english bur "bower", cottage".

BOUGH BEECH

Boubeche	1396 PAT
Bowbeche	1440/4 Ing. Aqd. (List of Inquisitions). Perhaps from old-english **boga** ("bow"), **bogen** "bowed, curved" plus **bece** "beech-tree".

BREECHES WOOD

de la Breche	1270 ASS. old-english **braec**, "strip of uncultivated land".
BROOKERS FARM	perhaps Pet. Broker 1327 SUBS
BROWNINGS perhaps Brounyng	1362 FF
CLOUT's FARM Clout	1348 SUBS

DEAN'S FURZES, DEAN'S WOOD

The Deane	1584 (index to Brit. Mus. Charters). Old-english **denu** "valley".
FRIENDEN	I have identified this place
de frindenne	1239 Registrum Roffense
de freyndenne	1240 circa Reg. Roff
Frayndenn'	1240 ASS.
(Hyl) frynden	1297 AD (Catalogue of Ancient Deeds)
Hylfrenden	1297 "

With Helfrethingdenn - 814 Birch's Saxon Charters 346 - one of a cluster of swine-pastures of which **HEVER**, situated at a distance of only less than 3 miles, is the only one that can be safely identified. Note the remarkable resemblance of the 1297 forms with the Charter Form. Very likely Karlstrom is right in his suggestion that the name is an - **ingdenn** - derivative of an old-english personal name (**Hel(p)frith**, as equivalent to old High German **Helpfrith**. Names containing Help- are evidenced in old-english. As a matter of fact names in - **ingdenn** are often derived from a personal name base. I suggested that as an alternative, the first element may be a compound of old-english **hyll** "hill" and **fyrhthea** "firth, wooded land", and that the name may accordingly have meant "pasture of a man in a hilly wood", or the like. This interpretation is probably too complicated to be plausible. Besides we expect a "Frithhill" rather than a "Hillfrith"; in a compound of the two elements **hyll** is no doubt the primary, **frith** the secondary element. The loss of the first syllable is probably best explained by assuming that it was by popular etymology associated with **hill,** which was left out of the name because the rest of it was considered sufficient as a designation of the place.

GASSON'S WOOD.	Will **Gasson** (in Hever) 1648 Arch. Cant. XX. 43.
GILLRIDGE	probably from old-english gylden "**golden**" hrycg "**ridge**"
GILWYNS	1278 Personal name
HALE	old English heall "**hall**" healh "**corner**"
PILBEAMS	Manorial name probably original name meant a piece of wood
POLBROOK	Old-english pol "**pool**" broc "**brook**"
SLATERS FARM	de Slightre 1278
CHESTED	de Chepstede 1240 ? market-place
VEXOUR	This name is obviously a compound of old-english feax "**hair**", here probably indicating a place covered with some sort of rough grass or shrubs and ora "**border**" "**bank**"

CHIDDINGSTONE in VERY early TIMES (by Dr. Gordon Ward)

For very many hundreds, even thousands, of years men have lived in what is now the parish of Chiddingstone, but of the earliest of them we know almost nothing. Our remote ancestors whose weapons were sharpened flints may well have wandered there: and certainly Iron Age man hunted on the banks of the Kent Water, and pressed up northwards across the Hoath and knew the meadows of Somerden and buried his dead on Chested Hill. The wealden clay served him for the making of rough pottery, and iron was everywhere. In due course, we shall perhaps discover his smelting-sites (which we should now call "bloomeries"). But all the pre-history of the Weald of Kent is still very obscure, and the written history of Chiddingstone does not begin until the year 814.

In that year Coenwulf, King of the Middle English or Mercians, reigned in Kent, which had been conquered by his predecessor Offa at the great battle of Otford. And Coenwulf made a grant of land to the Archbishop of Canterbury with the approval of his council of wise men. This gift was embodied in a charter which still exists and it tells us that the land was in part at Hever, but mostly at Bexley. It gives the boundary of the Hever land and the eastern boundary is called SPACHRYGG - which is in Chiddingstone.

SPACHRYCG

Very likely this strange name had once some definite meaning, but after 814 we hear no more of the place for more than 500 years. Then we learn that the tenement of Richard Blakeboy, **Spokereg**, is in the hands of the Lord of the Manor of Hever Brocas. This is in 1327. He seems to have put it out to farm again, and we hear of various tenants. In **1499** Margaret Hayward lived at **Spokeregge**, and paid a rent of 1/9d as well as a couple of hens and 1-1/2d which was a composition by which she was excused attendance at the hay-making. A little later it was in the hands of the father of Anne Boleyn, but we do not know who his tenant may have been. Presently it was added to Hever Park, and a note on a very old rental says "Nicholas Screven alias Dyer held a parcel of land called **Spokeredge**... the owner after him was Hayward, and after St. Thomas Bullein, Erle of Wiltshire; now the rent is extinct! All this goes very well with the information of the old Saxon deed which tells us that this place was the eastern boundary of Hever. But to find the exact site we must turn to the Tithe Map of **1841**. On this we find traces of it (under a strangely altered name) on Old **Pokerage** Mead, old **Pokerage** Hop Garden, and **Pokerage** Field. The meadow is now in Hever Lake, and the Hop Garden is park land, and so is Pokerage Field. They all lie together at the South Eastern border of the lake between the woodland and the water, in Chiddingstone Parish, but long removed from any practical interest to the men of Chiddingstone. Of the site of the mansion of **Spokeridge** there remains no trace.

THE DENS

The Weald is full of places like Spokeridge. Some have vanished, others have scarcely changed, a few have grown to great importance. In Saxon times they had a rather curious usefulness. The men who lived in the "upland", north of the sandhills on which Westerham and Sevenoaks stand - right away north as far as the Thames - had a mighty appetite for bacon. But it was the custom for pigs to be fed on oak mast - that is, acorns, and there were not sufficient oaks in far-away Bexley, Dartford, etc. Sot the Lords of these places acquired holdings in the Weald. These were such places as Spokeridge, - centres of cultivation and pig culture from so far back in history that we can hardly even guess when they began. In any case, it was long before there were any churches or parishes; and it may well have been in the Iron Age before the Romans came. Nor do we know who first started adding these "**dens**" as they were called, to upland manors whose Lords came down in the summertime and collected rents of small amount, and took one pig in ten of the year's increase, or even one in seven. Chiddingstone as we know it to-day, certainly originated in a group of dens, but we scarcely know to whom they belonged.

DOMESDAY BOOK

Domesday Book helps us a little. Nearly everyone will tell you that Chiddingstone isn't mentioned in Domesday Book, and it certainly isn't mentioned by name. But we are told that the King (the Conqueror) owned the great manor of Dartford, and that attached to it were "eight small and three large dens of wood." Very likely Spokeridge was one of the small one, and there is no doubt at all that **Cransted** was one of the others. It was a very important place. In 1280 it was "the Borough of Lord Roger of Cranstede", which sounds very well indeed; to be exact it was the centre of the Borough - which was sometimes called **Kingsborough**. It paid 66s 3d yearly to Dartford, no small sum in those days. There was also some land to the west of Weller's Town, which once belonged to Dartford, but its old name has been lost; and there is reason to suppose that **Stonelake** may have been another of the Dartford dens. Most of Chiddingstone, however, belonged to the manor of Sundridge. Domesday Book does not tell us how many dens went with Sundridge, probably because they were all grouped together, whereas those of Dartford were more scattered. But we are told that Sundridge collected a rent of 60 hogs. That may have meant that there were 600 new little hogs in Chiddingstone every year, in the Sundridge part of Chiddingstone only, - and if they had only acorns to feed on they must have needed considerable space in the woods. We have another entry about Sundridge in a document of the same date as Domesday Book (that is 1086), and called the Domesday of the Monks. It is kept at Canterbury, and tells us that Sundridge (and therefore most of Chiddingstone as well) "was held unjustly by (Earl) Godwin in the time of Edward (the Confessor) but (Archbishop) Lanfranc recovered it rightfully from the Bishop of Bayeux (who was also Earl of Kent) by leave of the King".

THE GROWTH OF CHIDDINGSTONE VILLAGE

Now we must go back a little. When Domesday Book was written Chiddingstone had a church, and at least some rudiments of a village street. The farms of the neighbourhood would need a place where they could meet together, another where they could drink together, a third where a horse might be shoed, - a fourth where leather could be purchased, and so on. Then there would be the parson's house, if he didn't happen to live in part of the church, - and the manor house, where the post office now is. These different facilities might be scattered about the parish, but they would tend to collect together near the Church and Manor House. In this way a village would come slowly into being, and it is likely that Chiddingstone had got as far as a manor house, church, ale house and smithy, when Bishop Odo had to give it up to the Archbishop about **1072**. The Church was a real Church with a parish of its own, and not a mere chapel to some other church. There is a record of it at Rochester, wherein it is called CIDINGSTANE, which is the very earliest record we have of its name. And every year the parson of Chiddingstane (that is how it would have been pronounced) must have gone to Rochester at Easter time and paid ninepence to the Bishop of Rochester. In return he brought back the "chrism", the oil used in the administration of the sacraments, renewed and solemly blessed every year at Rochester.

SUMMARY

Thus very briefly we can construct the early history of the parish of Chiddingstone. First a forest with wolves and deer, wild boar, fox, badger and lesser beasts, - with here and there the settlements of Iron Age man, - where now we find such farms as Somerden, Oakenden, Frienden, etc. Then a stage of rather firmer settlement when these places are permanently inhabited and are visited now and then by Roman officers on hunting expeditions; when the inhabitants go from time to time to sell vegetables and perhaps iron brooches (such as were found at Otford) to Roman soldiers passing on the great road through Edenbridge. Of course they would keep one eye open for the Roman taskmaster who might catch them for forced work on that same road, and vanish quickly by their own forest paths on the slightest rumour of his coming. The protection of the Roman Eagles was withdrawn in time, - but for a while the land enjoyed prosperity. It would be long before the Saxons found much to interest them in the forest, but sooner or later the urge for bacon brought about the changes already mentioned. Then came Saint Augustine, and the light of Christianity came to help and raise the forest dwellers, who were doubtless almost as primitive as their pigs. Someone long forgotten, some Saxon thane of Sundridge as like as not, built the first small church. The nearest dens were grouped into a Parish, and so the grouped stage was set for a thousand years and more of written history.

DARTFORD WEALD and CHIDDINGSTONE

from Dr.Gordon Ward

The domesday Evidence

We learn from Domesday Book that Dartford (Tarentefort) was then part of the ancient demesne lands of the King, and that it had "eight small and three large dens". Where were these dens? Probably we shall look with best success in the neighbourhood of the Hundred of SOMERDEN. Entries in Domesday Book tell us that King William acquired other lands which were certainly in the neighbourhood. These were portions of the woodland of other upland manors and are described in Domesday under 10 manors, of which the last is:

10 In summerdene Robert Latin has of the new gift of the Bishop, in the King's hands, under Richard de Tonebrigge, 10 villians with 3 teams and wood of 50 hogs.

The Bishop in question was Odo, Bishop of Bayeux and half brother to the Conqueror, but nevertheless in prison at this time for various offences... it is clear that such relatively small portions may well have been thrown into the royal manor of Dartford for convenience of administration. We must therefore remember that a wealden holding described in the 13th century or later as part of the manor of Dartford was not necessarily any part of it before these "new gifts" of the Bishop came into operation. One naturally wonders whether the Bishop knew anything about them - but that is another matter which we must not turn aside to discuss.

Extents of Dartford Manor

There are three main sources from which we expect assistance in tracing the wealden portions of upland manors, that is manors of which the headquarters were beyond the bounds of the forest (once called Andred but later the Weald), and which had detached possessions which were often many miles distant. These are:-

(a) Rentals & extents of Upland Manors which make mention of wealden portions or tenants.

(b) Rentals of wealden manors which show, usually under the heading "Rents Resolute", various payments due to upland courts.

(c) Records of non-manorial courts, i.e. the courts of Hundreds and Boroughs and courts which held "view of frank pledge."

Of Dartford Manor, at least two extents have found their way into print. The first is of the year 1253 (K.A.S. ii 311) and is comprised in the report of an enquiry as to the value of the manor of Dartford. It includes:-

"Item, there are certain members pertaining to the said manor, viz. Cranestede, with its pertinencies, and it renders 66s 3d per annum of rent of assize; and Chislehurst etc. etc..."

The second is seven years later (K.A.S. iii.249) and is the return to a writ ordering a valuation of the manors formerly held by "William de Fortibus, Earl of Albemarle". This contains the words:-

> "Item, of rent of assize in Craneford, at the four terms in equal portions, 66s.3d.

One supposes that Craneford is an error for Cranestede, an error which might easily happen, since those who made answer to the writ seem all to have been from upland Dartford, and might well be hazy as to the proper name of a distant wealden portion. Moreover the King himself was probably much more interested in the 66s.3d than in the precise name of the holding which owed this sum. This, it must be admitted, is anticipating an argument yet to be developed: for we have not yet adduced any evidence to show that one name or the other is the more correct, or that the place in question was in the Weald. But it is perhaps permissible to state that no such place is discoverable in upland Dartford. On the other hand there is undoubtedly a place, once of considerable importance, and then named Cranstead or Granstead, in the Hundred of Somerden. Since there is some evidence connecting this place with Dartford, we will consider this next.

The Perambulations of 1280

In the year 1280 there was made a perambulation of the bounds of the Lowy of Tonbridge. The Lowy was an ill-defined area centering on Tonbridge, in which the Lords of Tonbridge claimed a civil and criminal jurisdiction exclusive of that of the surrounding hundreds. The claim was based on an alleged grant of such rights - they were very profitable rights - by William the Conqueror to that Richard de Tonebrigge who fought for him at Hastings and was indeed a kinsman and trusted councillor. But the area of the Lowy was composed of wealden possessions of many upland manors, the more important of which belonged to the Archbishop of Canterbury. There were accordingly many and bitter disputes as to the bounds of the Lowy and as to the rights of the Lord of Tonbridge therein. The perambulation of 1280 was one of the attempts to define the bounds. But those who perambulated also reported on the tenure and status of various places which were within the bounds but which had some claim to be outside the criminal and civil jurisdiction. Such a claim is allowed to-day in respect of Embassy buildings in London. These are indeed within the bounds of England and yet are outside its civil and criminal jurisdiction, owing obedience in this respect to distant Kingdoms which are not within the bounds of England, nor owe to it any manner of allegiance. A contemporary copy of the report of these perambulations is in the Chapter House Library at Canterbury (MS T 32). It includes the following paragraph dealing with one of these included areas which, for purposes of petty justice, claimed to be without:-

"Item, they say that the whole borough of the Kyngelomde in La Leghe, which is within, is the Barony of Derteford, and used to attend the Borough of Lord Roger of Cranstede until John of Stanigrave by force made them attend at Hyldenn, in the time of Henry the King and Richard the Earl.".

This extract shows that certain lands existed in Leigh which were held of the Barony of "Dartford, i.e. were part of the manor of Dartford and owed quit rents (which we might better call **ground** rents) to the Lord of Dartford Manor. But police court jurisdiction was exercised over these lands that, over those who lived on them, by the "Borough of Lord Roger of Cranstede, This last is also called more shortly Cranstede or King's Borough, and is one of the subdivisions of the Hundred of Somerden. this must be discussed later. The importance of the above quotation now appears in the evidence it gives:-

(1) That a place called Cranstede (not Craneford) was connected in some way with Dartford Manor

(2) That this place was very remote from the upland part of this manor, being in fact so distant that the people of Leigh could conveniently attend Courts held there.

At the same time it will be noted that the same people of Leigh did not live within the Borough territories, but were at most a detached portion of it. This suggests that they may have inhabited one of those areas of which the Bishop of Bayeux made a new gift to the King before 1086.

The Borough of Cransted

It was quite usual for the area of a Hundred Court's jurisdiction to be divided into Boroughs. These were called "Tithing Boroughs", which have nothing at all to do with church tithes, and their representative was called a Decimus, or Ten-man. There were such Boroughs in the Hundred of Somerden, for example, Frienden, Chiddingstone, Penshurst, Stanford and Cowden. But there is also in existence another subdivision of the Hundred. This is best described in the words of the Hundred Rolls of 1274. The relevant extracts as quoted by Furley (History of the Weald, Vol. 2, part 1, p.127) are:-

"The Hundred of Sumerdene: Two parts of this Hundred are of the liberty of the Lord the Archbishop, and one borough only, called Grensted, appertains to the King, rendering 3s 6d a year---- The tenants of Durkinghol formerly attended the King with the Borough of Gransted, and they have now withdrawn through the bailiffs of the Earl of Gloucester... The tenants of Exore and Wigginden did suit at the Hundred of Sumerdene, and were wont to scot and lot with the Borough of Gransted, and they have withdrawn themselves by (the persuasion of the baillifs of) the Archbishop of Canterbury. John de Duttindene and his brother have done the same. The tenements of Appleton and of Chekesland, and the tenants of Cherecote, Everherst and Stonlake were anciently in the Borough of Gransted, and attended the King, and they are withdrawn by the Archbishop of Canterbury."

Furley was probably working from the printed Hundred Rolls which are exceedingly inaccurate where place-names are concerned. This accounts for the appearance of "Grensted" for "Cransted". On an earlier page he gives extracts from the Plea of Rolls of Henry III where, under the Hundred of Sumerdene, we read:-

"William, son of William de Berkfold, and Matilda his sister, children of three years, were found burnt in the house of their father in Cransted. **Judgement:** Misfortune. And the vill of Cransted buried the aforesaid dead without view of the coroner; therefore in mercy."

This extract gives the usual spelling, and also tells us for the first time that Cransted was a "**vill**", a name which is used as equivalent to a borough in various records, but in others as corresponding to a manor.

The next point to be considered about this Borough of Cransted is that it seems at a later date to have held its own courts separate from those of Somerden Hundred. Amongst the Sydney papers (Add. MSS.33898) are some extracts of Court Rolls of Honour of Otford, and these include many Rolls of Somerden Hundred from 1460 to 1503. Various Boroughs attend but never that of Cransted. On the other hand we find amongst certain records in the hands of Mr. Herbert Knocker, that the lands which we shall presently find to have been within the Borough of Cransted in the 13th century, were answering in the 17th to a Court held for Kingsborough. It is not proposed to carry further the question of the exact status of the courts held for this Borough, since this would take us too far from our purpose of identifying the wealden part of Dartford Manor. That it should have come to be called "King's Borough" is natural enough, since Cransted was then no longer a place of any importance and this borough undoubtedly belonged to the King.

Cransted

The house or farm named Cransted was shown on the maps of the 1869/70 Ordnance Survey but now no longer exists. The site is now included in the park of Hever Castle, but is in Chiddingstone Parish. It had an entrance road from Bow Beech via Gravelpits, and this still remains. Between Cransted and Chiddingstone (alias Cransted) Mill, north of the river Eden, lay Cransted Mead. This last field-name is still in use. The association of mansion, common meadow, and mill, all having the same name leaves little doubt that here was the original centre of Dartford Weald. It may also be noted that these were certainly Clinton lands at a later date. The Courts of Kingsborough (**alias** Cransted Borough) were held at Bow Beech. It was always considered necessary to hold manorial or other courts within the manor or borough for which they were summoned. Sometimes they were later adjourned to an inn which did not happen to lie within the manor, but they were never summoned to meet there. We may therefore assume with good reason that Bow Beech was within the Borough of Cransted; and also since there is no other holding interposed, within the original wealden portion of Dartford. All this area was also included in the "Clinton" lands held "of the Barony", but there is no other clue to the extent of Cransted Manor(if ever it was a manor) at present available to the writer. The area seems somewhat too small to be equivalent to the "eight small and three large dens" of Domesday Book. Some other part of Dartford Weald remains to be detected.

We have evidence that Kingland (also called King's Land) in Leigh was part of the Barony of Dartford. This was very near what was later called Sinderhill, then for many years Gilwyns, and now again Cinderhill - with a slight difference in spelling. Close to this were Cherecote, Everhurst and Stonelake, with, to the east of these, Durkinghol, Applestone and Chekesland remain unidentified, but the way in which they are mentioned rather suggests that they were in the same locality. One can hardly doubt that this multiplication of names in a small area points to these as the eight small dens of Domesday Dartford.

We have also evidence that part of the forelese of the Court of Chiddingstone Burghersh once belonged to Dartford. This suggests a holding somewhere near Gillridge and Watstock in Chiddingstone, extending over the road to the west and including part of the forelese, which last extended from Wellers Town southward almost to Lew Cross.

We have now three possible areas of Dartford Weald:-

a) Cransted proper - including Cransted & Bow Beech
b) The Kingland, Cerecote & area, including part of Leigh
c) An area somewhere near Watstock & Gillridge

It seems quite possible that we have still to identify one more large den. At a guess, one would place this near Bore Place, Sharp's Place & Sidcup - all old holdings - which do not seem to have any representation at Hundred Courts, unless through the Borough of Cransted.

Both east and west of the boundaries of Chiddingstone Parish were the wealden portions of other manors. Within Chiddingstone were various lands which we have provisionally allocated to Dartford, and certain lands of which nothing has yet been said. These last include Chiddingstone Village with the land to the north of it as far as Somerden Farm, and other land to the south bounded by Rensley Heath and the Cowden border. Below Rensley Heath is another area which was apparently the Borough of Frienden, which was included in the Archbishop's share of Somerden Hundred.

These various lands at present unallotted may well have been the original wealden portion of Sundridge Manor. They certainly pay quit-rents to Sundridge Manor to-day, or have enfranchised themselves. But so also do the Dartfordlands. Herein is a difficulty. How is it that Clinton **lands held of the Barony** (and in this way distinguished from those held of Sundridge) how is it that these lands now pay to Sundridge instead of the Barony???

An assumption which would be correct in many cases would be that an heir of Dartford married a Lord of Sundridge, or vice-versa, and the two wealden portions were thus thrown together for convenience of administration.

In conclusion a word about Exore and Wigginden, which were withdrawn from the Borough of Cransted, and might therefore seem to have some claim to consideration as parts of Dartford Weald. Both are in the parish of Cowden. Exore is now called Riccards, Wigginden has been lost. Both were well-known as holdings of Lewisham manor long

Cransted Borough, it was probably because this was nearest, and not because they were in any way connected with Dartford.

We know that:- There was a subdivision of Sumerden Hundred known as "The Borough of Cransted" otherwise "Kingsborough", and a subdivision or Member of Dartford manor which had the same name. Although one is an administrative area and the other a manorial building, it may well be that both had reference to the same area. To identify the two satisfactorily we ought to be able to produce records of places in that area paying rent to Dartford. Such evidence is very slight.

Somewhere about 1470 a division was made between three heirs, of the lands of Sir John de Clynton in Chiddingstone and neighbouring parishes. The record of this division is now in the Sevenoaks Library. It shows that the possessions were divided:-

a) Lands, apparently "in hand"
b) Rents from tenants

Among the latter we find one tenant paying "Dertefford Rent" of an amount not specified. There is no other similar entry, for all other rents are specified as "so much cash", "so many hens" etc. Among the lands in hand several large areas are said to be "held of the Barony". Others are held of named manors but the Barony is nowhere further defined. The lands in question are around that part of Chiddingstone in which Cransted House was situated, and include a "water mill with two other houses there built", which can hardly be any other than Cransted Mill, later called Chiddingstone Mill, of which there are many records. It is only a question of probability that this "Barony" is the "Barony of Derteford", to which lands belonged in Leigh in 1280, but the area was one of 120 acres, and it is difficult to see what other Barony might have been in question.

Another record which connects Dartford & Chiddingstone occurs in a Rental of Chiddingstone Burghersh Manor for the year 1383. Among the "Rents Resolute", i.e. the outgoing rents to overlords of whom portions of this manor were held we find:-

"Item, the Court of Dertford for half the forlese before the gate of the Court......viii d qr. To the same court for half an acre in bournemede per annum........ob. It is possible to identify these holdings, but they lie to the south-east of Chiddingstone Street, whereas Cransted lies to the North-west. It therefore seems possible that here again a "new gift of the Bishop" is in question, and that this land "before the gate of the Court" originally belonged to some manor other than Dartford when Bishop Odo was in disgrace. In this case it would not be expected to be part of that district called Cransted in the Dartford manor e tents, although it might well answer for police court purposes to the Borough Court to which the name of Cransted was attached. For lack of exact proof this is a personal opinion:- That a wealden portion of Dartford was, in 1066, situated at and around Cransted in Chiddingstone, and that was the original area of the Borough of Cransted to which, on Odo's disgrace, were added outlying portions taken from the wealden portions of other manors. But it is equally possible that some or all of such outlying portions were really parts of Dartford Weald originally, but were not in territorial contiguity with the part named Cransted.

THE SITE OF THE MANOR HOUSE OF CHIDDINGSTONE BURGHERSH

- by Dr. Gordon Ward

We learn from surviving records of the Manor that in 1383 the "scite of the manor with the Forlese" was leased to Richard Chapman, - and also that the sum of 8 1/4 was owed to "The Court of Dartford" for "half the Forelese before the gate of the Court". These two records seem to refer to the Manor House, and tell us that at that date it was no longer the residence of the Lord, - a fact confirmed by the leasing of the demesne lands to various persons in comparatively small parcels.

The Forelese was presumably a part of the waste or heath (which may have been brought under cultivation) opposite the entrance to the Manor House. The Manor House of Nizels had a similar forlese only recently enclosed and so, no doubt, had other manors.

It may probably be deduced from these two entries that the manor house was still standing, but we learn nothing of its position. But we may learn something from the names of the fields which Richard held - all were demesne land and he held nothing else in the manor - namely:-

Horneslond	Stoneslond 24 acres	Herefeld 40 acres
Berefeld 5 acres	Tenacres	

The next evidence of importance is that afforded by the commentary on an ancient pedigree of the family of Seyliard of Dalaware. The commentary was written in 1591 and the whole is published in "Miscellanea Genealogica at Heraldica". The following sentences deserve mention -

> "This Sir William Borowashe alias Burghershe, that maryed one of the daughters and heyres of Peter de Chedyngston of Chedyngston in Kent, Bylded uppon his haulffe of the manor of Chedyngston A stately house wher de dwelled and his part was called by him Chedingston Burghershe ali' Borowashe".

Sketch showing position of Moats of Ancient Burghersh Manor House

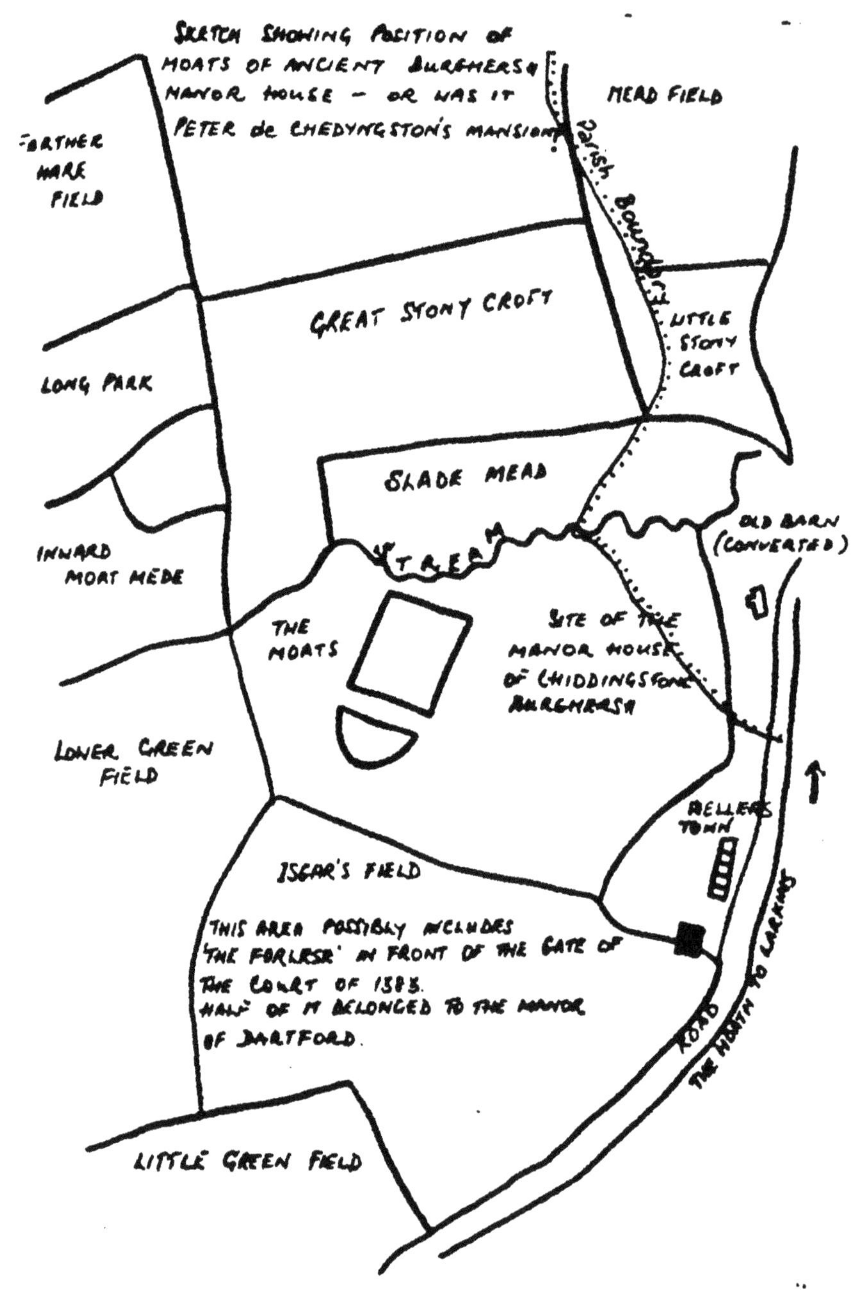

"Sr Barthelmewe Burghershe alias Borowashe did lykwise dwell uppon the manor of Chedyngston Burghershe in Kent".

"The house of the manor of Chedyngston Borowashe ys clene falen downe, but the grett motes remayne as a token of the statly byldynge".

According to Hasted (111.218) this Bartholomew - a "mighty stronge man" says the pedigree - sold this manor about the 43rd year of King Edward III i.e. 1369/70. It is probably from this date that the slow decay of the great house in the hands of tenant farmers commenced.

In 1630 we find Thomas Seyliard of Delaware leasing to Richard Beecher of Penshurst certain parcels of land of which those of importance to us at the moment are:-

"Long Parke
Moat Meadows
Green Field
Isgars Field - 38 acres in Chiddingstone

These are specified as being part of the demesne lands of Chiddingstone Burgherst. All these names remain on a map of 1742 - and they adjoin Harefield & Stony Crofts, which remind us of the Herefeld and Stoneslond, which Richard Chapman farmed with the manor house in 1383. Another map from the same source, i.e. from the muniments of Sir Henry Streatfeild, shows us next to Moate Meadow a field called **"The Moates"**, - and drawn in it are two moats, the one quadrangular, the other shaped like half a full moon.

To find this site one must approach Chiddingstone from the north, over Vexour Bridge and up to the Oast houses of Larkin's (which was once called **Lovekin's**) Farm. There avoid the road to Chiddingstone Street, and go straight on down into the valley until the road crosses a small stream. Following this stream to the west one comes to the moats, but they are on the south side of it. The Half-moon moat is almost dry but its shape is evident. The quadrangular moat is difficult to identify. Its northern side is the stream, and there **are** traces of other sides, but five hundred years of work by a restless stream have almost destroyed all that one could recognise.

It would seem that the existence of moats, **two** moats, together with the evidence cited, should be almost enough to fix the site of the old manor house of the "mighty stronge" Bartholomew of 1370. But there are difficulties. These are two in number:-

1). In 1615 Thomas Seyliard leased a mansion house in Chiddingstone Street, to Thomas Waters, and it is said to be part of the Manor of Chiddingstone Borowash alias Burgherst. This deed is endorsed "Burgherst Court". Moreover in 1727, a Court Baron was held at "the accustomed place, viz Burgherst court in the town of Chiddingstone".

2) Although the moat meadow already mentioned lies in the demesne of Chiddingstone Burghersh, the moats themselves lie in land stated in 1651 to be part of the demesnes of Chiddingstone Cobham.

The first objection is not on the face of it serious. If one manor house was "clene fallen downe" by 1600, it is not surprising that some house should have come to be regarded by the people as the manor house in 1727. The second objection is more serious - since it might be that there was a manor house Chiddingstone Cobham which also had moats.

We have therefore, if possible, to associate these moats more closely with Chiddingstone Burghersh than hitherto.

It will be remembered that in 1383 Richard Chapman had, inter alia, "the scite of the Manor, half the forlese, and Herefeld".

In about the year 1420 (the rental is undated) William Hunt held the Mote, half Court Green, and Herefeld. It is true that he did not hold it of Chiddingstone Burghersh, but of the old Manor of Rendesley, out of which most of Chiddingstone Manor seems to have been carved. (Such holdings of more than one manor are commonplaces of manorial history in West Kent). It seems legitimate to conclude that the Forlese before the Gate of the Court in 1383 and the Court Green of 1420 were the same. Nor does it seem too much to identify them with the lower green field of a map of 1742. a glance at the map will show that it is not unreasonable to suppose that these two, with Isgar's field, formed the Court Green of 1420. And it lies before the gate of any house built in Moat Field.

Questions of this sort are largely a matter of inference. Inference is largely a matter of bias or opinion. Each much form his own conclusions. A further identification of the Chapman and Hunt holdings is afforded by the fact that in 1473 one of the name of Hunt had a **Tenacres & Berecroft**, apparently the Tenacres & Berefeld of Chapman in 1383. But the Hunt family did not live at the Mote House - it it still stood. There is much evidence that they lived in a house known as **LONGHOUSE**, and this had **Catsfield**, (still so called) to the south end and the churchyard of Chiddingstone to the north. This must surely be the old Streatfeild Mansion, now the Post Office, or an earlier one on the same site. It is probably also the Burghersh Court of 1727. It **may** even be the old residence of **Peter de Chiddingstone,** before ever the Manor was divided, and before the new house with its moats came into existence.

And so matter must be left. A few probabilities and several guesses make one suggest that the moats were those which surrounded the Burghersh Manor House, but only more documents and more careful examination of them could show how those same moats came to be regarded as part of the sister manor of Cobham, or what exactly was the origin of LONGHOUSE in Chiddingstone Street!!

OLD HOUSES AT CHIDDINGSTONE - by Dr. Gordon Ward

It is said that Peter of Chiddingstone had two daughters who were his heirs, and that, on his death, their husbands divided between them his lands in Chiddingstone.

One half became the manor of **Chiddingstone Burghersh**, and the other the Manor of **Chiddingstone Cobham**.

Certainly Peter knew a certain William de Burghersh - an old form of "Burwash", the family came from Sussex - for William and Peter together witnessed a deed at Edenbridge in the year 1275. Certainly, also, the story is an old one, for an unknown author wrote in the time of Queen Elizabeth:-

> "This Sir William Borowashe, alias Burghershe, that maryed one of the daughters and heyres of Peter de Chedyngston of Chedyngston in Kent, bylded uppon his haulffe of the manor of Chedyngston a stately house wher he dwelled, and his part was called by him Chedingeston Burghershe, alias Borowashe".

The whereabouts of this stately house shall be our first enquiry. It no longer exists. Even in 1591, when the above extract was written, the author added:-

> "The house of the manor of Chedyngston Borowashe ys clene falen downe, but the grett motes remayne as a tolken of the statly byldynge".

It is these great moats which give us a clue, for we have various other references to them in the important series of deeds preserved by Sir Henry Streatfeild. The stately mansion can hardly have been built earlier than 1275, for Peter was then alive. In 1383 we find it shelters only a tenant farmer for "the scite of the manor with the Forlese" was let to Richard Chapman. The Forlese are the "foreleas" i.e. the mead-ows in front of the house: they are described as being "before the gate of the court". They were also called the Court Green, and as late as 1742 were known as Lower Green Field and Little Green Field. Now they seem to have no distinguishing names, the Green Fields being described as the "hop garden by the Slip". A third portion of the Forlese had the curious name of Isgar's Field.

But traces of the moats remain, and one can gain some idea of the position of the house. James Beecher made a map in 1703 and Humphrey Giles another in 1742. Mr. Giles was lavish with acreage when it came to moats, though accurate enough otherwise. The tiny pond by the stream in fact represents the similunar moat, the other has almost vanished.

The decay of this stately house was probably due to the great success of Sir Bartholomew Burghershe, who was "a mighty stronge man", and the last of his family to live there. But his son's heir was a daughter, and marriage took her away from Chiddingstone. Thus the stately house and the old family disappeared from Chiddingstone - more than 500 years ago.

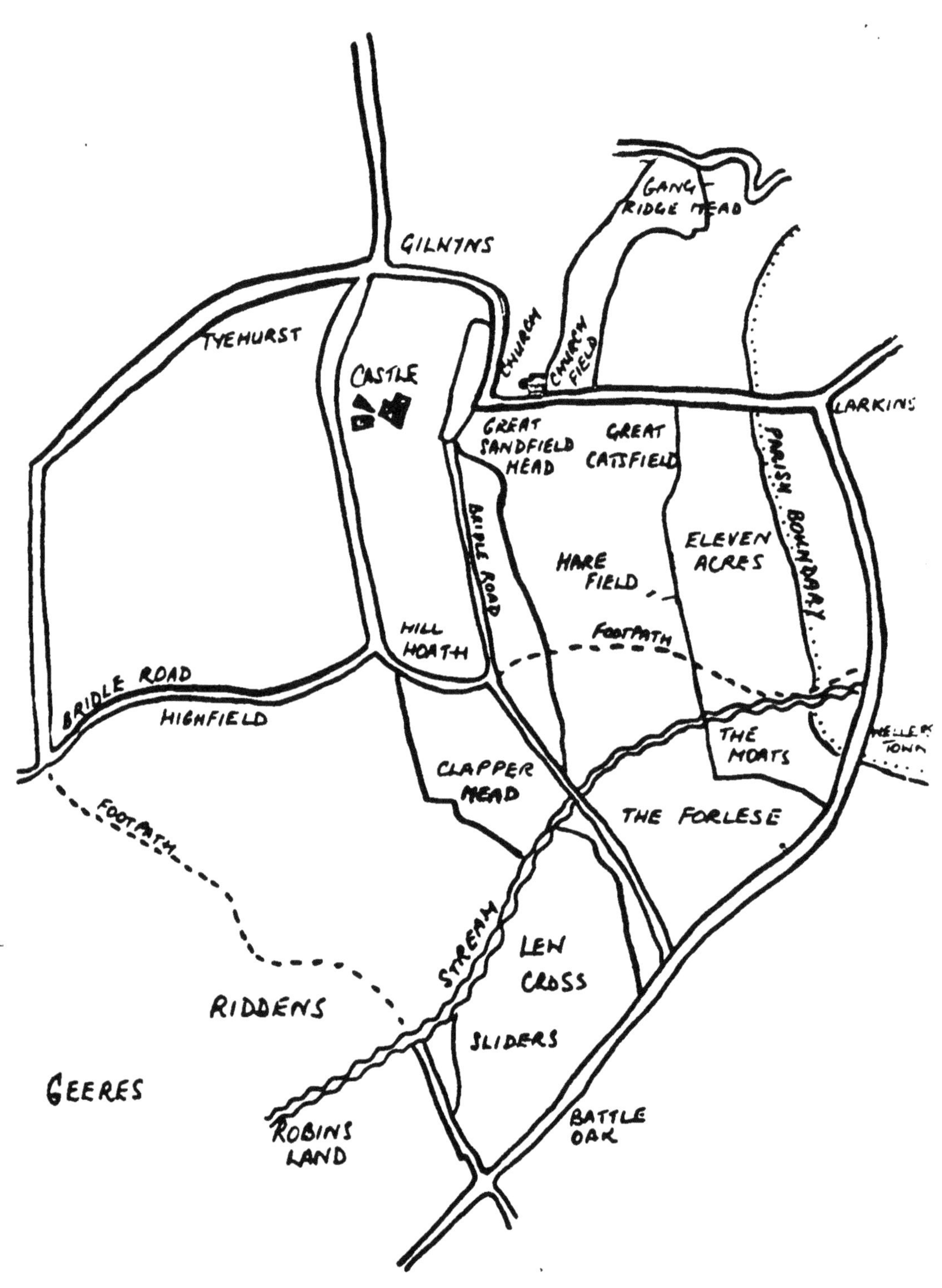

GANG RIDGE MEAD
GILNYNS
TYEHURST
CASTLE
CHURCH
CHURCH FIELD
LARKINS
GREAT SANDFIELD MEAD
GREAT CATSFIELD
PARISH BOUNDARY
BRIDLE ROAD
HARE FIELD
ELEVEN ACRES
FOOTPATH
HILL HOATH
BRIDLE ROAD
HIGHFIELD
THE MOATS
CLAPPER MEAD
THE FORLESE
FOOTPATH
STREAM
LEN CROSS
RIDDENS
SLIDERS
GEERES
BATTLE OAK
ROBINS LAND

THE SECOND MANOR HOUSE OF CHIDDINGSTONE BURGHERSHE

But although the house vanished, the Manor remained. There was still need for manor courts, which registered changes of tenancy and regulated the dues to the Lord. Particularly important was the due called a "Heriott", a tribute to the Lord of the best beast on his farm at the death of every tenant. At the same time the incoming tenant paid a "relief" i.e. an extra year's rent.

And the Courts dealt with trespasses and disputes, and were serious meetings with proper formalities. The only person who had little to do with them was the Lord of the Manor. He was never present, and neither he nor his representatives made decisions as to fines etc. All this was done by the tenants, the freeman of the Manor, according to the custom of the Manor. That was always the phrase used - "according to the custom of the Manor" - and that custom was almost as old as the word Chiddingstone, of which we will speak presently.

But first let us seek to identify where the Courts met after Burghershe court had "clene fallen downe".

In the year 1615 Thomas Seyliard leased a "mansion house" in Chiddingstone Street to Thomas Waters, and this deed is endorsed "Burgherst Court". Moreover, in 1727, it is stated in the official roll of the proceedings of the Court that it was held "at the accustomed place, namely, Burgherst Court in the town of Chiddingstone". There is no reasonable doubt about which house it was that Thomas Seyliard (of Delaware near Edenbridge) possessed at Chiddingstone Street. It is now called the Post Office, but it has had other names as well as Burgherst Court. For a hundred years or more - 1453-1537 deeds - it was called LONGHOUSE and, at times, "HUNTS" from the name of the then owner. Here is a description of the property in 1453:-

> "A messuage called Longhouse with a garden in the vill of Chedyngstone, abbutting to land of Thomas Wilmot on the west, to a field called Cattefeld on the south, to the messuage of Roger atte Wode on the east, and opposite the churchyard of Chedyngston towards the north, all of which came to me William Durkynghole on the death of my mother Joane".

This was written when William Hunt obtained the house and he lived there until his death in 1485. He was burried "in the church yard of Blessed Mary at Chedyngston", and he left 20 pence to the "pavimentum" of the said church. Each of his daughters had 20 shillings and an ox aged three years, his two houses going to his sons.

Adjoining the Post Office, and apparently part of the one house, is another with a fine entrance. In the front room of this may be seen panelling of the 17th Century, and over the fireplace the initials and date "G.I.B. 1638". There is some doubt about this dwelling, but it may be noted that in 1635 Richard Beecher paid 18 pence a year to the Manor for a house in Chiddingstone Street. He had a son George. George was a very uncommon name and it is almost certain that it was this George who put up the panels in 1638, and had his initials carved on them. The central initial "I" was probably that of his wife. The letter "J" was usually written in this way, and her name was doubtless Joan. This pleasant habit of making a single monogram of husband's and wife's initials was usual then. It may often be seen on the trade tokens of the period, when tradesmen had their own minted small change because the State was too busy to issue any.

To the east of the Post Office, at the end of the row, is another ancient house. This is now joined to the Post Office by a residence not shown on a map of 1703 and so quite modern, as we count time in Chiddingstone. This is evidently the messuage of Roger atte Wode referred to in the dead of 1452. It belonged to John Wodde in 1537. These names afford an interesting example of how proper names arose in the past. It is rather unusual to find such a name as "atte Wode", i.e. at the wood, so late as 1453 but in the 13th century it was usual. Alternatively he might have been described as Roger de la Wode. Frequently the same man is described as one time as "de", at another as "de la", at still another as "atte" Wode, Hale, Ware etc. But these extra syllables were not as a rule incorporated in the name. Delaware is an exception, but the change from "atte Wode" in 1453 to "Wodde" or "Wood" in 1537 represents the usual process.

This old house at the end of the row has certainly undergone alterations since 1453, but it is likely that many of the old beams remain. These old wooden houses with their enormous beams were practically indestructible except by fire or the deliberate effort of man, i.e. so long as they were inhabited. Sometimes the wood was preserved by the action of open fires in the centre of a hall, from which the smoke ascended to the ceiling and eventually found its way out. Such smoke stained beams may be seen in the roof of the Beecher house already mentioned. It is unfortunate that there seem to be few records of the house of Roger atte Wode, he seems to have been farming Cattesfield, which is behind the house, about 1420.

THE LITTLE HOUSE AT THE CHURCH GATE - By Dr. Gordon Ward

It was no uncommon thing in the old days to find a little house at the Church gate. It seems even to have been the rule. There was a "Simon atte Cherche gate" in Shoreham in 1291, and he was son of "William of the Church". But both of them were laymen, and such houses do not seem to have belonged to the parson or churchwardens. There is a house at the church gate in Shoreham to-day, and another at Otford.

Still more typical of our old cottages is that at Fordwich near Canterbury. But the little house at the Church Gate of Chiddingstone vanished long ago, when it was thought convenient to widen the highway. And with it one supposes there also came to an end the strange provision made by the will of Richard Streatfeild.

This Richard Streatfeild, yeoman and ironmaster of Chiddingstone, was a great man in his day. He was Lord of the Manors of Leighton in Cowden, and of Chiddingstone Cobham. That he was a man of wealth is shown by the fact that there was owing to him at his death no less than £584 - a great sum in those days, for he died in the last years of Queen Elizabeth. We have also an inventory of his possessions, as follows:-

Household Goods	£59. 4. 0
Farm & Cattle	204.11.0
Iron at Pilbeams	506 15 2
Iron at Chiddingstone	723 8 8

Together with the debts owing, these make a total of £2,078. 3. 8 - and it has to be remembered that most of his wealth was probably in land. The little house at the Church Gate was one of the least of his possessions. He left to the Parson & Churchwardens of Chiddingstone and to their successors for ever:-

> "the little house at the church gate for and to the onelye use heerafter expresses That ys to saye for one of the poore of the said parish of Chiddingstone to dwell in for ever, and to be appointed from time to time by the Churchwardens and chiefe of the saide parishe. so as the said dweller in yt shall allwaies paye yeerely vi s viiid for and towards the maintenance and amendinge of the Clocke in the Churche of Chiddingstone aforesaid. Provided allwaies that if the said clocke shall want repairing or emendinge in such sort that it shall not go by the space of one whole year together that then my will and mynde is that the dweller in the said house shall pay the said vis viiid unto my son Henry Streatfeild and his heirs for ever".

It would be interesting to know how this arrangement worked, but it is characteristic of ancient records that they stop short just where one would wish them to continue. The next available record of the little house is in an account book dealing with the sales of wood. Under date 27 March 1690 we read:-

> "The widdow Goulsmith and Eliz. Everest at ye church gate for halfe a hundred of ffaggetts 00. 3. 00
> Ten years later Elizabeth Everest has passed away and we find:-
> "1706. Widdow Clarke and Elizabeth Goldsmyth on the parish account 200 fagots...0.18.0
> Why the price of faggots should have increased by 50% in so short a time is

So Richard Streatfeild has gone, and his remains lie beneath an iron slab in the centre aisle: and his iron works are long closed, and the foundations of the little house are underneath the road. But still there remains a record to tell us of long ago - and still there remains the family of Streatfeild of Chiddingstone.

THE BUILDING OF THE POOR HOUSE ON SOMERDEN GREEN - By Dr. Gordon Ward

Before the year 1601 the poor of Chiddingstone lived in such houses as they could find, and were given relief in money. Thus, in 1598, we find in the Overseer's books:-

To Henry Benet, an impotent aged man	4s 8d
To Widow Everest, sicke and poore	9s 10d

Sometimes the parish had to repair the houses of the old folk, including Widow Everest. In 1600 two such items are mentioned:-

Item, for building old Lambard's house	20s
Item, for setting up of a lodge for the Widow Everest, etc.	5s. 6d

These entries are not spelt in this way in the original books, because the Elizabethans had their own ideas on such matters and wrote "ould lambards howse" and "wyddow Everest" and so on. But it is wearisome to read such spelling nowadays, and all the quotations which follow have been altered accordingly. It was very likely the fact that two houses had to be repaired in 1600 which decided the parish to build a house for the poor. But it was a big expence for the ratepayers, and it seems that some of the money had to be borrowed. A gentleman named John fuller gave ten pounds. This was probably John Fuller of "Chaundelers" (it is called Chantlers on the latest maps) who married Thomasine Holmden of Edenbridge in 1572. Since he had been married nearly 30 years he was probably getting on in age, and he does not seem to have lived to see the Poor House completed. Robert Streatfeild gave three pounds. He was quite a young man living at Chested - which, like Chantlers, is really in Penshurst parish, although it always seems to be part of Chiddingstone for ordinary purposes. Peter Woodgate did not give money, but contributed bricks and probably acted as clerk of the works. He was one of the Overseers who built the Poor House and was an elderly man who had long lived at Truggers, but had possibly by 1601 moved to his newly built house called Stonewall. Finally there was the sum of £3.13.0 from a general assessment of the whole parish ("thouroughe the hole parishe"). The whole amount so collected was £17. 9. 7d. All this is duly set forth in the accounts under the following heading:-

> A note of the receipts and disbursements for the building of one house on Somerden Greene for the relief of the poor of the parish of Chiddingstone in the year 1601 by Peter Woodgate and John Pygott, churchwardens, and Andrew Combridge, William Wallis, Robert Goldsmith, and Matthew Tye, Overseers for the poor in the year aforesaid. Taken and allowed by John Hawkins gent and Thomas Waters,. Churchwardens, and Thomas Willoughby gent, William Dursty, William Beecher and Thomas West, Overseers for the year following, 1602.

After the receipts follow the disbursements. The frame and iron work, that is the wooden frame which was first erected was supplied by Christopher Cooper at a cost of £7. 4. 0. It has lasted well, for it stands firm to-day, much more firm than the woodwork of many modern houses. Christopher Cooper also charged 12d for digging stone, and 35s 10d for "carrying timber, stone and other necessaries towards the building". But Thomas Holland the mason was responsible for squaring up the stone on which the timber frame was set up and his charge was 27s. The great blocks of Kent rag are still in place and do much credit to his memory.

The next person employed was John Harris, who supplied the lathes and plaster. Here is his account:-

Item, to John Harrys for six bundles of rods	12d
Item, for lathes and prigs	18s. 5d
Item, for lathe nails	8s. 2d

"Five hundred of bricks" together with those supplied gratis by Peter Woodgate, completed the material for the house, and there only remained the thatch to cover it. Thomas Bassett did the thatching for 12s, and Christopher Cooper supplied the material for 11s 4d. There were still a few expenses remaining to be met. It was necessary for the parish to have a good title to the land and this involved the payment of one shilling for "the Coppy out of the Court role for the howse", that is, for a copy of the entry on the official records of the manor. There were also "extra-ordinary charges in the law" amounting to the large sum of £3. 4. 0d. Possibly there was some sort of official opening ceremony, or it may have been the laying of the first stone; However that may have been, there is a note that the very moderate sum of 6d was spent on "bread and beer", presumably on some such special occasion.

The final cost of the whole building was £16. 6. 1d, which seems little enough, but as there seem to be practically no payments for labour, it is possible that much of this was provided at the cost of neighbouring farmers and yeomen.

But, after all, some of our old friends did not go and live there; for in 1604 we find:-

Given Father Lambert (buld Lamberd") for relief	5s. 1d
Given Mother Everest for relief	8s. 4d

FORGES IN CHIDDINGSTONE PARISH (From "Wealden Iron" by Ernest Straker)

ASHURST

Par. Ashurst and Chiddingstone, Kent. 3/4 mile north of Church of Kent Water Place-Name "Forge Feilds" (one in each parish), Hammerfield.

John (or Thomas) Stacie, had, in 1574 and in 1588, a forge and furnace at Ashurst. In 1609/10 Thomas Browne, of Ashurst, Co. Kent, gunfounder, deposed that he had delivered to divers persons since 1591 about 463 tons of Iron Ordnance. He was the father of the prominent Stuart gunfounder, John Browne.

The furnace was situated on the Medway, a little way below the corn-mill, which is still at work. At the furnace the bay has entirely disappeared, and the pond silted up to the general level of the flat water-meadows, but no doubt the furnace was somewhere near the present mill-race. There is a little slag in the banks and gateways and larger pieces have been dug.

The bay at the forge, although now much reduced in height, is still visible, but there is no clue as to which side of the stream the building was placed, and only very little cinder.
Note by Dr. G.W.: (This is PILTBEAMES furname of Rd. Streatfeild, 1601).

BOUGH BEECH

Furnace in Hever Parish 1-3/4 miles north of Hever Church.
Place names. Furnace House - Furnace Field - Furnace Bank. Pond Mead.

There appears to be no record of this furnace. It is on the Weald clay, two or three miles to the north of the nearest source of ore on the Hastings sands, but there are several large marlpits near it, which may have contained pockets of ferruginous stone. It is shown on Andrews map, 1769, in a wrong position.

This is the most northerly of the Wealden furnaces.
Note by Dr. G.W.: At Work 1470

Remarks:- Does Andrews Map of 1769 show **BOUGH BEECH** furnace in the wrong place?? Was there not another further down the stream from that described by Mr. Straker, and just inside Chiddingstone Parish? Place-names! On Tithe map of 1841 are four fields running down the stream from the parish boundary to the north as far as the site of **Cransted House - Banky-Field, Great Pond Field, Second Pond Field, Third Pond Field**. At the top of "Banky" and the bottom of "Second Pond" the bays (gigantic ones) still stand! Were not the original Streatfields of the 16th century iron-masters and rich men thanks to their forge or furnace at Cransted?? The stream runs just inside Hever Park boundary, but the bays can be clearly seen from Cransted Lane! The face of nature has been much altered all over Hever Castle Park but these bays were too cumbrous to remove!!

MONUMENTS IN CHURCH (Hasted)

MIDDLE AISLE: Iron Plate & inscription for Richard Streatfeild, died 1601 Stone with brass plate (incription in black letters) for Richard Streatfeild of Cransted, died 1584 A like stone for William, son of Thomas Birchensty, of Sussex, by Anne, coheir of John Fremling, who left two daughters, Anne and Catherine, died 1637.

SOUTH AISLE: Memorial to Anne, widow of John Bassett of Edenbridge, who left 3 daughters and 2 sons, died 1714. Thomas Bassett of Cowden, son of Michael Bassett of Chiddingstone, died 1714.

ON A PILLAR In body of Church, a monument to Henry Streatfeild, gent, late of Great High Street House, the eldest son of Richard Streatfeild of the same, died 1709, and is buried under the iron plate in the middle aisle, erected by Henry his eldest son, and for Sarah his wife, died 1716.

IN THE CHANCEL A memorial for Richard Nurse, rector of Chiddingstone, died June 10, 1765 age 65

Another with a brass plate for Margaret Waters, widow, first married to John Reeves of London, died 1638. - His daughter Frances, was wife of John Seyliard Esq.

On a Pillar a hatchment of Thomas Streatfeild, gent, died 1628.

On the North side: called **Bore's Place Chapel**, against the wall, is a brass plate & incription for Strode Hyde Esq. of Bore Place, Died 1742.

On the south side of the altar, an escutcheon & inscription for John Shefferden, gent., who married Frank, daughter & co-heir of Thomas Streatfeild of this parish, died 1645.

An Altar Tomb for Frances, daughter of John Reeve, married (1) Thomas Streatfeild by whom she had 4 sons. (2) John Seyliard, by whom she had w sons. died 1650.

In the South Chancel a memorial for Thomas Woodgate, citizen & ironmonger of London, son of William Woodgate of this parish, gent, died 1706. He married Susannah, daughter of Thomas Seyliard of Penshurst, by whom had 2 sons & 4 daughters.

Against a pillar a small monument for W. Streatfeild gent., late of Burgherst Court, second son of Henry Streatfeild, gent. of High Street house, died 1724, without issue.

On the same Pillar, an escutcheon, with an inscription for Richard Streatfeild gent., of this parish, died 1676.

The CHAPEL on the North side called Bore's Place Chapel, was built by Sir Robert Read in 1516, and was dedicated to Saint Catherine, in which he founded a chantry by his deed, dated 1517. (This deed is in Augmentations Office Papers).

By virtue of the Commission of Enquiry into the value of Church Livings within the diocese, taken in 1650, by order of the State, issuing out of Chancery, it was returned that in Chiddingstone there was a parsonage, with a house and 5 acres of land, worth £110 per annum, master Thomas Seyliard then incumbent, who received the profits of the parsonage for his salary, and that the late Archbishop of Canterbury was donor thereof.

CHARITIES (Hasted)

Richard Streatfeild Esq. of Chiddingstone gave by will in 1601, a house for poor people to live in, close to the Churchyard, now vested in his heirs, and of the annual produce of £1. 10. 0d, and also lands in this parish, for the use of the poor, vested likewise in heirs, and of the like annual produce.

John Pelsett of Penshurst, gave by will in 1602, lands in Cowden for the use of the poor, vested in Cary Saunders of Croydon, and of the annual value of £1.

Thomas Nevill of London, gave by will, in 1633, lands in Romney Marsh for the like use, vested in the Girdlers Co., and of the annual produce of £1.

Robert Goodhugh of Tonbridge, gave by will in 1662, lands in Tunbridge, for the use of the poor, vested in his heirs, and of the annual produce of £1.

Anne Hyde of London, gave by will in 1637, for the benefit of the poor of Bore's Place, in this parish, vested in her heirs, money to the amount of £5.

Margaret Hyde of Halnaker in Sussex, in 1698, assigned over by indenture, for poor people to dwell in, two tenements in this parish, vested in Henry Streatfeild, of the annual produce of £3.

Henry Streatfeild Esq of Chiddingstone, gave by will, in 1708, lands in this parish, for the use of the poor, vested in his heirs, of the annual produce of £2.

CHURCH PORCH **(Memorials of Old Kent) - Ditchfield & Clench.**

The Porch of Chiddingstone Church is of a much more interesting character (than that of Ashurst), and has been described in Bloxam's **Gothic Ecclesiastical Architecture**. It is a particularly good example of the combination of classic detail with the forms of the departing Gothic style. The arch is semi-circular, with a keystone and capitals to the jambs, all moulded in the renaissance style, but the whole is placed within a square-headed dripstone in the perpendicular manner. The corbels under the springing of the gables are formed into classic trusses: and in the centre of the **gable** is a well-finished sundial, over which is carved the date, 1626. The upper part of the porch is now covered with ivy, so that the gable-cross is hidden, but Bloxam describes it as a "cross of the form heraldically termed **bottonee**, or trefoiled at the extremities, and this cross is of a date coevel with the porch".

PLAN OF CHURCH AND CHURCHYARD

Plan of the Church and Churchyard of **CHIDDINGSTONE** in Kent with an account of what houses the Pews in the Church have belonged to time out of mind and do now belong to as far as is known or can be found out by the most diligent enquiry

And alsoe

An account of what messuage farms & lands etc. have kept and maintained time out of mind and doe now keep & maintain the Marks and Bounds round the Churchyard.

All

Which accounts were taken from the Information of several of the oldest and most knowing of the Inhabitants both men and women, and such others as could give a certain account of the ye same

when

Dr. Edward Tenison was Rector, Richard Chapman and Edward Cronk Churchwardens. Thomas Turner and Mr Robert Streatfeild Overseers of the said Parish.

Anno Domino
1724

Above is a book in Chiddingstone Church in handwriting of Mr. Henry Streatfeild: on front page:- "Presented to Chiddingstone Church by Colonel Sir Henry Streatfeild, G.C.V.O., C.B., C.M.G.

May 1935

Extracts from ARCHAEOLOGIA CANTIANA referring to CHIDDINGSTONE

Vol.1. Letter from Archbishop WARHAM to Lord Rochford & others of the Council 22nd April 1526. (Giving a detailed account of his interview with deputies from the Commons of Kent, who desired to have their loan-money again).

... On Tuesday in Easter-week, last came to my manor at Knowle, a multitude of yeoman of the country to the number of 100... desiring to speak with me.... I offered to see a committee of 5 or 6... When the said 6 persons were come before me.... they said they and their neighbours were poor and needy and desired to have their loan-money... they had persuaded the masses to stay at home and only 2 or 3 from each parish had come.... And at all this communication were present: Sir Edmund Wotton Knt, Master Thomas Willoughby, sergeant-at-the-law, & Richard Clement of the Mote esquire.

At Otford, the 22nd April 1526

Vol.V. p 28 Temp Henry VIII

Two Chief Justices and 1 Chief Baron who afterwards became Chief Justice, flourished in this reign... The second Chief Justice was Sir Robert Read, who resided at Bore Place in Chiddingstone, which he left to his daughter Bridget, who married Sir Thomas Willoughby, a Judge of the Common Pleas in the same reign, who lies buried in the church of this parish

Vol. X p 153. To Knight the Black Prince. Hundred of Somerden

De Johanne de Sepham pro.j.quaterio j.f. quod idem Johannes tenet in Penshurst et CHYDYNGSTONE cum parte in VIELSTONE (Lullingstone) in Hundredum de Coddeshethe. X. s.

Summa X.s. pro.j.quarterio j.f.

Hundred de Maydenstane

De Domino Bartholomeo de Burghersshe pro.j. quarterio f.quod

Radulphus de Dyttone tenuit in Shoforde (alia the Mote) de eodem Archiepicio

X. s.

(page 230)

Robert de Burghersshe was Warden of Cinque Ports 1290, 1297, 1298.

Lord Warden & Constable of Dover Castle in writs relating to Faversham 1300 & 1301.

Vol. XI. p. 398.

Kent Contributors to a loan to the King A.D. 1542.

5. Sir Thomas Willoughby, knight c.li. (£100)

Vol.XII

Holders of Fees in Kent 1253.

Hundred of Somerden.

422. Piscopus Reffensis tenet Manorium de Stanes cum baronia sua.

423. Laurencius de Broc tenet dimid. feod. in Stanes de Willelmo-Butailes.

Hundred of Acstane

443. Reginaldius do Cobham tenet j.quarter. feod. in Orkesdene de Willelmo de Eynesforde

Vol.XIV p.198

Archives of Faversham. A.D. 1301/24

(4) Constabularius. Sir Robert de Burghersshe was Constable of Dover Castle & Warden of the Cinque Ports 1300, 1301, 1302, 1304 & 1305. He is described as Lieutenant of Sir Stephen de Pencester, "Constable & Warden in 1296." He summoned Jeffery Bocton (Boughton) Abbott of Faversham to appear at Shipway and answer for trespasses committed. As the Abbot declined to attend, he was arrested and sent to Dover Castle. The Archbishop thereupon cited the Warden in his Ecclesiastical Court and, on Sir Robert refusing to plead, he was condemned. The King, however, compelled the Archbishop to reverse his sentences.

Bartholomew, son of Sir Robert, lived at Plumstead. He was knighted at the taking of Carlaverock, and was Warden of the Ports under Edward III.

Another Robert de Burghersshe appears to have succeeded Edmund of Woodstock as Warden in 1330.

Vol. XI. p.64

In 1355 John de Cobham appears on the Council, together with **Sir Reginald de Cobham of Sterborough**, for debate on the proprietary of submitting the disputes with France to the arbitration of the Pope. ...The virtue of hospitality is often spoken of on monuments and on that of Sir Reginald de Cobham, 1402, **second Baron Cobham of Sterborough**, in Lingfield Church, we find it expressed by "dapsilis in mensis". in 1389, Lord Cobham, about to die without a direct heir, executed an elaborate deed of entail which included several members of the family. In the following year a storm burst upon him..... Lord Cobham fleeing to Charterhouse Monastery, renounced the world. But he was extradited and committed to the Tower. He was condemned to be hanged, drawn and quartered, and all estates confiscated, but converted to banishment to Jersey. **Two** Lords Cobham were in exile at the same time, for **Sir Reginald and Lord of Sterborough**, was included in the condemnation. Henry IV started from Vannes in Brittany (north of Loire mouth) and landed in Yorkshire, and among the few knights in his train was **Sir Reginald Cobham.** There followed the surrender of Richard II's crown.

Vol.XIII p.11 Notes on Kentish Earthworks

The following I have left for future examination:
Camp Hill, near Penshurst (close to Chiddingstone Causeway which is a suggestive name).
Fines 16th & 17th Edward II (1324/25)

Vol. XV No **748**. At York - between John **Itum** & Alice his wife, pl and Nicholas de hanley, **defts**, of 2 messuages 4 tofts, 2 mills, 400 acres land, 8 acres meadow, 40 acres wood, and 10 sh. rent, with appurts., in Pencestre, **Chidyngston**, Couden, and La Lye. Right of Nicholas, who, for the admission, grants to John & Alice for their lives, with remainder after their deaths to Robert, son of Philip de Coleuill (Coleville) and to the heirs of his body: but, if none, the after the death of Robert to remain to the right heirs of the aforesaid John.

18th Edward II - 1326 - At Westminster - between **THOMAS de COBEHAM** & Idonea his wife (by William de Passeleye in place of Idonea) pltfs. O and Henry de Gerounde, deft., of 1 messuage, 1 toft, 2 mills, 1 carucate & 80 acres of land, 180 acres pasture, and 40 sh. rent, with appurts., in Penesherst, **Chydyngeston**, Halghestowe, and in the Vill of All Saints in Hoo. Right of Henry, who, for the admission, grants to Thomas and Idonea, and to the heirs of the body of Thomas: but if none, then after the deaths of Thomas and Idonea to remain to William de Passelete and to the heirs of his body, but if none, then after his death to remain to John his brother and to the heirs of his body: but if none, then after the death of John, to remain to the right heirs of the aforesaid Thomas.

Vol.XV **A Kentish Roll of Arms - A.D. 1317/27.**
COBEHAM de **STERBOROUGH** - On a chevron 3 estocles.
Sir Reginald de Cobham, who died 1257, bore 3 estocles, or mullets, on a chevron, as did his nephew, Sir Regional of Sterborough.

Vol XVI **p.227 PECHE** of Lullingstone. **John Pecche** was a citizen, clothier, and alderman of London who, in the year 1354, obtained from **Bartholomew, Lord Burghersh,** - by purchase probably - the extensive manor of Malorees, which runs into 4 parishes of Willesden, Paddington, Chelsea & Fulham.
p.37

STAFFORD commanded the van in the great English victory at Cressy. It is to him and Sir **Reginald Cobham** that history owes the record of the slain, which was returned by them and 3 heralds who searched the field, as:

11 great princes
80 bannerets
1200 Knights
and over 30,000 men of all arms

Vol.XVIII **p.17 KENTISH ADMINISTRATIONS. 1564/67**

No. 121. PIGOTT, William, of Chydingstone deceased, granted to his brother John, 3rd June 1567.

Vol. XX **p.6 KENTISH ADMINISTRATIONS, CHIDDINGSTONE PARISH**

Cumbridge John	Andrew, his brother	1611
Ashdowne John	Joan, widow	1612
Beecher Henry	Joan, widow	1612
Everest Robert	Bennette, widow	1612
Faierbrother Joan (widow)	Thomas, son	1614
Ashdowne John	John & Matthew sons Joan widow being dead)	1617
Hawkins John	Agnes, widow	1619
Wells Walter	Silvester, widow	1619
Brett Thomas	Edward Lant, kinsman	1627
Maninge George	Elizabeth, mother	1630
Morrice John	Mary, widow	1638
Walters Elizabeth (widow)	John Reeve, son	1639
Reeve William	Margaret, widow	1647
Streatfeild Henry	Susan, widow	1647
Hollumby **alias** Nicholas, Silvester.	Dorothy Hollumby **alias** Nicolas, widow.	1648
Streatfeild Susanna	Richard & Stephen, sons Thomas Slayter & Anne his wife, daughter	1648

Vol. XX **p.165 Kent Fines Temp Edward III**

At Westminster, between William Moraunt pltf. & William Herleston, dft, of 5/8 rent withappurts. in Chidynggeston. William H. admits it to be the right of William M. and his heirs, and receives 40 sh. for the concession.

Vol XX **p.268**

John Pelset (who left bequests to the poor of several Kentish parishes) in described in his will of Feb. 1558 as "servant & bailey to the Rt. hon. the Lord Sydney".

Vol XXI **p.293 Parish Registers of Edenbridge**
sir John **Seyliard**, Barronett, of chiddingstone was buried ye 19th day of December 1667.

Vol. XXII **p.112**
The family of Hyde (see elsewhere)

Vol. XXIII **p.137 CHIDDINGSTON,**

Dedication our lady	Sep. in cancello beato Marie de Chedingstone coram summo altare John Woode, rector, 1486 (3 Milles)
Lights etc. St.John Baptist	Sep. in corpore ecclesiae beate Marie Verginis de Chedingstone in australi parte inter altare taneti Johannis Baptiste et hostium ejusdem ecclesiae. John Asshedown, yoman 1488 (12 Milles)
St.Katherine	To be buried in the parish church afore the aulter ther of St. Kateryne by Isabell late my wife. John Alfeight (Alphew)

Vol. XXIV. **p.198**
Thomas Willoughby letters to Sir Francis Walsingham - Willoughby cousin to Lord Cobham

Extra Vol. 1907p.11 - Testamenta Cantiana

Corpus meum ad speliendum in cancello Beate Marie de Chedingstone coram summo altare ita quod pedes mei attingant ad medium altaris predicti. Ad usum ejusdem ecclesie duos libros vocatos legents ac unum pax argenti et unum calicem argenti.
John Woode, rector 1486. Proved 1487 (P.C.C. 3, Milles)

To the parish church of Chedingstone a sewte of vestments of whyte damaske. To Robard Reed my chales of sylver and ouergilt w. the patent and pax brede of siluer and ouergilt of the cone syde.

John Alphey, 1488 (P.C.C. 18 Milles)

To the reparation of the parish church of Chedyngston and for a grayle to be bought for the same church to the helpe of diuine service there, tenne marks. (He wished to be buried at Charterhouse, and mentions "my place of the Bore at Chiddingstone) Sir Robert Rede, knight, 1518. (P.C.C. 13, Ayloffe)

Vol..XXVIII **p.105**.....After the death of Sir Geoffrey Boleyn, Earl of Wiltshire.... The Ormonde property, which was not limited in **tail male**, descended in due course of law to Mary Boleyn, and so did property which the late Earl had himself acquired, as for example the Manor of Henden, which adjoined Hever, and which consisted of portions of the parishes of Hever, Brasted & Chiddingstone. **Henden** was however exchanged in 1541 by Mary Boleyn with the King for a manor in Yorkshire.

Patent Rolls of 1540 mention a grant by the King to "Mary Boleyn, daughter and heir of Thomas, Earl of Wilts, of all his lands in Hever". This is perplexing in as much as the King in the same year granted Hever to Anne of Cleves. But there were certain lands in Hever, as there were also in Brasted, which though detached from Henden Manor, formed pat of it, and should properly have passed with it. The Patent Rolls refer to these **lands in Hever**, and not to the **Manor of Hever**, which, if conveyed, would have been so described.

Vol. XXXI p. 197. Chyddingstone.

Also we present that John Ashdowne, yeoman. late of Chiddingstone in the sayd countie of Kent by his last will bering date the 22 daye of August 1590 **did** give the sum of iii li. vi. s viii d issuing out of one tenement and certayne lands containing by estimation xii acres in Chiddingstone aforesaid now in the occupation of William ffathers to be dystrybuted and payd to pore maydens maryages of Chiddingstone by the dyscression of Henrye Pygot and Richard Stretfeld his overseers of his will which said overseers have receved that sayd iiili vis viiid and also dystrybuted it according to the sayd will..

He also left to Ann his wife one tenement and lands in Chiddingstone during her widowhood, she paying a sum to the overseers, who should repair the tenement with it and what was over to the poor etc. etc.

Also refers to Anne Ashdowne & John Ashdowne.

Vol.XXXVIII p.157

It is well-known that Joan, wife of John de Mohun, Lord of Dunster, and daughter of Bartholomew, Lord of Burghersth, was the founder of a chantry at the altar of St. mary Undercroft, Canterbury Cathedral in the year 1396, at which date her tomb and effigy were already in the place they still occupy, though she did not die until 1404; but that she had a much earlier connection with this part of the Church has hitherto escaped notice.

p.170. Bartholomew, Lord Burghersh, a brother of Lady Joan, was in the retinue of Prince Edward at Crecy & Poitiers. He died in 1369 and was buried in the Lady Chapel of Walsingham Abbey. His daughter Elizabeth married Edward Lord Despenser.

Vol XL p.100

No. 126 Robert Rede. Hasted ascribes to Sir Robert Rede of Chedingstone, Chief Justice Common Pleas (1507) the arms..gu:. on a fess wavy... three cock pheasants.

p.102 No. 147. Sir Regional Cobham GU ON A CHEVRON OR 3 ESTOILES SA. The arms of de Cobham, Baron of Starborough. Borne by Sir Reginald de Cobham K.G. (Baron 1342) at the 2nd Dunstable Tournament.

Vol. XXXI p.171

The **Hundred of Somerden** is attended by tything men from \the tythings of boroughs of Stanford (Principally in Edenbridge), Cowden, Chiddingstone, Frinden Borough, (in Chiddingstone) and Penshurst.

By 1670 Penshurst has become subdivided into the Boroughs of Penshurst Town & Penshurst Upland, and Groombridge appears. Sherborne Borough **alias** Hallborough (in Penshurst) and **Kingsborough** (in Chiddingstone) also appear as separate boroughs with separate courts leet or views of frankpledge.

The whole of the above names are still found as land tax parishes, except that Frindsborough and Chiddingstone appear as Chiddingstone North and Chiddingstone South. Charcott (in or near Leigh) now appears as a land tax parish, though not as a borough represented at the Somerden Hundred Court. And excepting the land tax parishes of Hallborough and Groombridge (now in the Tonbridge Land Tax Division) the whole of the hundreds of Westerham, Somerden and Codsheath with Kemsing and Seal, are now grouped together as the Sevenoaks land tax division.,

p.173. The Sundridge of Domesday is unique. The court rolls extant make it quite clear that the Manor of Sundridge not only comprised the whole of the parish of that name, but the bulk of the present parish of Chiddingstone, a portion of Hever, and possibly of other parishes; but some portion of Chiddingstone, as well as of the adjoining parishes, may well have represented the Wealden portion of other upland manors.

Broxham, in Edenbridge, was a severed portion of the upland manor of Bromley, extending into Westerham, Hever and Chiddingstone.

OFFICIALS OF CHIDDINGSTONE PARISH THROUGH THE AGES

DATE	CHURCH WARDENS	OVERSEERS
1598	Andrew ? Wm. Everest	John Ashdowne: Thos. Waters: John Pigot
1599	Richard Streatfeild: Bartholomew Mose	Wm.Gibson, gent: J. Woodgate: J. Nicholas. H. Piggot
1600	J. Ashdowne : George Beecher	J. Ashdowne Jr: Peter Woodgate: R. Homes: E. Whash
1601	Peter Woodgate, J. Pygott	A. Combridge: M. Tye: Robert Goldsmith: Wm Wallis
1602	John Hawkins, gent: Thos. Waters	Thos. Willoughby, Wm.Bursty, W. Beecher
1603	Robert Everest: Henry Piggott	John Sydley gent: Thos. Everest, T. Woodgate
1604	J. Ashdowne: Richard Homes.	R. Ashdowne: J. Medhurst, George Beecher, R. Sevenoc
1605	Thos. Bassett, E. Pullinger	Bart. Moore, Water Woodgate, P. WQells, E. Goldsmith
1606	Drewe Wood, Richard Jessop	Thos. Wickenden, Wm. Woodgate, Water Bassett, - Everest
1607	Wm. Birstye, Robert Goldsmith	W. Webster, J. Day, Richard Goldsmith, G. Beckett
1608	Gerrard Gattland, William Woodgate	W. Taylor, G. Hollamby, S. Wells, Wm. Beach
1609	Richard Goldsmith, Walter Woodgate	R. Nicholas, T. Stace, H. Beecher, T. Saunder
1610	John Medhurst, R. Hollamby	H. Cruttenden, M. Overy, J. Speed, H. Moldye
1611	Gilbert Beckett, Edward Goldsmith	E. Everist, P. Everist, J. Pyggott jun., N. Purcel
1612	Wm. Taylor, Martyn Overy	F. Hurley, Walter Tye, H. Ashdowne, J. Smith
1613	Henry Streatfeild, J. Nicholas	Edmund Beecher Humfry Marshall, J. Carter, F. Pelling
1614	Edward Everist; John Speed	H. Ashdowne; J. Stephens, Gyles Everist, G. Wood
1615	John Hawkens; T. Everist	Samuel Godin, G. Wells, W. Stanfoord, T. Hollamby
1616	John Hawkens; Thomas Brett	J. Hollambie Jr., T. Everist, H. Care, R. Ashdowne
1617	Peter Everist, J. Daye	Jeromye Heaver, S. Bourne, J. Pollenger, J Care
1618	Walter Tye, John Pygott	J. Bassett , R. Reade, T. Huddlow, Westerman
1619	R. Ashdowne; Samuell Godden	G. Beckett, W. Fathers, W. Hollamby
1620	Henry Streatfeild, R. Hollambie	R. Beacher, G. Goldsmith, T. Winter, T. Chapman
1621	Wm. Woodgate, George Beecher	J. Beacher, R. Moare, T. Levitt, J. Bassett
1622	Walter Woodgate, Richard Beecher	T. Ashdowne, W. Wickenden, H. Cosen, T.Moure
1623	William Birstye, J. Hollamby	W. Everist, R. Farrington, W. Wallis, R. Smale
1624	J. Beecher, Henry Care	N. Piggott, Robert Stuberfeild, J. Pullinger, M. Winter
1625	Peter Everist, J. Ashdowne	E. Wickenden, Penticost Bassett, R. Beecher
1626	W. Woodgate sn. R. Hollamby	J. Savadge, W. Woodgate jun. R. Tydman, A. Wood
1627	Wm. Woodgate, Richard Hollamby	J. Savadge, A. Medhurst, J. Speed, T. Cotty
1628	R. Ashdowne; George Beecher	M. Rivers, T. Copper, H. Ashdowne, J. Piggott
1629	W. Everist; W. Wallis	W. Tye, J. Fremling, W.Chary, R. Goodhee
1630	R. Ashdowne, Clement Basdow	J. Medhurst, E. Young, R. Moare, T. Saunder
1631	J. Fremlyn, J. Savadge	C. Basden, R. Ashdowne, N. Cruttfield, R. Saunder
1632	Robert Smale, John Care	R. Farrington, R. Wanmore, Walter Woodgate, J. Hoad

REFERENCES TO THE PLAN OF THE CHURCH OF CHIDDINGSTONE IN KENT, BEING AN ACCOUNT OF THE PEWS IN THE SAID CHURCH AND WHAT HOUSES THEY BELONG TO, SO FAR AS IS KNOWN OR CAN BE FOUND OUT BY THE INFORMATION OF SEVERAL OF THE OLDEST INHABITANTS & OTHERS, BOTH MEN AND WOMEN, TAKEN IN THE YEARE 1724.

SOUTH SIDE OF PARISH NAMES OF HOUSES	Landlords	Tennants	Men's Seats	Women's Seats	Servants' Seats Men	Servants' Seats Women
High Street House	Mr Henry Streatfeild	Himself	9	9	11	10
Lockskinners	"	Late James Saxby	34	42	-	-
Highfield House	"	John Small	38	59		
Tower Hill	"	John Wells	31	60		
Withers (**Hill Hoath House**)	"	Knight & Clarke	26	48		
Heldhouse (**House at Hill Hoath**)	"	Sam Scott	27	60		
Chiddingstone Shop	"	Thomas Smith	22	44	53	
Tyhaw	"	George Chapman	31	48		
Gilwins (**Gillwins**)	"	Wm. Halcomb	37	45		
Burgherst Court	Mr Wm. Streatfeild	Himself	12	12	13	
Hunts	"	Richard Chapman	20	41		
House in the Town	Mr Thos. Streatfeild	Himself	14	14	16	15
Chiddingstone **Mill House**	Mr Robert Streatfeild	John Durrant	37	47		
A little House neare the Mill (**Old Mill House**)	"	John Baker	-	-		
New Tye	Mr Wm. Streatfeild	Widow Woodgate	25	28		
Brookers	"	Himself	24	28		
Skipreed	"	John Grove	29	47		
Oakenden	Mr Richard Streatfeild	John King	38	47		
Stone Wall	Mr John Woodgate	Mr William Woodgate	20	42		
House near Stone Wall	"	Alex Kingswood	26	28		
" " " "	"	John Bassett	-	-		
Maynards near Stone Wall	"	Late Henry Care	-	-		
Frienden (FFrienden)	The Heirs of Mr Thos. Woodgate	John Head	37	42		
Knights	Mr John Woodgate	J. Kingswood Jnr	-	-		
Gillridge (Gilridge)	Mr Stephen Woodgate	John Ingram	35	30		
A House in the Towne	"	Wm. Pope & Thos. Egleton	29	28		
Trugers	Heirs of Mr Thos. Woodgate	Wm. Hoath	21	43		
Geers (**Gears**)	"	Richard Care	23	49		
A House at Renleigh's Hoath	"	John Pinn & Widow Egleton	31	32		
Batts (Great Batts)	John Ashdowne	Thomas Turner	34	44		

SOUTH SIDE OF PARISH NAMES OF HOUSES	Landlords	Tennants	Men's Seats	Women's Seats	Servants' Seats Men	Women
Skinners	Henry Pigott	Himself	24	44		
A House near Skinners	"	Thos. Cooper	27	-		
Chestnut Tree (**Chestnut**)	John Ashdowne	Himself	36	28		
Renleighs Manor House	Earle of Leicester	J. Kingswood Senr.	39	30		
Watstock (**Hobshill House**)	Mr John Seyliard	John Ffloyd	19	28		
House at Hobb's Hill	Mathew Everest	Himself	25	30		
Bassetts Mill (**House**)	Michaell Bassett	John Peerless	22	43		
Prankham (sic)	"	Henry Piggott Junr.	35	45		
Pilbeames (**Pillbeames**)	Edmund Medherst	Himself	24	46		
A House in Bradney Lane	"	Richard King	31	-		
Lower Buckherst	John Turner	Jeremiah Dives	38	**49**		
A House near Lew Cross	John Constable	John Merchant & Wm. Best	21	28		
Cobham Mannor House	Richard Leggatt	John Longherst & Wm. Cronke	25	59		
The Rock House (The Five Bells)	Thomas Weller	Himself	23	45		
Willetts at Hill Hoath **House at Hill Hoath**	The heirs of William Willett	John Daniell	31	59		
The Smith's Forge or Butt House	John Cronke	Robert Palmer	38	46		
Sliders Bridge	Richard Chapman	Joseph Smith	21			
(**Stakehallyes at Cares Corner**)	Henry Cox	Himself	39			
A House by Cares Corner	Henry Cox & Thos. Butcher	John Martin & Thos. Butcher	26	**28** **30**		
A House near Oakenden	John Parker	William Medherst	38	47		
Pottings - **Potings**	Daniell Williams	Edward Monk	-	-		
A House at Renleighs Hoath	John Bywood	Widdow Harrison	39	32		
Lew Cross	John Tye	Himself	29	32		
A House at Cares Corner	- Medherst	John Cripps & Thomas Eagleton	-	-		
A House near Trugers	John Cronke (**Wheelwright**)	Himself	-	-		
A House at Hilhoath	Thomas Winter	Himself	-	-		
A House near Ffinch Green	Robert Curd	-	-	-		

NORTH SIDE OF PARISH NAMES OF HOUSES	Landlords	Tennants	Men's Seats	Women's Seats	Servants' Seats Men	Servants' Seats Women
(Boar Place) **Bore Place**	Mr John Hyde	John Wickenden	8	8	8	8
A House in Boar Place Yard	"	John Day	34	42		
Sharps Place	"	John Boakes	19	17		
(Ivye House) **Ivy House**	"	Edward Cronke	34	45		
(Milbrook House) **Millbrooke House**	"	William Medhurst	22	44		
Bushes	"	Thomas Boakes	27	47		
(Baylys) **Baileys**	"	Late John Speed	19	43		
Boar Place Mill **(house)**	"	Richard Nye	-	-		
Swingate House	"	Widdow Denton	-	-		
Somerden **Green** House	Mr Henry Streatfeild	George Beaven	36	45		
(A House at Somerden Green) **Brookers**	Mr William Streatfeild	Himself	36	42		
(Salmons) **Hilders**	Mr Thomas Streatfeild	Widow Edward Everest	35	43		
(Danes) **House near Hilders**	"	Late Edward Monk	27	-		
(Hamerhaw0 **Allens**	"	John Smith	-	-		
A House near Somerden Green	Mr Stephen Woodgate	Robert Hollamby	-	-		
Cransted **House**	Sir William Humphreys Bart	Edward Humphrey & Wm. Holder	21	46		
(A House at Bowbeech)	Mr John Seyliard	William Edlow	35	41		
A House near Bowbeech Green	Mr Thomas Pettey (?)	Robert Abraham	35	**42**		
A House near Bowbeech Green	Mr William Heath	John Lamb	36	43		
Polbrooks	"	John Smith & widdow Beecher	29	43		
Kiln House	Mr Thomas Spence	J. Jacob & J. Debton	-	-		
(Dickers at Bowbeech Green)	John Cronke carpenter	Himself carpenter	23	45		
House at Bowbeech						
Sheffields **(at Bowbeech Green)**	"	William Winter	39	30		
Old Sheffields	"	John Jessup	-	-		
Clinton Brook	"	William Cackett	-	-		
(A small House at Bowbeech Green)	"	Jeremiah Collier	-	-		
(A House at Bowbeech Green)	Widdow Medherst	Herself	24	46		
"	John Piggott	Widdow Tye	27	30		
"	"	Thomas Kingswood	-	-		
The Chequer (at Bowbeech)	William Lee	Himself	29	30		
(Hilders) **House at Hilders**	John Cole	"	25	**45**		
Stonelake	Richard Hayward	Thomas Wallis	37	28		
A Little House neare Stonelake Lane	"	William Fullman	-	-		
	Richard Round	Thomas Smither	24	28		
(Coles) **Coals**	John Hollamby	Himself	19	46		
Hail House	Thomas Burgess	**(Widdow Findall) Spencer**	36			

NORTH SIDE OF PARISH NAMES OF HOUSES	Landlords	Tennants	Men's Seats	Women's Seats	Servants' Seats Men	 Women
Great Brownings	William Jewell	William Mugridge	36	46		
Little Brownings	Widdow Beecher	Widdow Sales	-	44		
(A House in Hail Lane)	Richard Walker	Edward Holms	36	-		
"	William Cowlard	Fortunatus Terry	29	-		
Great (Ffranks) **Funks**	Widdow Green	George Pinn	-	44		
Bassetts	John Turner	John Parsons	-	-		
(A House neare Bassetts)	Thomas Gilbert	Himself	-	-		
Blackhouse	(John Humfrys) **John Turner**	Edward Palmer	-	-		
(**A House near Sedcubs**)	Widdow Swaysland	Robert Sales	-	-		
(Causeway House) **Causeway House**	Widdow of Thos.) Shoobridge)	Humfry Medherst	**31**	32		
(A House near the Causway)	Widdow Turner	Herself	-	-		
"	Henry Mecomb	Henry Upton	-	-		
A House neare Cowpers Corner	Mr Tatton	Edward Tooth	-	-		
"	Thomas Weller	Thomas Merchant	40	**49**		
"	John Ffloyd	John Cooper:John Nye	-	-		
(A House near Winkherst Green)	George Allen	James Lee	-	-		
(A House near Hail Lane)	John Goldsmith	William Ashdowne	-	-		
Pudding Millhouse	"	Richard Best	-	-		
A House near Broxham Pound	John Moyce	George Easted	-	-		
Churchwardens	Churchwardens	Churchwardens	65			
House at Cooper's Corner	**Trustees for**	**Thomas Lee ye poor**				

EMBOLDENED are corrections from an M.S. list inset in this book. The list is not in the hand of Mr Henry Streatfeild, with the exception of 2 additions to list.

References to the 1724 Plan of the Church, showing the number of Houses whose occupiers have a right to each pew in the Church.

1.	The Communion Table
2.	The ffont
3,4	The Reading Desk & Pulpitt
5.	1 The Parish Clerk's Seat
69,6,7	1 The Parsonage House
8.	1 Boar Place
9,10,11	1 High Street House
12,13	1 Burgherst Court
14,15,16	1 Mr. Thomas. Streatfeild's House in the Towne
17.18	1 Sharp's Place
19	4 Watstock, Sharp's Place, Baylys, Coles
20	2 Hunts & Stonewall
21	4 Trugers, John Constables house near Lew Cross, Slider's Bridge,Cransted
22	3 Chiddingstone Shop, Bassett's Millhouse, Milbrook
23	3 Geers, Rockhouse, John Cronk's house at Bowbeech Green
24	5 Brookers, Skinners, Pilbeams, Widow Medherst' House at Bowbeech Green & Camphill
25	4 New Tye, Cobham Manor, Hobshill, Hilders.
26	3 Withers, Mr John Woodgate's House near Stonewall, and Henry Cox's and Thos. Butchers house at Cares Corner
27	5 Heldhouse, Henry Piggott's house near Skinners, Bushes, Danes, & John Piggott's house at Bowbeech Green.
28	8 New Tye, Brookers, Mr. Stephen Woodgate's house in the Towne, Chesnut Tree, Watstock, John Constable's house near Lew Cross, Stonelake & Camphill
29	6 Skipreed, Mr Stephen Woodgate's house in the Towne, Lew Cross, Polbrooks, The Cheque at Bowbeech & Wm. Cowlard's house in Hail Lane.
30	8 Gilridge, Renleighs Mannor House, Hobshill House, Henry cox & Thomas Butcher's house at the corner, Sheffield, John Piggott's house at Bowbeech Green, the Chequer at Bowbeech.
31	6 Tower Hill House, Tyhaw, the heirs of Thos. Woodgate's house at Renleighs Hoath, Willett's at Hillhoath, Causeway House. Edmond Medherst's house in Bradney Lane.
32	4 The heirs of Thos. Woodgate's house at Renleighs Hoath, John Bywoods house at Renleighs Hoath, Lewcross & Causeway House.
33	
34	4 Lockskinners, Batts, Mr. John Hyde's house in Bore Place yard Ivye House.
35	5 Gilridge, Prankham, Salmons, Mr. John Seyliard's House at Bow Beech, Wm. Heath's house at Bowbeech Green.

36 7 Chestnut Tree, Somerden Ho, Mr Wm Streatfeild's House at Somerden Green, Mr Thos Petley's Ho, near Bowbeech Green. Hail Ho. Great Brownings, Richard Walker's House in Hail Lane

37 4 Gilwins, Chiddingstone Millhouse, Frienden, Stonelake

38 5 Highfields Ho, Oakenden, Lower Buckhurst, Smith's Forge House, John Parker's House near Oakenden

39 4 Renleighs Manor House, Henry Cox's Ho. at Cares Corner, John Bywoods ho, at Renleighs Heath, Sheffields at Bowbeech Green.

40 1 Thos. Wellers house near Coopers Corner

41 2 Hunts, Mr John Seyliard's House at Bowbeech

42 6 Lockskinners, Stonewall, Frienden, Mr. John Hyde's Ho, in Bore Place Yard, Mr. Wm. Streatfeild's Ho, Nr. Somerden Green, Mr. Wm. Heath's House at Bowbeech Green

43 6 Trugers, Bassetts Millhouse, Baylys, Salmons, Mr. Wm Heath's House atBowbeech Green, Polbrooks

44 6 Chiddingstone Shop, Batts, Skinners, Milbrook Ho. Little Brownings & Great Franks

45 Gilwins, Prankham, Ivye Ho., Somerden Ho, John Cronke's House at Bowbeech Green, Hilders, Rockhouse

46 6 Pilbeams, Smiths Forge Ho, Cransted, Widdow Medherst Ho. at Bowbeech Green, Coles, Great Brownings

47 5 Chiddingstone Mill Ho, Skipreed, Oakenden, John Parkers Ho, near Oakenden, Bushes.

48 2 Withers, Tyhaw

49 3 Geers, Lower Buckhurst, Thos.Wellers House, Nr Coopers Corner

53 3 Lockskinners, Chiddingstone Shop, Stonewall

59 3 Highfield, Cobham Manor House, Willetts at Hillhoath

2 Tower Hill, Held House, 65 Churchwardens Seat 66 The Vestry

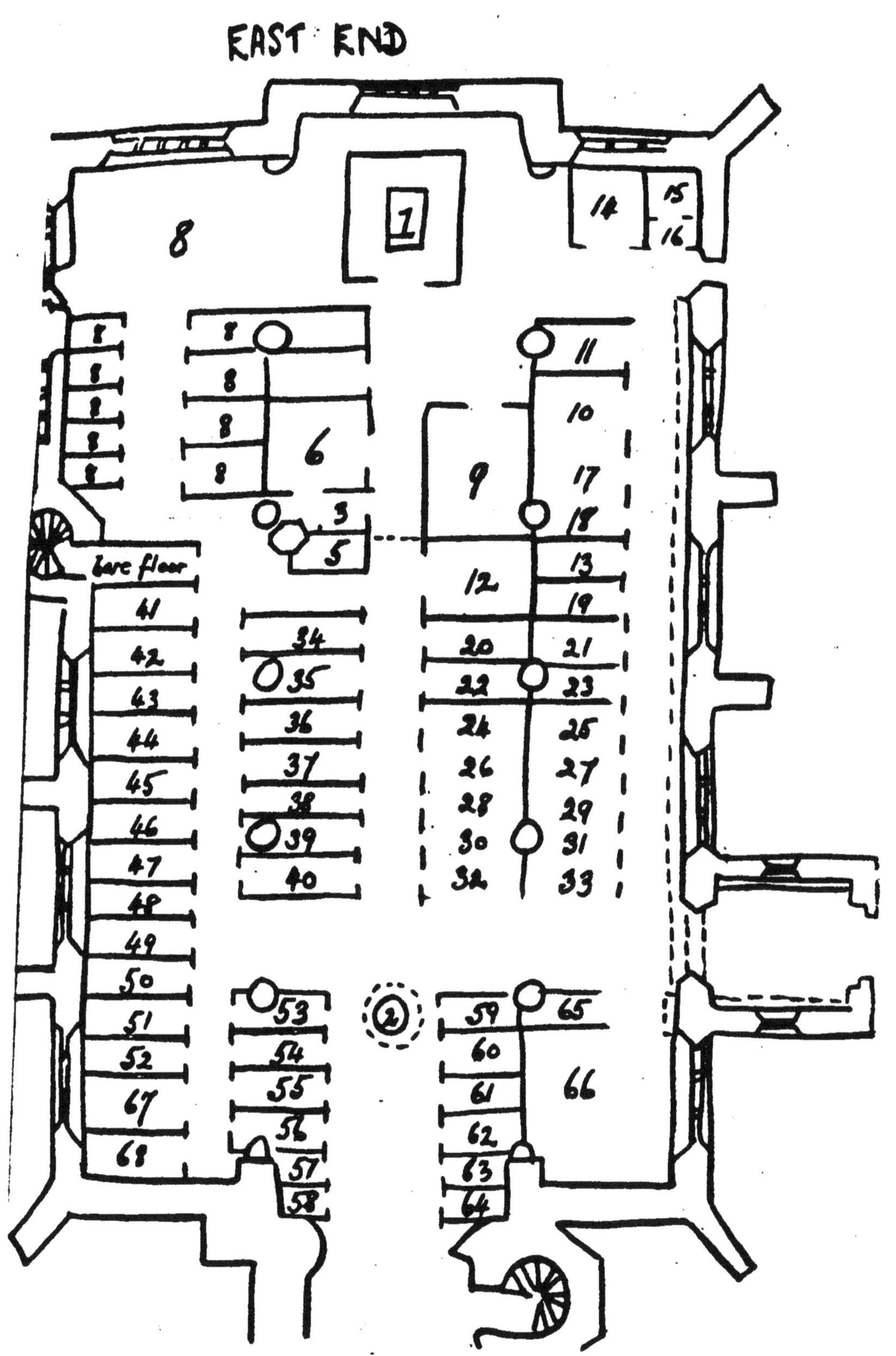
EAST END
1
2
3
5
6
8
9
10
11
12
13
14
15
16
17
18
19
20
21
22
23
24
25
26
27
28
29
30
31
32
33
34
35
36
37
38
39
40
bare floor
41
42
43
44
45
46
47
48
49
50
51
52
53
54
55
56
57
58
59
60
61
62
63
64
65
66
67
68

MAINTENANCE OF CHURCHYARD BOUNDARIES IN 1724

These Boundaries were marked, and between, each householder had to keep the Boundary in order

Mark No.	ft	in	Owner	Name of Farm	Occupiers
1			Parish	A tenement belonging to Parish	
2			A cage, and house for the stocks		
3			A hedge on north side maintained by Rector		
4			Two walls on south side, by all the houses and lands on the south side of the river (except Mr. Seyliard's WATSTOCK FARM)		
5	3	6	Mr. John Seyliard	Watstock	John Ffloyd

THE EAST END OF THE CHURCHYARD

Mark No.	ft	in	Owner	Name of Farm	Occupiers
6	10	-	John Hyde	Sharpes Place	John Boakes
7	10	-	"	Boar Place Farm	John Day
8	13	-	"	Boar Place Farm	John Wickenham
9	10	-	"	Milbrook Farm	Wm. Medherst
10	4	-	Thos. Burges	Hail Farme	Late widow Findall
11	2	6	Widow T. Shoobridge	Causway Farm	Humfry Medherst
12	10	6	J. Hollamby	Cles Farm	Himself
13	8	6	J. Goldsmith Hollamby	Farm nr Hail Lane	W.Ashdowne & J.
			Widow Green	Great Franks Farm	Geo. Pinn
			Widow Swayland farm nr. Sedcubs		Robert Sales
14	11	9	William Jewell	Great Brownings	William Mugridge
			J. Turner	Mountjoys	Himself
			J. Turner	Bassetts Farm	J. Parson & Himself
15	5	-	William Heath Beecher	Polbrooks	J. Smither, widow & himself
16	4	3	William Cowlard	Farm in Hail Lane	Fortunatus Terry & Edward Shoobridge
17	4	6	Widdow Beecher	Little Browning Farm in Hail Lane	Widow Sale
18	8	-	Henry Streatfeild Streatfield	Somerden Farm	Geo.Brown & Wm
19	6	9	Richard Hayward	Stonelake	Thomas Wallis
20	6	-	John Hyde	Bushes	Thomas Boakes
21	9	-	John Hyde	Ivyhouse Farm	Edward Cronke

MAINTENANCE OF CHURCHYARD BOUNDARIES IN 1724 (cont'd)

THE WEST END OF THE CHURCHYARD

22	8	6	Thomas Spence	Kiln Farm	John Jacob, John
			Wm. Lee	house and land called The Chequer	Denton & John Reeve
				Nr. Bowbeech	himself
			J. Humfry	Blackhouse in Hail Lane	Edward Palmer & John Turner
23	9	3	Mr. Tatton	Nr. Coopers Corner	E. Tooth, J. Cranwell
			Thos. Weller	Farm " "	T.Marchant & self
24	6	6	Heirs of Richard Goodhugh	Camphill	T.Smithers J Ashdowne
25	9	9	Thomas Petley T.Streatfeild	Nr.Bowbeech	R.Abraham:
			Widow Danes	farm	late Edward Monke
		(? last should be "Mr.Thomas Streatfeild's widow Danes farme")			
26	3	3	Widow Medherst	at Bowbeech Green	Herself
27	8	6	John Cronke	Bowbeech Green	Himself
			" "	Sheffield's Farm	late John Speed's now Wm. Winter & self
			John Coles	Hilders Farm	Himself
28	7	3	John Piggott	2 farms at Bowbeech Green	Widow Tye
29	10	-	Thomas Streatfeild's Widow	Salmons (?Hilders)	Edward Everest
			Williams Streatfeild	Nr. Somerden	Himself
30	7	9	John Seyliard Ffloyd	at Bowbeech	Wm. Edlow, John
31	11	3	William Heath at	Bowbeech Green	J. Lamb & Himself
32	9	9	Sir William Humfry Holder	Cransted	Edward Humfry, Wm & Robert Streatfeild
33	7	0	John Hyde	Baylys	Late in occupation John Speed
34	10	6	All the parish		
35	6	-	Richard Walker	Farm in Hail Lane	Edward Holms

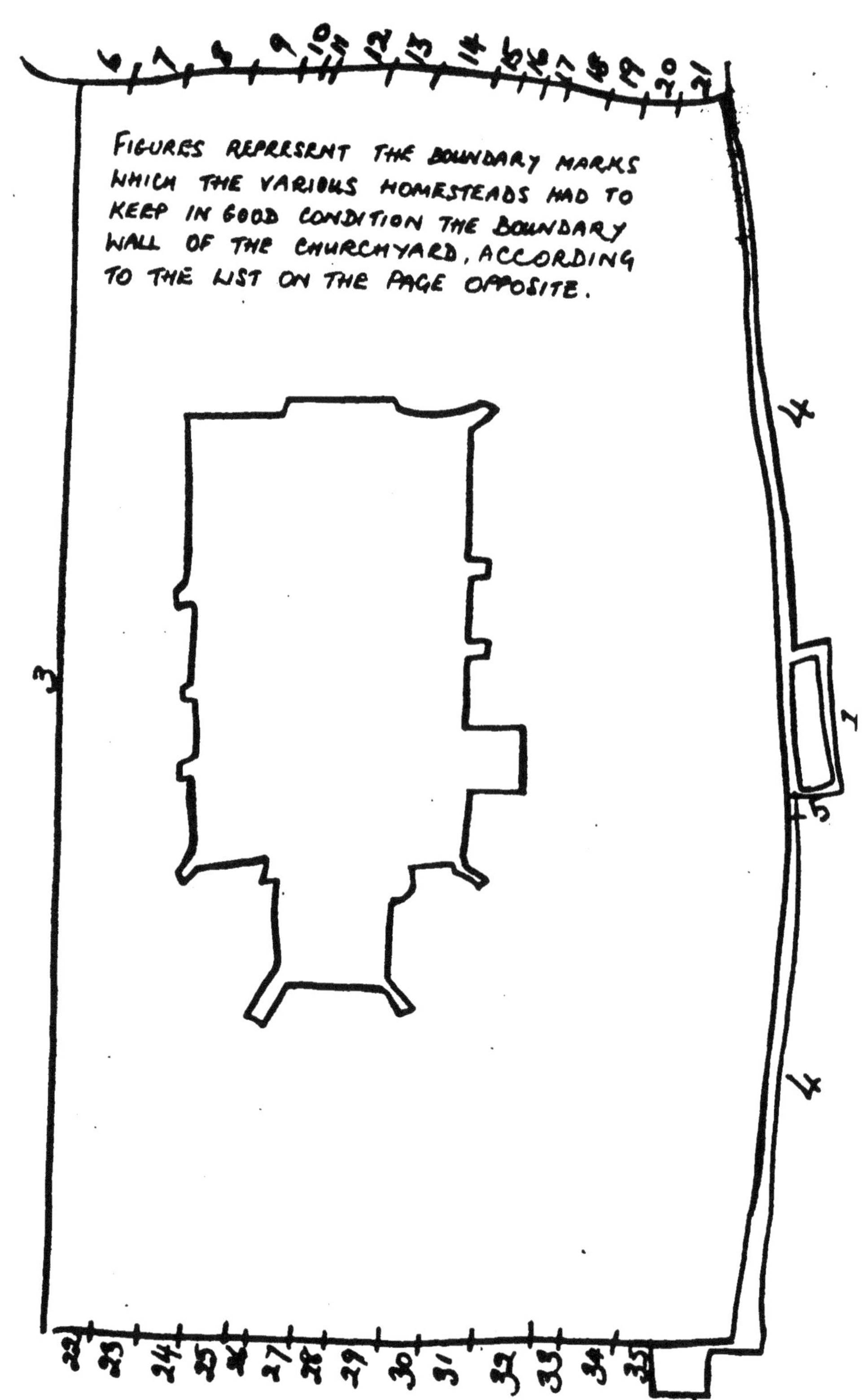
FIGURES REPRESENT THE BOUNDARY MARKS WHICH THE VARIOUS HOMESTEADS HAD TO KEEP IN GOOD CONDITION THE BOUNDARY WALL OF THE CHURCHYARD, ACCORDING TO THE LIST ON THE PAGE OPPOSITE.
6 7 8 9 10 11 12 13 14 15 16 17 18 19 20 21
4
1
5
4
3
22 23 24 25 26 27 28 29 30 31 32 33 34 35
2

A COPY OF THE DUPLICATE FOR THE LAND TAX FOR THE YEAR 1709

CHIDDINGSTONE NORTH

	£.	s.	d.
Mr Hyde or Thos. Chapman	5	12	0
Mr Hyde from his Woodland	1	12	0
Richard Overy	6	8	0
Thomas Boakes	8	8	0
Thomas Boakes	1	16	0
Thomas Burges or Tenant	3	4	0
Henry Waker or tenant	2	4	0
Sam. Searles	2	4	0
William Hatton	5	4	0
Thomas Wallis	2	16	0
Edward Palmer		16	0
Edward Croncke	8	8	0
Henry Streatfeild Gent	1	0	0
Robert Steatfeild	3	0	0
Robert Abraham	5	0	0
Robert Pearles	5	8	0
John Floyd	5	4	0
Widdow Medhurst	1	8	0
John Pye	2	0	0
John Tye	1	0	0
George Finch	3	12	0
George Children	5	16	0
Widdow Lee		8	0
John Cronke		16	0
do		12	0
John Hollamby	4	16	0
Thomas Reeve or tenant	3	0	0
Will Cowlard or tenant	1	4	0
George Children	1	16	0
Thos. Shoebridge, Thos. Wallis & Thos.Beckett	1	0	0

	£	s.	d
Stephen Streatfeild,gent	2	0	0
do for Mr Michael	2	8	0
Widdow Searles	2	16	0
John Overy	10	12	0
George Allen	6	0	0
do		12	0
William Hearnden	2	0	0
James King		12	0
William Edlow		16	0
John Speed	4	8	0
William Cole		16	0
Edward Everest	2	8	0
Edward & James Munck	4	8	0
Outbounders			
Thomas Streatfeild	2	16	0
John Turner	1	16	0
do		16	0
Abraham Thornton		16	0
Robert Martin	2.	0	0
do		16	0
Richard Turner	3	4	0
do	2	8	0
do		1	0
William Holmden	3	8	0
John Ashdowne	4	0	0
John Medhurst	1	0	0
John Ashdowne		4	0
Edward Shoebridge		12	0
Avery Lambert	4	12	0
Thos. Beckett	1	4	0
do		12	0
Thos. Bassett	1	12	0
Heirs of Edward Lambert	2	16	0
Thomas Weller	2	4	0
Mr. Streatfeild for part of the lodge		12	0
Michael Cronck		6	0
Wm. Wickenden or tenant		10	0
John Woodgate	4	0	0
John Boret		4	0
Richard Saxby		4	0
	£179	0	0

GEO.CHILDREN)
&)Assessors
EDWARD CRONCK)

JOHN HOLLAMBY)
&) Collectors.
GEORGE FINCH)

A COPY OF THE DUPLICATE FOR THE LAND TAX FOR THE YEAR 1709

CHIDDINGSTONE SOUTH

	£	s	d
Mr Edward Tennison, Rector	12	0	0
Henry Streatfeild, gent	15	0	0
do.	3	12	0
Wm. Woodgate Esq.		8	0
Richard Chapman, tenant			
Henry Streatfeild	9	8	0
Sam Arnold, ten. Streatfeild		12	0
Robert Streatfeild & Thomas Webb	5	0	0
John Croncke tenant Hy Streatfeild	3	4	0
Thomas Waller do.		12	0
Henry Streatfeild, gent		12	0
Richard Woodgate for GIULDIDGE	5	16	0
William Woodgate Esq.	18	0	0
Nicholas Piggott, tenant	1	4	0
to Hy. Streatfeild			
John Ashdowne	6	8	0
Henry Piggott	5	12	0
do for a tenant at			
Hill Hoath	2	0	0
John Findall, tenant to			
- Woodgate Esq.	6	18	0
Stephen Streatfeild of NEW TYE	4	8	0
John Floyd, tenant to			
John Seyliard, gent.	6	8	0
Henry Saxby, tenant to heirs			
of Thos. Streatfeild	1	0	0
do. tenant Hy. Constable	2	16	0
John Speed	1	0	0
Widdow Woodgate & John			
Longhurst	1	0	0
Henry Streatfeild for land to be			
purchased of Wm. Walkin		18	0
William Woodgate	8	12	0
Heirs of Richard Streatfeild			
for SKIPREED	3	16	0
" OAKENDEN	1	12	0
Joell Woodgate or tenant		16	0
Wm. Baker tenant to John Luck	4	0	0
John Cronck, wheelwright		6	0
Edmund Medhurst	4	4	0
Thos. Bassett for PINKHAM	4	14	0

	£	s	d
Thomas Bassett	6	16	0
Heirs of John Everest	3	8	0
Heirs of Sam Rivers		14	0
Joseph Cox	1	0	0
do		4	0
Robt. or Thos. Turner	1	8	0
James Saxby, tenant			
to Hy Streatfeild	6	12	0
Richard Chapman	1	2	0
John Saunders		6	0
Richard Ashdowne	2	10	0
Henry Carr, tenant			
to Rchd. Ashdowne		10	0
Thomas Eldridge		8	0
John Knight, tenant			
to - Hards		16	0
Robert Palmer, tenant			
to John Croncke		8	0
John Kingswood tenant		6	0
to Earl of Leicester			
OUTBOUNDERS			
Earl of Leicester	3	0	0
Mrs Woodgate	3	4	0
Sir George Rivers	4	0	0
or tenant John Findall			
Hy. Saxby, tenant to	7	16	0
John Seyliard			
Robt. Curd or tenant	1	8	0
John Bourn tenant to		8	0
heirs of Rt. Skinner			
Widdow Dennis tenant			
to heirs of Thos.			
Streatfeild	3	0	0
Wm. Streatfeild		12	0
Richard Saxby		12	0
Thomas Bridger	1	0	0
James Friend		4	0
The Lord Waldgrave			
Heirs of John Thorpe		12	0
" of Richard			
Streatfeild		12	0
Robert Curd		16	0
Heirs of Edmund Burges		4	0
Sir Geo. Rivers for a mead			
called THE PANNS		12	0
	£199	16	0

Wm Woodgate)
)
&) Assessors Henry Pigott Collector
)
Henry Piggott)

An ASSESSMENT MADE 30 MARCH 1733 for Repairing the inside of the Church of CHIDDINGSTONE, and for Bread & Wine for the Communnions, by Wm. Woodgate Esq. and Wm. Mugridge, Churchwardens, @ 4½d in the pound.

NAME	as TENANT to	LANDS	AMOUNT S.	D.
Mary Hyde, widow	-	Woodlands	2.	3
John Hyde Esq.	-	BORE PLACE HOUSE	9.	3
John Hyde Esq.	-	& Lands	12.	6
John Boakes	John Hyde Esq.	"	15.	3
Henry Adams	"	"	2.	9
Abraham Floyd	"	"	20.	0
John Head	"	"	4.	6
Richard Wye	"	BORE PLACE MILL	2.	6
Wid. Medhurst	"	-	20.	0
" "	Beecher's heirs	-	4.	6
Thos. Streatfeild, gent	-	LITTLE SOMERDEN MEAD		4½
Mr Wm. Streatfeild	-	His House & Land	3.	3
" "	Hy. Streatfeild Esq.	-	4.	1½
Robt. Streatfeild	Mr Chas. Hoskyns	-	7.	0
Mr William Heath	-	Farm at Boughbeech	12.	6
" "	-	Pollbrook's Farm	4.	1
Henry Beadle	Mr Petley	-	6.	3
Geo. Medhurst	Mr Seyliard	-	6.	3
" "	-	His House & Land	2.	1½
Richard Burfoot	Sir Wm. Humphreys	CRANSTED FARM	10.	0
Edward Everest	Mrs Streatfeild, widow	-	14.	0
John Cronck	-	Lands late Medhursts	1.	0½
" "	-	Tenemt. & lands at Clinton Brook	1.	3
" "	-	Tenemt. & lands late SPEEDS	2.	3
" "	John Cole	-		9
Widow Tye	John Pigott	-	2.	0
" "	" "	-	3.	9
William Lee	-	His House & Land	1.	3
Mr Wm. Streatfeild	Mr Round	-	6.	0
Wm. Muggridge	Mr Jewell	-	10.	7½
" "	John Turner	for BURNT HOUSE lands	3.	0
" "	-	Humphry's house & land	1.	4½
John Turner or his tenant		-	1.	3
Mr John Streatfeild	-	DUNG CROFT		9
John Hollamby	-	His house & land	5.	0
" "	John Goldsmith	-	4.	6
" "	-	KILN FARM	3.	9
Thomas Wallis	-	John Haywards Farm	4.	4½
" "	-	Lands late Hollamby's	2.	9
" "	-	Part of JESSOP'S Land		4½
Mr Weller	-	His house and lands	5.	0
Edward Shoebridge	Wm. Cowlard	-	1.	6
John Beckett or Humphrey Medhurst	-	-	1.	6½
Edward Holmes	Richard Wakerell	-	3.	0
John Cole	-	His house and land	1.	9
William Weller	-	His house and land	2.	6
			16.	6s.10½

Assessment of 1733 - cont.

NAME	as TENANT to	LANDS	AMOUNT	
			S.	D.
Widow Pinne	Mrs Green	-	3.	0
" "	Mrs Swaysland	-	1.	4½
Jeremiah Collier	John Moyce	-	0.	0
John Hollamby	Mr John Streatfeild	-	2.	3
THE OUTBOUNDERS				
John Earl of Leicester	-	-	3.	0
Robert Streatfeild, Gent	-	Part of Gravel Pits	2.	10
Richard Burfoot	Sir Wm. Humphreys	Part HEVER LODGE	1.	0
Henry Beadle	Mr Petley	BROADAY	3.	4
John Cackott	Geo. Allen's heirs	-	1.	0
John Wickenden	John Hyde Esq.	-	3.	4
George Turner	-	Part of MOORDEN	3.	6
Richard Turner	-	-		4
John Turner	-	Part of ROSES		10
Richard Turner	-	Land late Thos. Barrs	1.	1½
Thomas Oliver	Mr Arthur Children	HALE OAK	3.	4
Samuel Waite	Mr Stephen Woodgate	SEDCOBS & Part of CHESTED FARM	3.	4
Mr Wim. Streatfeild	-	Part of CHARKET	4.	6
William Hoskyns Esq.	-	Woodlands		6
William Weller	Mr Hoskyns	-	2.	11½
Edward Lambert	"	-	2.	0
John Ashdown of Hever	-	-		6
Thomas Sale	-	FORE HAWES & other land	2.	4
Simon Medhurst	-	Part WICKHURST		10
James Cranwell	-	Part CHITTENDEN	4.	6
Thos. Bassett of VEXORE	JOHN NICCOLL	-		7½
" "	Mrs Northey	-	1.	4
" "	-	WILMOT LANDS	1.	10
Mr John Streatfeild of Vexore	-	-	3.	3
John Wells	Mr Seyliard	-	1.	0
Wm. Wickenden	John Hawes	-		4
" "	-	His own land		8
Richard Pagden	John Bassett	-		4
		£15.	5.	1

ASSESSMENT 30th MARCH 1733 for OUTSIDE of Church of Chiddingstone and for Bread and Wine etc. by Wm. Woodgate gent & Wm Mugridge Churchwardens, after the Rate of 4d in the £ for the Inhabitants and 3d for the Outbounders.

Assessment of 1733 - cont.

NAME	as TENANT to	LANDS	AMOUNT S.	D.
Henry Streatfeild	-	House & Land	7.	6
" "	-	HIGHFIELDS etc.	2.	6
" "	-	HILL HOATH HOUSE & Land	3.	9
" "	-	GILWYNS	3.	9
" "	-	HELDE HOATH house & land	1.	0
" "	-	BENGELAND FIELD		4½
" "	-	WILLETS HOUSE & LAND	1.	3
George Rose	Henry Streatfeild Esq.	-	27.	6
Thomas Smith	"	-	3.	9
Thos. & Richard Chapman	Mr Sidney Streatfeild	-	16.	6
Thomas Streatfeild, gent	-	His house & land	2.	3
" "	-	Lands called WAKLYNS	1.	7½
Mr William Woodgate	-	House & lands	26.	3
Mr Stephen Woodgate	-	GUILDRIDGE	9.	0
John Best	Mr Stephen Woodgate	NEW TYE TENEMENT	8.	9
Mr William Streatfeild	-	House & land	5.	0
" " "	-	SKIPREED	5.	0
" " "	-	OAKENDEN	2.	6
" " "	Mr Wm. Woodgate	-	1.	6
Henry Piggott	-	House & land	5.	10½
Thomas Turner	Henry Piggott	-	9.	6
Thomas Perch	-	House & land	5.	3
Matthew Everest	-	House & land	4.	1½
" "	Michael Bassett	PRINCKHAM	6.	9
Michael Bassett	-	The MILL & other lands	9	4½
William Hoath	John Woodgate (alias Longley)	-	13.	0
John Head	Mr Wm. Woodgate	-	9.	0
" "	Mr Stephen Woodgate	SILCOCKS MEADS	3.	9
Jeremiah Dives	John Turner	-	6.	6
James Saxby	Lady Seyliard	-	3.	0
John Saxby	-	WATSTOCK & SCOTLAND REED	114.	0
Robert Palmer	John Cronck	-	1	1½
John Cronck	-	BRIDGEFIELDS	1.	3
" "	Mr Constable	-	4.	9
" "	Mrs Leggatt	-		9
			£16. 6. 10½	

Assessment of 1733 - cont:

Name	as Tenant to	Lands	Amount S	D.
Wm Cronk & John Longhurst	Mrs Leggatt	(Manor House?)	1	9
Thos. Weller	-	His house,shop etc	1	6.
Thos & Richard Chapmen	-	House & land	2	0.
" " "	-	Lands late John Saunders		6.
John Durrant	Mr Robert Streatfeild		10	6
Robert Palmer	"	"Hope Mead	7	0 1/2
Richard King	Edmund Medhurst	"	2	4 1/2
Henry Cox		"Tenement etc.wherein he now dwelleth		6
James Knight	Henry Cox		2	4 1/2
William Cronck		His House & land at Rendsley Heath		9
Thomas Butcher		His tenement		9
John Tye		"His tenement		6 1/2
Robert Gurd (or his tenant)		"	2	3
Widow Arnold	"	Tenement at the Hoath		0
John Hilton 7 1/2	Earl of Leicester	"		
Edward Monk	Heirs of Daniel Williams	"	0	0

The Outbounders

Name	as Tenant to	Lands	S	D.
Thomas Butcher	Sir George Rivers Bart	-	3	4.
Robert Streatfeild gent		Part of EEL-PANNS	8	8 1/2
John Saxby		Part SALMONDS	10.	0.
Robert Gurd		Lands late Richard Ashdownes		10
"		His tenement	1	2
William Bourne	Robert Curd & Widow Falkner			6
Robert Streatfeild,gent	Sir William Humphreys		8	4
"		Piece of Mead late used by James Friend		4
Richard Burfoot	Sir Wm. Humphreys			4 1/2
Thomas Burfoot	"		1	0
Thos. Wells	Henry Streatfeild Esq		2	6.
John Best	Mr. William Streatfeild	Bourn Mead		6
Robert Ingram	Mr.Stephen Woodgate	Part of Buckhurst		7 1/2
John Peerless	Mr. Madix			2 1/2
Thomas Weller (or his tenant)				2
John Boakes		Lands near MARSHOPE		2
Oliver Thorpe		FRIENDEN LANDS		8
" (or his tenant)		FRIENDEN WOOD		3
			£14. 6	5 1/2

AN ASSESSMENT made 23. Oct, 1730 for the Relief of the Poor at Chiddingstone by Edward Cronck and William Streatfeild, Churchwardens, George Rose and Edward Everest Overseers for the Poor after the rate of 12 pence in the pound as followeth:-

(details of lands, etc, names etc., are much as in 1733)

Yielded £36. 5. 6d.

The same persons made a rate for same purpose on 11 March 1730 (N.S. 1731) at 12d in the £.

Signatories: William Streatfeild & Thos Smith Churchwardens
John Durrant, Thomas Weller & Fran Aylmer Curate

THE MANORS OF THE PARISH OF CHIDDINGSTONE

Chiddingstone Burgersh. (formerly called BURWASH COURT).

1288 **Robert** de Burgersh made constable of Dover Castle & Warden of Cinque ports
1304 Summoned to Parliament among Barons of Realm
1306 Died possessed of manor. **Stephen** son & heir.
1307 Grant of **free warren** of demesne lands.
? Succeeded by Bartholomew; married Elizabeth de Verdon; took part with king's favourites, and after their defeat at Boroughbridge was made prisoner and sent to Tower, whence released -
1326 by Queen Isabel & Prince Edward III, and made constable of Dover Castle and Warden of Cinque Ports
1327 New commission granted for above offices
1331 Seneschal of Ponthieu
1335 Warden of all king's forests south of Trent
1337 Admiral of the seas westward of Thames
1338 Confirmation of free warren for his demesne lands in this parish
1342 Another charter of free warren for his lands here
1343 Again made constable of Dover Castle
1346 Fought at Cressy
1349 Lord Chamberlain of King's Household
1355 Constable of Tower of London
1327-1355He was summoned to Parliament
1355 Died - leaving 2 sons & 1 daughter - Bartholomew, Henry & Joan. Bartholomew married Cicely, daughter & heir of Richard de Weyland
1350 created Knight of Garter on its initiation. Continually employed in French wars, at Poitiers. His arms can still be seen on roof of cloisters in Canterbury.
1369 Bartholomew de Burgersh conveyed this manor to Sir Walter de Pavely K.G.
1395 Conveyed to family of VAUX of Northampton circa.

Temp. Henry
1422/1461 This Manor wa alienated to John Alphegh (or Alphew) of Bore Place.
1489 John Alphew died - leaving two daughters. Margaret inherited and married Sir Robert Read
1507 Read made Chief Justice - executor to Henry VII (arms still in window in Serjeants Inn).
1501 Edmund - only son of Sir Robert & Margaret Read died & buried in Chiddingstone Church. There were 4 daughters.
1518 Sir Robert Read died. This Manor with his other estates in Chiddingstone went to his daughter Bridget, wife of Sir Thomas Willoughby, who became entitled to his seat called Bore Place, and other estates in this Parish.
1537 Sir Thomas Willoughby made Chief Justice and knighted
1539 Procured disgavelment of his lands

1545	Sir Thomas Willoughby died and was burried in Chiddingstone Church with Bridget his Wife. His arms still remain in a window in Serjeants Inn.
1572	Sir Thomas Willoughby - a grandson of above - was Sheriff of Kent.
&	He married Catherine - daughter of Sir Percival Hart of Lullingstone
1589	Several sons and daughters
?	Percival Willoughby succeeded
1603	Percival Willoughby knighted by James 1.
??	He married Bridget, daughter of Sir Francis Willoughby of Wollaton Hall, Notts. Elected to serve in lst Parliament of James I for Notts - ancestor of Henry Willoughby, Lord Middleton.
??	Percival Willoughby alienated this manor to John & Robert Seyliard of Delaware, Brasted.
??	From above this descended to John Seyliard Esq., who was created a
1661	Baronet.
??	Sir Thomas Seyliard inherited who conveyed
1700	with Delaware to Henry Streatfeild Esq
??	Henry Streatfeild died & bequeathed this manor to his youngest son Thomas Streatfeild Esq. of Sevenoaks.
1762	Passed to Thomas' nephew Henry Streatfeild Esq., of High Street House.

1340	**Reginald** de Cobham (grandson of Reginald de Cobham & William de Hever) charter of **free warren** in his demesne lands within the lordship of Chiddingstone. Soldier, Ambassador, Reputation for wisdom & fidelity.
1356	Fought at Poitiers. Admiral of the King's fleet westward of Thames.
1342-1361	called to Parliament
1361	Died of pestilence, leaving Joan, widow surviving.
1369	Joan de Cobham died and was buried in St.Mary Overy, Southwark
1369	**Reginald** de Cobham succeeded (son of Reginald & Joan). He was Lord of **Starborough Castle** and his family was called hereafter "**Cobham of Starborough**". He was summoned to Parliament. Twice married.
1402	Reginald died - his second wife Alianore surviving (she was widow of Sir John Fitzalan, alias Arundel
1402	**Reginald** - son of above, succeeded. Twice married
1445	Reginald died
1445	His eldest son succeeds. **Sir Thomas Reginald Cobham** - married Anne, daughter of Humphrey Stafford, Duke of Buckingham.
1471	**Sir Thomas Reginald Cobham** died, leaving only daughter Anne, who married Sir Edward Borough of Gainsborough, Lincs. (descended from Hubert de Burgh).
1543	Act of Parliament passed bastardising children of this marriage
1550	**Thomas** died - leaving by the 2nd wife Alice, 2 sons & other chilren
1572	William, Lord Burgh, one of the peers who judged the Duke of Norfolk
1582	William, Lord Burgh died, having children by Catherine, daughter of Earl of Lincoln, Sir John Borough who predeceased. Also Thomas & 3 daughters.
1582	Thomas, Lord Burgh, succeeded, and resided like his ancestors at Starborough Castle
1586	Made Governor of the Brill - then ambassador to Scotland & KG
1597	Thomas, Lord Burgh appointed Lord Deputy for Ireland
1595	Having expended large sums in the service of Queen Elizabeth, he was compelled to sell this manor, with that of TYHURST (in this parish) to **Richard Streatfeild** Esq. of High Street House, in this parish
???	**Richard Streatfeild** married, Anne, daughter of a Fremling, by whom he had 3 sons, Henry, Silvester & Thomas, and one daughter Margaret.
1601	**Richard Streatfeild** died. **Thomas** youngest son of above, inherited this manor. (**Henry** inherited Tyhurst)
???	Henry had a son **Richard**, whose son **Henry** was of High Street House and acquired this manor from his aunts - the daughters & co-heirs of Thomas.
1709	**Henry Streatfeild** died owning Chiddingstone Cobham, and Tyehurst and was succeeded by his son:-
1709	**Henry Streatfeild** who married Miss Baird and left by her a son
???	**Henry Streatfield** who
1752	Married **Miss Anne Sidney**
1762	Henry Streatfield died leaving widow, 2 sons & 2 daughters
1762	**Henry Streatfeild** inherited High Street House, Tyhurst & Chiddingstone Cobham Manors.

RANESLEY (or RENDESLEY) - (Near boundary of Penshurst - owners in ancient deed spelt Rendesley and Rennesley).

Bore Place and Milbroke

Temp Henry III

1216-1272 Estate of a family called **BORE**

Temp. Henry VI

1422-1461 John Bore sold to John Alphew, who rebuilt Bore Place

1489 Family of Ranesley became extinct and sold to John Alphew

1489 **JOHN APHEW** died leaving two daughters -. Margaret married **Sir Robert Read.** He lived at Bore Plce and much enlarged it.

1518 Died without sons - eldest daughter Bridget married married **Sir Thomas Willoughby**, and had this seat of Milbroke and his other possessions in Chiddingstone for her share. Sir Thomas Willoughby resides at Bore Place and improved it.

1547 In possession of **MRS ANNE BOND** - Her heirs conveyed it to **Nathaniel Studley**, of Emborne Minster, Yorks whose only son succeeded and conveyed it to Christopher Knight of Cowdham - on whose death it passed to **Michael Knight** of **WESTERHAM**

??? Sold by Knight to Robert, Earl of Leicester, after which it continued in his descendants like the rest of his estates in this parish.

Temp.James I

circa

1606 **Sir Percival Willoughby** - grandson of Sir Thomas sold Bore Place & Milbroke to Mr. Bernard Hyde of London - a Commissioner of Customs of Charles 1.

Temp. Civil War 1647/54???

Circa

1750 A descendant of Bernard **HYDE** sold to Henry Streatfeild of High Street House

1762 Henry Streatfeild died and bore Place and Milbroke vested in eldest son Henry Streatfeild.

BOWZELL (or Boresell) - (lies mostly in Chevening Parish)

Part of possessions of Cobhams of Sterborough Castle

1362 Reginald de Cobham died possessed of above

1370 Joan de Cobham died possessed of above

1472 Sir Thomas Cobham died - his daughter married Sir Edward Borough of Gainsborough Lincs

1526 Sir Thomas' daughter died, having survived her husband

1598 Sir Thomas Burgh, Lord Burgh, K.G., died possessed of manor leaving 4 daughters - who some years later

??? sold it to the **THOMAS'S** of Whitley, Sevenoaks:-

??? thence it passed to the Watersons

??? from which line by a female descendant to the Bonnels whose descendant

1784 **JAMES BONNEL** sold it to Rev Richard **RYCROFT**, rector of Penshurst and a Baronet

Sir Nicholas Rycroft, son of above, succeeded

The Family of Ashdowne

The Ashdownes were an old Chiddingstone family. They figure in one of the visitations of Kent (date uncertain) as being descended from Henry Ashdowne of Chiddingstone and Agnes his wife, the daughter of Peter Manning of Chiddingstone, a lady of 12 quarterings. Their eldest son Bartholomew married Maria, daughter of Henry Pratt of Oundel, Northants. The Ashdowne Arms are: "Argent, a lion rampant gules, collared or and linqued azure".

John Ashdowne the elder of Chiddingstone, Lord of the Manor of Lewisham, Cowden (as to one moiety), left issue by Joan, his wife:-

(1) John the younger of Hever, married Sarah, daughter of Richard Streatfeild, relict of John Woodgate of Stonewall: left issue Henry, buried at Chiddingstone 1657, and Sarah, daughter and heiress, married Henry Streatfeild.

(2) Ann, married Henry Pigott of Chiddingstone, and left issue Nicholas & four daughters.

(3) William, succeeded to the Manor

(4) Richard, who left issue Anne, John and Henry, the latter of whom had left to him by his grandfather in 1677 an annuity of £14 towards his expenses at school and at the University.

Sarah Woodgate, the only daughter of John Woodgate of Stonewall, married John Ashdowne of Rendsley Heath. The marriage licence, dated 2nd June 1663, describes her as of Penshurst, maiden, aged 19, with consent of her mother; John Ashdowne was about 26. It took place at Penshurst llth June 1663. This licence was obtained on the same day as that of her brother William. From the parish Registers of Hever, it appears that the Ashdownes lived at Hever Place, and Hever Lodge.

Pedigree of the BEECHER of LONGHOUSE (alias Burghersh Court)

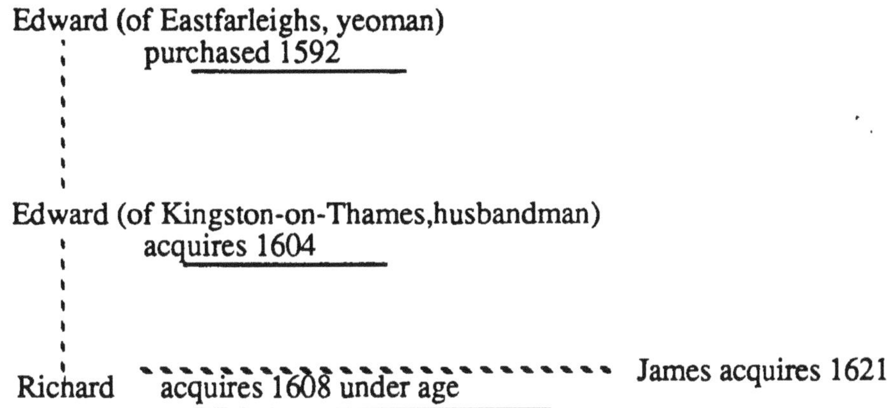

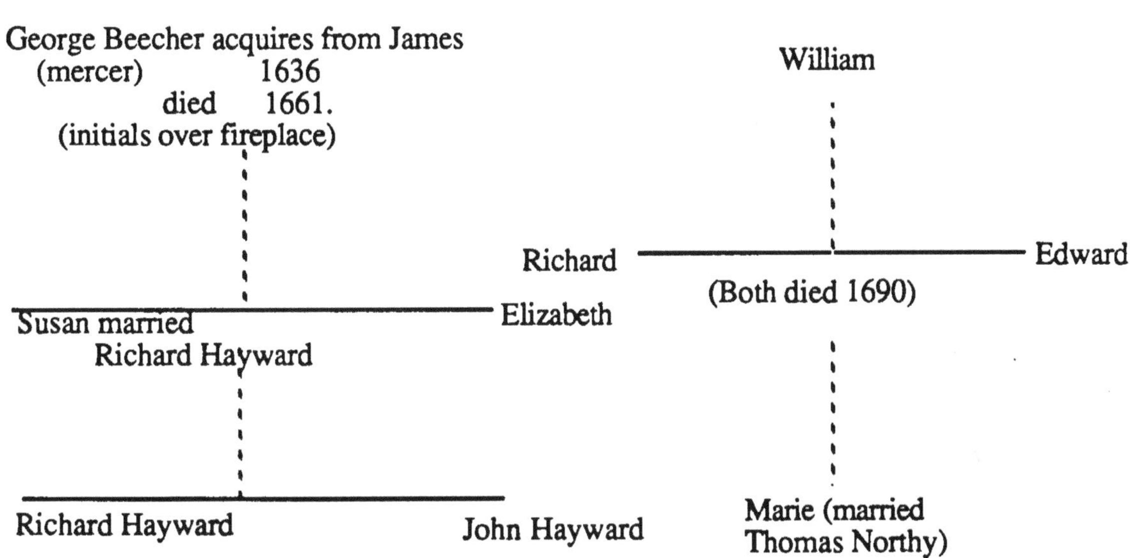

The Family of BEECHER

The **Beechers** were an old family of Penshurst. One of them was Alderman and Sheriff of London in 1570. He died in 1571, leaving issue by Alice Heron his wife (sister of Sir Nicholas Heron of Edgecombe) Edward; Bartholomew who died in Ireland; Henry married Edith, daughter of John Riche Apothacary to Queen Elizabeth; and three daughters.

Edward Beecher, the eldest, married Frances, relict of Francis Coppinger, and relict of **Thomas, Lord Burgh K.G.** Lord Deputy of Ireland. Seymer Coppinger, her second son and eventually heir to his mother, by will dated 1656, devised his estates to William Walter of the Trench, ancestor of the Walters of Tonbridge.

Another branch settled at Bletchingly. Henry, son of **James Beecher** of Chiddingstone married a Bletchingly girl and continued the family there. The family owned Vexour, and apparently at one time Chested also.

The Family of BIRSTY

The **Birsty's**, otherwise Birchensty's or Burster's, were lords of the manor of Birchensty in Ardlingly, Sussex, from a time of remote antiquity.

Thomas, fourth in descent from John Birchensty of Birchensty, was the first to use the surname in the contracted form of BIRSTY, and was likewise the first to remove from the family home. He was a man-of-law, and "Serjeant" to the hapless Anne of Cleves, who was banished to Hever Castle.

How Green, otherwise Hook Green, was held of the manor of Chiddingstone Burghersh and belonged originally to John Hynes, afterwards to John Seyliard, then to **Thomas** Seyliard, and finally to Ewry Seyliard, who sold it to **Thomas** Birsty, who left it to his second son Thomas. The **third** son of "Thomas the Serjeant" was **William Birsty** of Chiddingstone, who was one of the principal inhabitants. He was buried in the Nave at Chiddingstone, where there is a brass to his memory inscribed:-

> "Gulielmus filius Tho de Birchensty
> Com. Sussex ex Anna una cohaeredum
> Johannis Fremling duas relinquens filias,
> annam et Catharinam obift XX die mensis,
> Maij Ao Dni MDCXXXVIj",
> Aetatis LXViij"

above are the Birsty Arms.
Administration of his estate was granted in 1637 to Anna Birsty, relict.

Pedigree of the Family of Burghersh (or Burgherst)

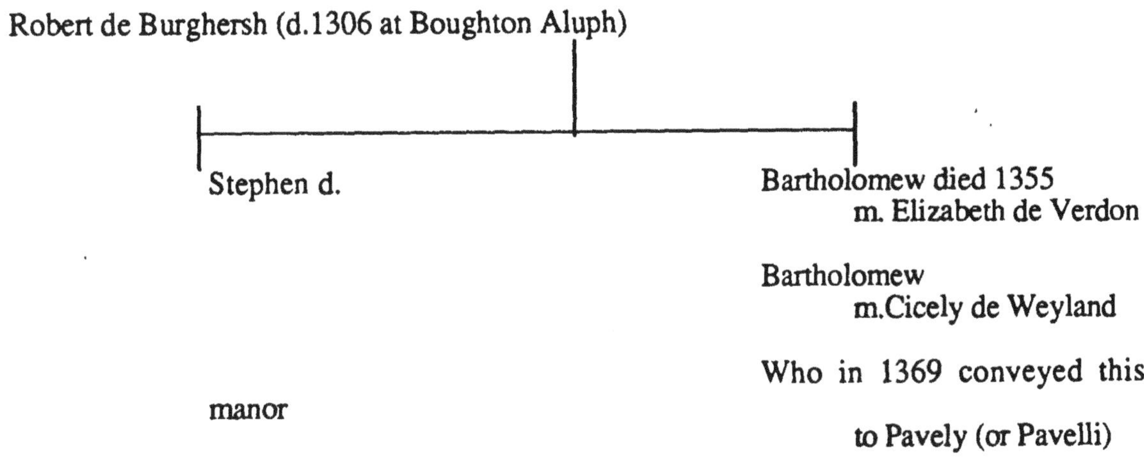

A Pedigree of the Family of Burghersh

(found amongst the Streatfeild papers relating to the Manor of Chiddingstone Burghersh - written in a 16th Century handwriting).

Tempore R.R. henrici secundi 1154-88	Sr,. Stephen Burghershe Knight	
Rich primi 1188-98	Sr.Herberd Burghershe Knight	
henrici tertii 1216-72	Reginald de Burghersh	Sir Walter de Burghershe Knight second son
	Dr.Robert de Burghershe -	Margaret Badelsmer sister of Sir Bartholomew Badelesmere Lord Badelsmer
	Sir Bartholmewe Burghershe or Borowashe -	Margaret Badelsmer sister of Sir Bartholomew Badelesmere Lord Badelsmer
	Sir Bartholmewe Burghershe or Borowashe - knight; he was of the order of the garter	Elizabeth Verdon second daugher and one of the heyres of Theobalde Lord Verdon of Alton Castell
Thomas Elizabethe Borowashe	Elizabeth Burghershe or Borowash, daughter & heyr of Sir Barthelmew Burwashe was fyrst maryed to the Lord Spencer	

Sir Thomas	Secondly to Sir Thomas	
Grene kt.	Grene Knight	
2nd husband	Thirdly to William Pawlyn =	William Pawlyn Esquier
and of Eliz-	Esquier	third husband of
abeth Boro		Elizabeth Burghersh
washe		

Note:- the compiler of above pedigree neglected to mention Bartholomew Burghersh the younger, who was the father of the **"Elizabethe Burghershe" or "Borowashe"** mentioned above.

Note: by Dr. Gordon Ware:-

> Stephen B. in 1 Edw. 11 had charter of free warren here 1307/8
> Bartholomew de B. had charter of free warren here 1338 & 1342.

Family of Burghersh. (Dict. of Nat. Biography)

Burghersh, Bartholomew, Lord, the elder (died 1355) was the 2nd (or perhaps 3rd) son of Robert, Lord Burghersh, and succeeded to his father's title and estates on the death of his elder brother, Stephen. He was the nephew on the mother's side and namesake of Bartholomew, Lord Badlesmere, one of the most powerful of the barons. He married Elizabeth, one of the three co-heiresses of Theobald, Lord Verdon, an alliance by which his wealth and power were increased.

Lord Badlesmere was a bitter enemy of Thomas, Earl of Lancaster, and we find Burghersh taking an active part in the unhappy contests of parties in Edward 11's reign as an adherent of his uncle, whom in 1317 he accompanied in an expedition to Scotland.

In October 1321, when Leeds Castle, Kent - the gates of which had been shut against Queen Isabella by Lady Badlesmere - surrendered to Edward, who had with unwonted spirit raised a force of 30,000 men to avenge the insult offered to his wife, Burghersh, who was one of the garrison, was taken prisoner and incarcerated in the Tower of London. This imprisonment was probably the means of saving him from the fate of his uncle after the disastrous battle of Boroughbridge. He was spared to aid in the overthrow of the unfortunate sovereign. On the landing of Isabella, on 24 Sept. 1326, his brother Henry, the Bishop of Lincoln hastened to join her, and with Orlton, Bishop of Hereford, took the initiative in the measures which speedily led to Edward's deposition and murder.

The important post of Constable of Dover Castle and Warden of the Cinque Ports, which had been held by his father, were given to Burghersh, and he held to the offices, with but slight intermission, till his death. In the unsettled relations between England and France, which lasted throughout the greater part of Edward III's reign, the responsibility devolving on the holder of these offices, which implied the command of the chief channel of communication between the two countries, was of the highest moment, and it evidences the confidenced reposed in Burghersh that he should have held them almost continuously during so important an epoch.

The commission given originally in the name of Edward II, but really proceeding from the party conspiring only too successfully against him, was renewed by his son in the first year of his reign.

The first Royal Missive to him in this capacity, contained in Rymer, as an order to have 60 does taken from the king's park of Brabourne, and salted for the use of the Parliament about to meet at Westminster. This is followed by an order to use his authority to put a stop to predatory incursions on the French coast.

Burghersh evidently very speedily obtained the complete confidencde of the young king, which he retained uninterruptedly till the end of his life. His services were rewarded by large grants of land and manorial privileges, escheated to the crown, or in some other way falling to the sovereign to dispose of. The king dispatched him repeatedly on diplomatic errands. In 1329 he was sent to Philip of France to explain the reasons for the delay in the rendering of his homage, and in the same year as an ambassador to the Pope, to plead for pecuniary aid from the revenues of the England church, a tenth of which was granted to the King for 4 years. Rymer contains a series of royal orders issued to him in his capacity of Constable of Dover
Borowashe" mentioned aforehand.

Note by :Dr. Gordon Ward
Stephen B. in 1 Edw. II had charter of free warren here 1307/B
Bartholomew de B had charter of free warren here 1338 & 1342

Family of Burghersh. (Dict of Nat Biography).

Burghersh, Bartholomew, Lord, the elder (died 1355) was the 2nd (or perhaps 3rd) son of Robert, Lord Burghersh, and succeeded to his father's title and estates on the death of his elder brother, Stephen.

He was the nephew on the mother's side and namesake of Bartholomew, Lord Badlesmere, one of the most powerful of the barons. He married Elizabeth, one of the three co-heiresses of Theobald, Lord Verdon, an alliance by which his wealth and power were increased.

Lord Badlesmere was a better enemy of Thomas, Earl of Lancaster, and we find Burghersh taking an active part in the unhappy contests of parties in Edward II's reign as an adherent of his uncle, whom in 1317 he accompanied in an expedition to Scotland.

In October 1321, when Leeds Castle, Kent - the gates of which had been shut against Queen Isabella by Lady Badlesmere - surrendered to Edward, who had with unwanted spirit raised a force of 30,000 men to avenge the insult offered to his wife, Burghersh, who was one of the garrison, was taken prisoner and incarcerated in the Tower of London. This imprisonment was probably the means of saving him for the fate of his uncle after the disastrous battle of Boroughbridge. He was spared to aid in the overthrow of the unfortunate sovereign. On the landing of Isabella, on 24th September, 1326, his brother Henry, the Bishop of Lincoln, hastened to join her, and with Orlton, Bishop of Hereford, took the initiative in the measures which speedily led to Edward's deposition and murder.

The important post of constable of Dover Castle and Warden of the Cinque Ports, which had been held by his father, were given to Burghersh, and he held to the offices, with but slight intermission, till his death. In the unsettled relations between England and France, which lasted throughout the greater part of Edward III's reign, the responsibility devolving on the holder of these offices, which implied the command of the chief channel of communication between the two countries, was of the highest moment, and it evidences the confidence reposed in Burghersh that he should have held them almost continously during so important an epoch.

The commission given originally in the name of Edward II, but really proceeding from the party conspiring only too successfully against him, was renewed by his son in the first year of his reign.

The first Royal Missive to him in this capacity, contained in Rymer, as an order to have 60 does taken from the King's Park of Brabourne, and salted for the use of the Parliament about to meet at Westminster. This is followed by order to use his authority to put a stop to predatory incursions on the French coast.

Burghersh evidently very speedily obtained the complete confidence of the young king, which he retained uninterruptedly till the end of his life. His services were rewarded by large grants of land and manorial privileges, escheated to the crown, or in some other way falling to the sovereign to dispose of. The king dispatched him repeatedly on diplomatic errands. In 1329 he was sent to Philip of France to explain the reasons for the delay in the rendering of his homage, and in the same year as an ambassador to the Pope, to plead for pecuniary aid from the revenues of the English church, a tenth of which was granted to the king for 4 years. Rymer contains a series of royal orders issued to him in his capacity of Constable of Dover relating to prohibitions or licences to cross the sea when the peace of the country was threatened, and to make arrangements for the passage of the king and other distinguished persons. He was entrusted with other offices calling for vigour and practical wisdom. In 1337 on the assumption by Edward of the title of King of France, he was made admiral of the fleet from the mouth of the Thames westward. He was appointed seneschal of Ponthieu, warden of the Tower, and chamberlain to the king, in which capacity his presence is often recorded at the delivery of the Great Seal.

In one of Edward's grievous straits for money, he was entrusted with the pawning of the crown and other jewels. As keeper of the King's Forest to the south of the Trent in 1341 he was commissioned to provide timber for the construction.

The confidence imposed in Burghersh as a diplomatic agent was equally great. He was frequently sent, as may be seen in Rymer, - often in company with Bishop Bateman of Norwich - to treat with the Pope at Avignon, with Philip of Valois, with the Counts of Brabant and Flanders, and other leading powers, on the truces and armistices so repeatedly made and broken, and to arrange the often promised but long deferred final peace between the two contending nations. As characteristic of the Age, it is curious to find that under an excess of religious zeal, Burghersh, before the breaking out of the war with France, when the realm was comparatively quiet, had laid aside his arms and assumed the cross. Edward, unable to dispense with the services of so valuable a helper, when starting for Gascony in 1347, petitioned the Pope to release him for his vow.

Two years after Crecy we find him again taking part in the French wars, and dispatched to Avignon to treat with the Pope for a firm and lasting peace between the two countries. The next year (1349) he accompanied the Earl of Lancaster to Gascony to suppress the rebellion there.

In 1355, when Edward was leaving England for a fresh invasion of France, Burghersh was appointed one of the guardians of the Realm, but died at the beginning of August of that year. He was buried in the chantry of St. Catherine, which he had founded in Lincoln Minster for the soul of his brother Henry, Bishop of Lincoln, and their father, Robert Burghersh.
Monuments of all three, with effigies of the two brothers, are still to be seen.

Burghersh, Bartholomew, Lord, the younger, (d. 1369), the son of Bartholomew Burghersh the elder, adopted his father's profession of arms and rivalled him in military distinction. His recorded career begins in 1339, when he accompanied Edward III in his expedition to Flanders and took part in the first invasion of French territory.

We find his name also as attending the king on his third inglorious and unprofitable campaign in Brittany in 1342/3. In 1346 he was one of the retinue of the Black Prince, then in his 15th year, in the ever memorable campaign of Crecy, and in the following year was present at the siege of Calais, being rewarded for his distinguished services there by a rich wardship.

In 1349 he was in the campaign in Gascony.
On the institution of the order of the Garter in 1350, he was chosen to be one of the knights companions.

In 1354 he fulfilled a religious vow by taking a journey to the Holy Land. On his return home, he joined the Black Prince in the expedition - the largest and most formidable yet directed against France - in 1355. He was one of the most eminent of the commanders of the invading army, and had a leading share in the events of the campaign, especially in the Battle of Poitiers, 19 Sept. 1356. A daring exploit of Burghersh is recorded by Froissart shortly before the battle. In company with Sir John Chandos and Sir James Audley, and attended only by 24 horsemen, he made an excursion from the main body of the army, and falling on the rear of the French army, took 32 knights and gentlemen prisoners. His prowess and skill were again tried about the same time when, with a small foraging party near Berry, he was attacked from an ambuscade by a much more formidable force, which, however, he managed to keep at bay till relieved by the Black Prince.

During the campaign, his father, Lord Burghersh, died and he received livery of his lands as his heir. In 1359 he again accompanied Edward III on his last and most formidable invasion of France, ending in the decisive Treaty of Bretigny 8 May 1360. He was deputed to aid in the negotiation of this Treaty between "the first-born sons of the kings of England and France" at Chartres, for which letters of protection were given him. He and his brother commissioners were taken prisoners in violation of the bond and Edward had to interpose to obtain their liberation. During this campaign, Knighton records his successful siege of the Castle of Sourmussy in Gascony, in which he appears to have evidenced no common skill.

In 1362 he was appointed one of the commissioners on the state of Ireland. When, in 1364, King John of France, to make atonement for the Duke of Anjou's breach of faith, determined to yield himself back to captivity, to die three months after his landing at the Savoy Palace, Burghersh was one of the nobles deputed to receive him at Dover and conduct him by Canterbury to Edward's presence at Eltham.

In 1366 he was one of the commissioners sent to Urban V, who had rashly demanded the payment of the arrears of tribute granted by King John. His death took place in 1369. He was twice married:-

(1) To Cecilia, heiress of Richard Weyland
(2) To his cousin Margaret, sister of Bartholomew, Lord Badlesmere

He left an only daughter, Elizabeth married to Edward, Lord Despenser.

The Family of COMBRIDGE

John Combridge of Penshurst, ancestor of the Combridges of Walter's Green, Penshurst, left issue by Elizabeth, his wife (buried 21st Oct. 1568):-

1. Andrew Combridge, sen. of Chiddingstone, whose daughter and heiress Joanna, married 1602 William Woodgate of Stonewall.
2. Francis of Chiddingstone: married 1578, Abia, relect of Thomas Woodgate of Watstock, Chiddingstone. Buried 1583.
3. Robert - of Penshurst, died 1598

Robert Combridge sen. (brother of first-mentioned John) died 1584.
Left issue:-

1. Anthony of Newhouse, alias Harts, Penshurst, Married Abia, widow and relict of above mentioned Francis Combridge s.p.
2. Robert of Coldharbour died 1590
3. Oliver of Hawden otherwise Harden
4. Katherine, living 1590
5. Andrew of Coldharbour

A daughter of Oliver (No.3 above) married Gilbert Spencer of Redleafe, and died 1714.

PEDIGREE OF THE COBHAMS OF STERBOROUGH, SURREY

Henry de Cobham d.1225

John d.1251
m 1) dau. of Warine - 2) Joan dau. of Hugh Neville
Fitzbenedict

Reginald d.1257
William

John d. 1300 age 71
m. Joan de
Septvans

Henry
(Sir) of Roundall

Reginald (Sir) of Orkesden (Lullingstone &
Eynsford) m. Joan dau. & heir
of William de Hever

Henry d.1339
age 79
(lst Lord Cobham)

Reginald

John d. 1354
(2nd Lord Cobham)

John d.1407

Joan (grandmother of last John)
Baroness Cobham in her own
right. m. Sir Gerald Braybroke
& 4 other husbands.

Joan m. Sir Thomas Brooks

Reginald d. 1361
lst Baron m. Joan...
Sterborough

Reginald d. 1403
2nd Baron m 1) Eliz.le Strang
2) Alianore
Sterborough

Reginald d. 1445
3rd Baron m 1) Eleanor Culpepper
Sterborough 2) Anne

(Sir) Thomas Reginald d.1471
m. Anne dau. of Duke of
Buckingham

Anne d. 1526
m 1) Lord Mountjoy
2) Edward Burgh
and so the Burghs inherited
Chiddingstone Cobham Manor

JOHN 3rd Lord of Cobham Hall - seems to have held cordial relations with the Cobhams of Sterborough, who had promised endowments to the College of Cobham.

LADY JOAN, the widow of the lst Baron - (Sir Reginald de Cobham - who died in 1361) enjoined her son Reginald to fulfil the above-named obligation, and she leaves to John, Lord Cobham - 1 pax & crucifix, gilt cup, book called "Apocalypse" etc. John 3rd Lord Cobham was one of the executors of Sir Reginald - 2nd Baron Cobham of Sterborough - who died in 1403.

From Arch. Canterbury:-

In 1355. Sir Reginald de Cobham of Sterborough was of the Council to debate on the proprietary of submitting the disputes with France to the arbitrament of the Pope.

1402. Tomb of 2nd Baron in Lingfield Church, praises his hospitality.

FAMILY OF BURGH (Burke's Peerage)

SIR EDWARD BURGH, of Gainsborough, Lincs, - de jure Lord Strabolgi, Member of Parliament for Lincoln 1492; who was never summoned to Parliament as a baron. Married, 1477, ANNE, daughter and heir of Sir Thomas Cobham of Sterborough, and widow of Edward Blount, 2nd Lord Mountjoy. By an inquisition , 14th June 1510, he was found to be a lunatic with lucid intervals, and he and his wife to possess the manors of Chiddingstone Cobham and others in Kent. In an inquisition (post-mortem) 7 Nov. 1528, they were found to be seised of the manors of Oxted & Sterborough in Surrey. She died 26 June 1526, having had issue:-

Thomas, lst Lord Burgh

Henry - married Catherine, dau. of Sir Ralph Neville - and they had a daughter married Richard Vaughan.

Sir Edward Burgh died 20th Aug. 1528 - his son and heir was THOMAS, lst Lord BURGH (age 34 & more in 1528), who was knighted in 1513, and admitted to Parliament as Lord Burgh 2 Dec. 1529:-

Married - lst) Agnes. dau. of Sir William Tyrwhitt of Kettleby, Lincs
2nd) Alice, dau. of William London & widow of Sir Thomas Bedingfield & Edmund Rokewood.

Alice died 1558 (will dated 25 March 1558) prov 1559.
Thomas lst Lord Burgh died 28 Feb. 1549/50 having had issue with several daughters:-

1) Edward (Sir) who married about 1529, **KATHERINE**, dau. of Sir Thomas Parr of Kendal. Edward died during the lifetime of his father.
   Katherine married (2) 1533, John Nevill, Lord Latymer, who died 2 March 1542/3. (3) on 12th July 1543 - **KING HENRY VIII** - who died 28th Jan. 1547 (4) on 3rd March 1547 Lord Seymour of Sudely K.G. Katherine died 5th September 1548.

2) Thomas (Sir) who married Elizabeth, daughter of Sir David Owen, and left issue bastardised by Act of Parliament 1542/3.
3) WILLIAM, 2nd Lord.
4) Henry of Stowe, Lincs, who married Elizabeth, daughter of Richard Constantine of Bewdley.

WILLIAM, 2nd Lord Burgh - age 28 in 1550. Sat in Parliament 26th Jan. 1551/2 was one of the peers who tried the Duke of Norfolk in 1553. He married Katherine, daughter of Edward Clinton, Earl of Lincoln and by her (who was buried 14th Aug. 1621 had - with several daughters:-

1) Henry, slain in a duel at Holworth Jan. 1578
2) **THOMAS** - 3rd Lord
3) John (Sir) Admiral of England.

William, Lord Burgh, died 10th Sept. 1584, succeeded by Thomas, 3rd Lord Burgh - age 26 in 1584. Took his seat in Parliament 26 Nov. 1584 Governor of BRILL in Flanders 1587/97. Knight of the Garter 23 April 1593. Went on an embassy to Scotland 1593. Succeeded Sir William Russell as Lord Deputy in Ireland 18 April 1597. He married Frances, dau. of John Vaughan, of Sutton-on-Derwent, Yorks, and by her (who was buried 19th July 1647) had issue:-

1) Robert, 4th Lord
2) Elizabeth
and 3 other daughters.

Thomas died 14th October 1597 and was succeeded by **Robert** - 4th Lord aged 3 in 1597, who died 26th Feb. 1601/2, when the Barony of Burgh fell into abeyance.
Elizabeth Burgh, the eldest sister, married - after 17 Jan 1598/99:-

1) George Brooke M.A., Prebendary of York, 4th son of William 10th Lord Cobham. He was concerned with his brother Henry, 11th Lord Cobham, and others, in the Raleigh conspiracy, and was attainted and executed for high treason, and buried at Winchester 5 Dec. 1603.

2) before 24th Oct 1605, Francis Reade, 2nd son of Sir William Reade of Osterleigh, Middx., but by him had no issue.

By her lst husband she had, with 2 daughters, Frances & Elizabeth, an only son:-

Sir William Brooks, K.B. of Sterborough, Surrey & Cooling, Kent.
Bapt. lst Dec 1601, who by Act of Parliament 1609/10 was restored in blood, but not to enjoy the title of Lord Cobham without the King's special grace. He was made a Knight of the Bath 1625/6, and was M.P. for Rochester 1628/9.

Note: The barony of COBHAM was called out of abeyance; the effects of the Act of Attainder of 1602 on the barony, having been removed by Act of Parliament in 1916.

Pedigree of the HYDE Family

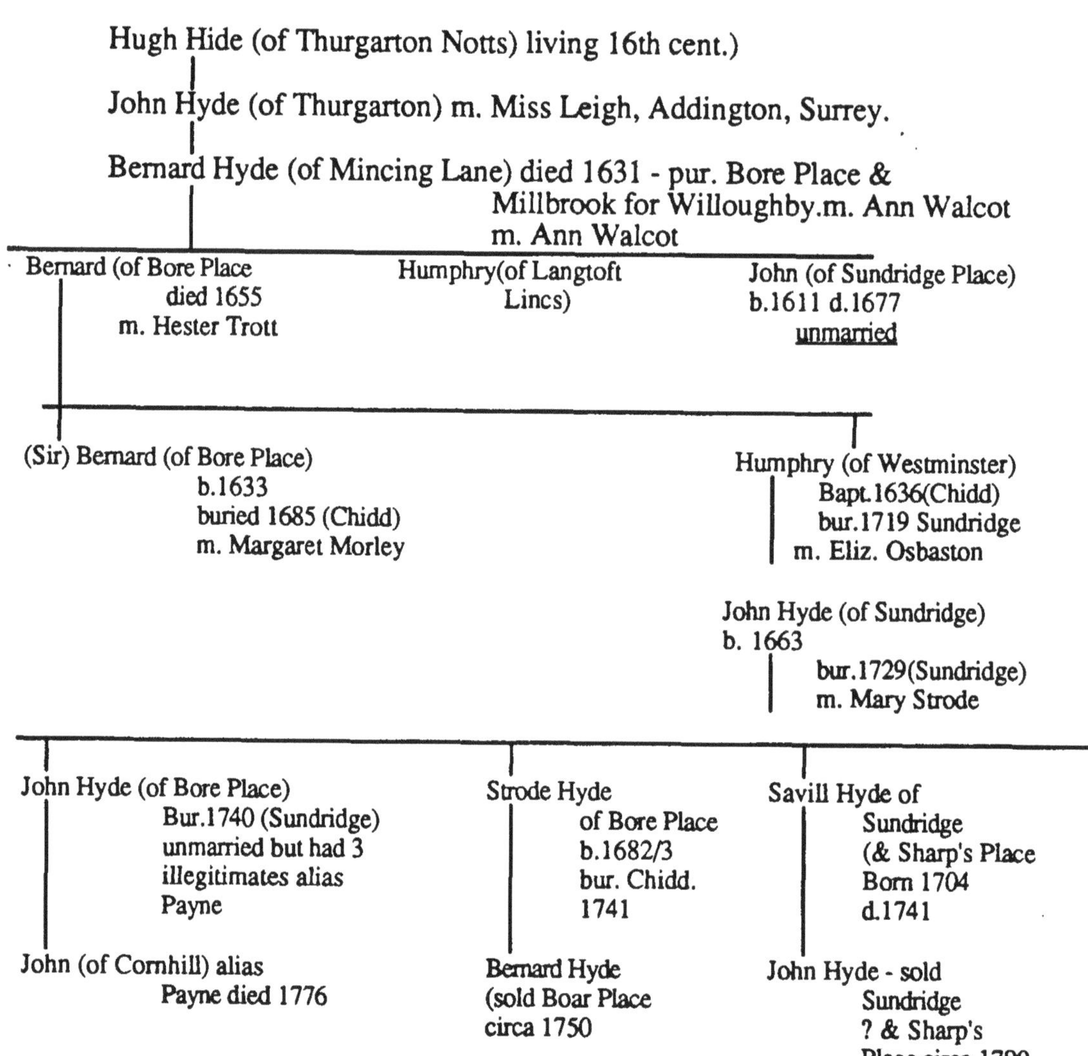

The Family of HYDE - Arch. Canterbury Vol. XXII p. 112

The Family of Hyde of Bore Place and Sundridge.

The following pedigree was entered at the Visitation of London in 1633 by "Anne Hide", widow of Bernard Hyde, a merchant of London:-

Hugh HIDE of Thurgarton in Nottingham, gent

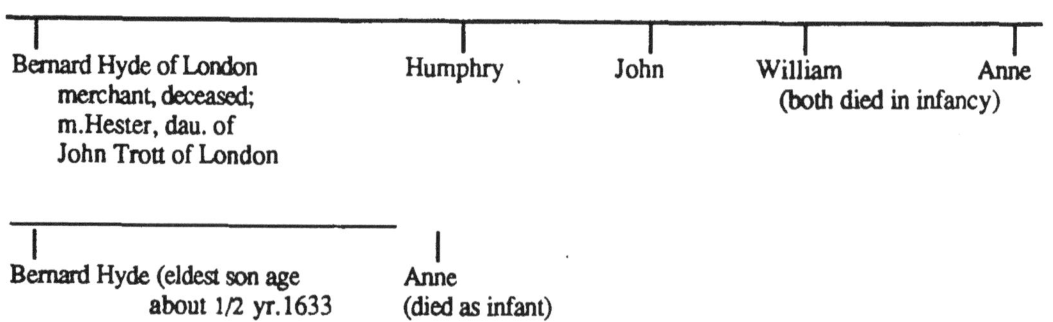

This coast and crest are exemplified under the hand & seal of Sir Wm. Segar, Kt Garter Principal King of Arms, dated 16th Sept. 1609.
Le Neve calls this last named Bernard Hyde, the son of Bernard Hyde and Hester Trott, "Sir Bernard Hyde of Bore Place, Kent," and named his wife "Margaret", daughter of Sir William Morley, of HALNAKED, Sussex, Kent", and he adds this note to the pedigree:-

> "Sir Bernard Hyde of Bore Place Kent, Kntd at .....30th April 1661. Sir Edward Byshe - Visit. of Sussex in Morley's Pedigree for Sir Bernard's wife.

I am not able to connect this family of Hyde with any of the name who were settled in Cheshire, Dorsetshire, Lancashire & Wiltshire. Nor have I attempted to trace the family in Nottinghamshire.

The Registers of Thurgarton do not extend back to the 16th Century; and no search has been made for the wills of the Nottinghamshire ancestors. Branches of this family were, however, located in Lincs and Leicestershire, and still remain in the latter county, though the family estates there have passed into other hands.

The HYDES possessed considerable estates in Kent. In Dr. Harris HISTORY, vol. 1 pp.304/5, 1719, is a view of Bore Place, Sundridge and Sharp's Place, the seats of John Hyde Esq., who was also Lord of the Manors of Sundridge, Wield, & Millbrook.

The earliest entry of any Hyde in the Chiddingstone Registers is in 1636, and in the Sundridge Register in 1665: in the Chevening Registers there are no entries of Hyde.

The following account of this family very considerably enlarges the Visitation Pedigree set out above:-

i. Hugh Hide of Thurgarten, Notts, Gent, the first-named in the Visitation Pedigree, living in the 16th Century, was father of:-

ii. John Hyde of Thurgarton, who married a daughter of ... Leigh, of Addington, Co. Surrey, and by her had issue:-

iii. Bernard Hyde of Mincing Lane, London, merchant, a member of the Salter's Company: one of the Commissioners of Excise of Charles 1: he purchased Bore Place and Milbroke of Sir Percival Willoughby, Kt., at the beginning of the reign of James 1: devisee of lands in Fulham, Richmond, and executor of the will of his "brother" Michael Meryall, citizen & salter of London, 1624.
He died in July 1631. By his will, proved 29 July 1631, he desires to be buried in St. Dunstan's-in-the-East, London, and left £100 towards repairing that church, and £5 to the poor of the parish. His wife is to occupy his capital house in Mincing Lane for her life, or she may have her dwelling in his house at Little Ilford if she prefer it. He gives his son, Bernard Hyde, £3,000 which Mr. John Trott is to give as part of his daughter's marriage portion, and all his cattle at Bore Place. He devises to his

son Humphrey Hyde in fee his lands in Langtoft & Boston, Co. Lincoln. He married Ann, daughter of Humphry Walcot of London (a Shropshire family) and by her had issue:-

1. Bernard Hyde of whom later
2. Humphry Hyde of Langtoft, co. Lincoln - the pedigree of whose family is given in "Blore's RUTLAND".

3. John Hyde of Sundridge Place, Esq., born 1611: died unmarried 27th May and buried at Sundridge 7 June 1677 aged 66..... During the Civil Wars he and Mr Bernard Hyde seem to have received the money raised in Chiddingstone and paid the same to the "Committee at Knowle" for horses, arms, soldiers etc. - evidently for the Parliament. (Chiddingstone Churchwardens & Overseer's Books).

4. William Hyde, died without issue
5. Anne, died without issue.

iv. Bernard HYDE, merchant of London, and of Bore Place; presumably a Parliamentarian in the Civil Wars, for which cause he raised and received money in Chiddingstone, conjointly with his brother John. In 1633 he gave a silver cup with paten cover, with his Arms, crest and initials engraved thereon, to Chiddingstone Church. He died in Ja. 1655, and was buried at St. Dunstan's-in-the-East, London. He married Hester, daughter of John Trott of London, merchant, and by her had issue:

1. Sir Bernard Hyde of Bore Place, born 1633: knighted 30 April 1661 by King Charles II. In 1669 he gave a silver flagon, and in 1675 a silver alms dish to Chiddingstone Church; each has the arms of Hyde impaling Morley engraved on it, and the inscription "Eccl'iae Parachiali de Chiddingstone in agro cantiano DDD Bernadus Hyde, Mil. De Bore Place", and the Year. He was buried at Chiddingstone 1685. He married about 1661, Margaret, daughter and co-heir (with her half-sister Mary, Countess of Derby) of Sir William Morley, K.B., of Halfnaked, Co. Sussex, by his second wife, Mary, daughter of Sir Robert Heath, Kent - by whom he had issue an only son, who died an infant, and was buried in St. Dunstan's-in-the-East, London, 12 May 1662. His widow survived him. Lady Margaret's will is dated 13 Oct. 1690, and was proved with several codicils 10 April 1701, by Sir Wm. Morley, Kent, and Mrs Cicely Osbaston, the Executors. She directs her body to be buried at Boxgrove in Sussex, where she was christened and her parents are buried at or at Chiddingstone, where her husband was buried: or at St. Dunstan's, near Thames Street, where her husband's parents and her only child are buried - which place she is nearest to at her death. She makes bequests to a very large number of relatives, who are named in the will.

2. Humphry, of whom later.
3. William Hyde, born Sundridge 28 July 1645
4. Charles Hyde born Sundridge 25 May 1649
5. Anne, died 24 Feb. 1695, buried at Norton, Co. Leicester: married to William Whalley of Norton, Esq., by whom she had 7 sons and 5 daughters.
6. Katharine, apt June and buried August 1637 at Chiddingstone
7. Elizabeth, Bapt. at Bore Place 29 Sept 1643. Married in 1664 Stanhope Whalley of Norton, Gent (lst cousin of above Wm. Whalley and had issue 2 sons and 2 daughters).

v. Humphry Hyde of St. Anne's, Westminster, and of the Middle Temple, gent., bapt. at Chiddingstone 1 Oct. 1636; was one of the intended Knights of the Royal Oak 1660, his estate being worth £600 per annum; he died 16th and was buried 22nd May 1719 at Sundridge - monumental inscription there. He left a charity of £6 yearly for the education of 10 poor children of Sundridge, payable out of his estate or farm called Gatton's, in the parish of Cliff, Kent. His will is dated 9 Aug. 1718 and was proved 8 June 1719. By it, he directs that he be buried in Sundridge Churchyard, near the bank of the wall of his uncle Hyde's monument, 10 feet deep; he devises Millbrook's farm in Kent to his son John Hyde for life, with remainder to his grandsons, John Hyde and Strode Hyde, successively in tail male... and he directs that the communion plate belonging to his chapel at Boar Place be continued there for the use of the said chapel.

He married at Little Ilford about 1662, Elizabeth, daughter of Francis Osbaston of Aldersbrook Hall, Little Ilford, Co. Essex (she was born 1645 and was buried at

Sundridge 20 July 1713) Monument inscription there. He had issue 5 sons and 5 daughters:-

1. John Hyde, of whom later
2. Bernard - probably died young. Bapt. Sundridge 1665.
3. William Hyde of St. George's Hanover Square; married 1703, Margaret and died in 1740.
4. Henry Hyde, M.A. of Cambridge, born 1681, buried 1706 at Sundridge
5. Edward Hyde of New Inn, London, Born 1687, died unmarried; buried 4th April 1726 at Sundridge. Monument inscription there:-

   "Humphry Hyde Esq., died 16 May 1719, aged 83,
   Edward Hyde, his son, died 29 Mar. 1736, aged 39."
6. Esther, buried Sundridge 1677
7. Margaret buried Sundridge 1678
8. Anne, born 1669, buried 1696/7 at Sundridge. Married 1690 to John Chaplin of St. John the Evangelist London and had 3 children all buried at Sundridge 1691/3.
9. Elizabeth born 1670 & died 1741.
10. Margaret - married twice and died before 1741.

vi. John HYDE of Sundridge Esq., Lord of the manors of Sundridge, Wield & Milbrooks, Co. Kent, and of 1/3rd of the manor of Otford... born 1663, and was buried 28 August 1729 at Sundridge, aged 66. Monument inscription there. His will proved lst Sept. 1729 by Mary Hyde his widow & executrix. He gives £5 each to the poor of Chiddingstone & Sundridge... to his eldest son John Hyde, his pictures at Bore Place & Sundridge and library of books, and directs that he be buried in Sundridge. He married Mary, daughter & coheir of Sir Nicholas Strode of Chevening, co. Kent, Knight & Barrister-at-Law (son of Sir George Strode of Westerham, Kent). He had issue 7 sons & 5 daughters.

1. John Hyde of Bore Place Esq., died unmarried & was buried in Sundridge 26 May 1740. He bequested £3,000 to his 3 natural children, all born on the body of Eliz. Payne: devises to his brother Savile Hyde - Edlows, Sleighter's (otherwise Theobalds) & Sharp's Place in Kent; and to his brother Strode Hyde for his life, Bore Place in Chiddingstone; the manor of Milbrooke & messuages there, with remainder to his nephew Bernard Hyde in tail male: and gives the residue to his brother Savil Hyde, whom he appoints executor.

The elder illegitimate son John Hyde (alias Payne), died in 1776 aged 52, a rich man, and owner of properties in St. Christophers (Leeward Islands, West Indies) and Grenada (Windward Islands).
The second Illegitimate son was baptised at Chiddingstone 10th Dec. 1734 and buried at Sundridge 15 April 1743. Following are the details of the illegitimate John Hyde:-
John Hyde, alias Payne, of Cornhill and of Upper Clapton, died 3 July 1776 age 52 Born 1724. A monumental Inscription at Sundridge Church reads:-

"John Hyde of Cornhill, London, Merchant, died 30 July 1776, aged 52. Humphry Hyde his brother died in April 1743 aged 10. Both were sons of John Hyde of Bore Place, who died in May 1740, and is interred in this chancel. Katherine, wife of above John Hyde, died Feb. 14 1807, aged 79".

He directs his body to be buried at Sundridge in the churchyard, near the Chancel door; and bequests £200 to the Minister & Churchwardens of Sundridge, the interest to be given to 12 poor families. To his wife his chariot & coach-horses, £20,000, and an annuity of £400 payable out of certain estates in the island of St. Christopher, and of £200 out of estates in the island of Grenada; and the residue to his son John Hyde.

2. Humphry HYDE bapt. Sundridge 1691, buried there 1716.
3. Strode HYDE - of whom later.
4. Francis HYDE, born 1698 at Sundridge
5. Bernard HYDE, buried at Sundridge 1701
6. Nicholas HYDE buried at Sundridge 1701
7. Savill HYDE of Sundridge, gent: devisee of Edlows, Sleighters (otherwise Theobalds) & Sharp's Place - all in Co. Kent, under his brother John's Will 1740. He seems to have inherited Sundridge, probably under marriage settlement. Bapt. Sundridge 1704, buried there 1741. Married 1730, Sarah Adamson of Goodman's Fields, Whitechapel, and had issue a son:- John HYDE of Sundridge and of Quorn Den Co - Leicester Esq. He pulled down Sundridge and erected a new house there in 1772. He had a large family of whom Savile John Hyde will be noticed hereafter. Soon after his decease in 1789 Sundridge Place was sold.

vii. Strode HYDE of Bore Place, Esq. devisee for life of Bore Place under will of his eldest brother John 1740. Lord of the manor of Milbrooks, Co. Kent: owned lands in Chiddingstone, Penshurst, Surrendon, Gillingham, Chatham and Hammersmith. Bapt. Sundridge 1692/3, buried in Chiddingstone 1741:- Monumental Inscription there:-

> "Near this place lies the body of Strode Hyde Esq., of Boor Place, who departed this life February ye 5th 1741/2, aged 50".

His will is dated 7 Jan 1741 and proved a month later by Elizabeth Hyde, his widow & executrix. He directs his body to be buried at Chiddingstone: devisees Boar Place, his manor of Millbrook, Surrendon, and his lands in Chiddingstone & Penshurst, to his wife Elizabeth Hyde for life, and then to his heirs: and to his son Bernard Hyde his lands in Hammersmith, Darland in Gillingham, and Chatham, & £25 per annum issuing out of Boar Place, Millbrook etc: and directs that the Communion Plate belonging to Boar Place be continued there for the use of the said Chapel.
He married Elizabeth... & had issue by her:-

1. Bernard HYDE - of whom later
2. Edward HYDE - died an infant
3. Elizabeth

viii. BERNARD HYDE of Southwark, gent: devisee in tail male of Boar Place, Millbrook etc., under the will of his uncle John Hyde 1740. He seems to have barred the entail, and sold Boar Place & Millbrook to Henry Streatfeild Esq. He died 1767/8 and was buried in Christ Church, Newgate, Srr Bernard Hyde was the last of the family who owned Boar Place and Millbrooks in co. Kent: and only a few years later his cousin John Hyde parted with Sundridge; and then all the old Hyde estates in Kent left the family.

The Family of **SEYLIARD**

The **SEYLIARDS** lived at Seyliards until Robert, eighth in descent from Ralph, made Delaware in Brasted his residence. the pedigrees drawn up by Hasted, Streatfeild, and Thorpe all conflict in the most essential particulars, but that here given is a compromise between the three:-

William Seyliard of Delaware, Hever (son of John Seyliard of Delaware and Alice his wife, daughter and heir of Richard Franklin of Reading) married Dorothy, daughter of William Crowndell of Tunstall, and died in 1595, age 39.

1. Sir Thomas Seyliard of Delaware
2. John Seyliard of Salmans, Penshurst.

Sir Thomas Seyliard of Delaware married Elizabeth Beaumont of Gracedieu and had issue:

Sir John Seyliard of Chiddingstone married the daughter of ... Brocket of Herts, and had issue

Sir Thomas of Boxley Abbey.

To revert to William's second son John Seyliard of the Petty Bag Office who purchased Salmans from Sir Thomas Willoughby in 1638; he was Feodary of Kent, and married Frances, daughter of John Reeve, and widow of Thomas Streatfeild, son of Richard Streatfeild of Chiddingstone. In the chancel of the Church at Chiddingstone there is a very fine freestone altar tomb, faced and topped with black marble, and along latin inscription to her memory:-....

> "... Viris duobus juncta, Thomas Streatfeild prius Deinde Johanni Seyliard, utrisq bonos Natalis sortitis et honestas familias Ambob' chara pariter et faecunda fuit..."

Facing the Nave are three achievements of arms; the first Streatfeild impaling Reeve the second /Seyliard impaling **Reeve**: the third Seyliard and 8 quarterings. The last letters on the monument are indistinct; but the arms are beautifully clear, having been repainted by the daughter of Harriet Streatfeild in 1814.

The granddaughter of John and Frances Seyliard married Thomas Woodgate, her name was Susanna. He died young in 1706, and an inscribed stone near the altar rail marks the spot.

Pedigree of Family of STREATFEILD of Chiddingstone

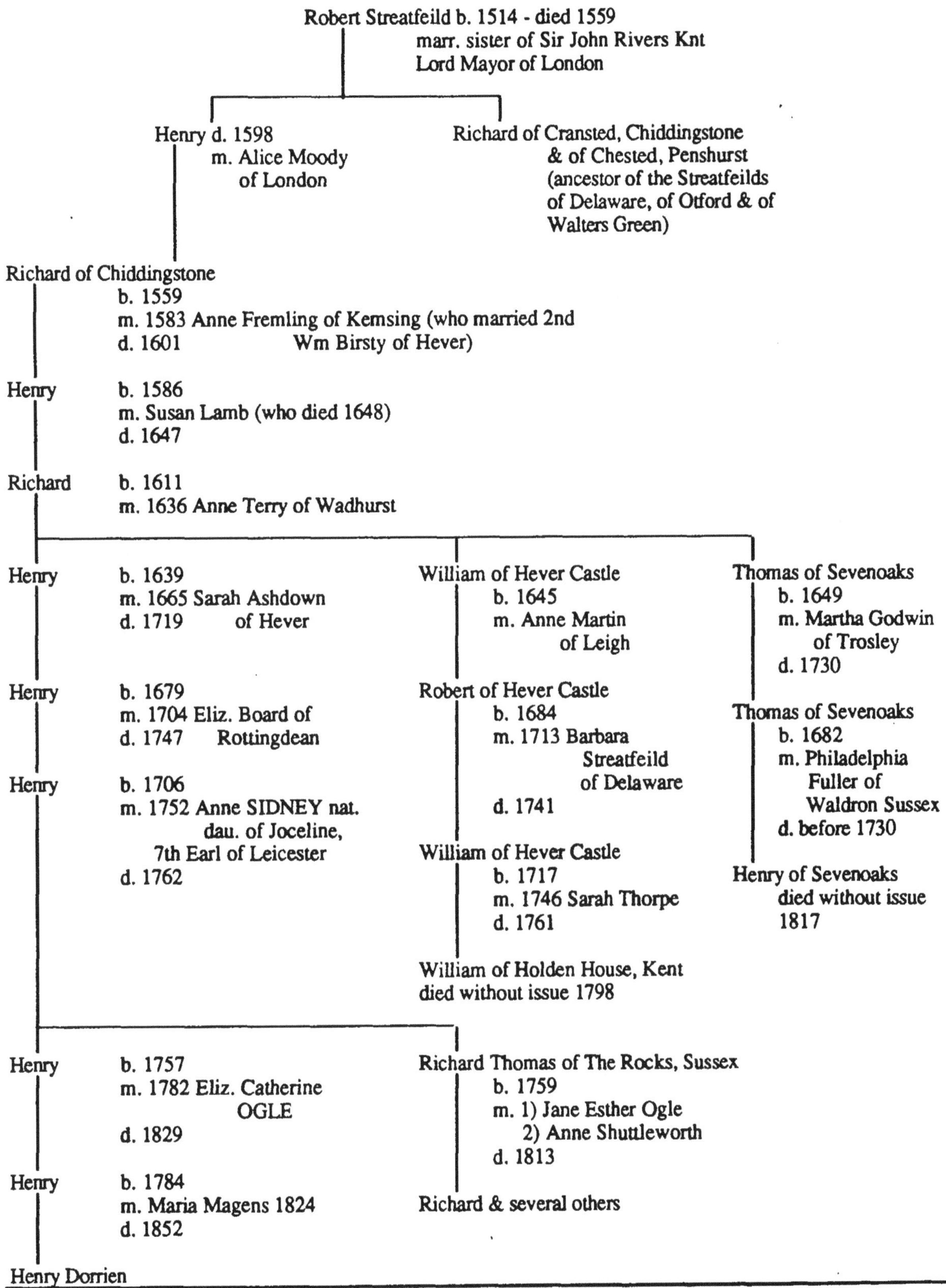

THE FAMILY OF STREATFEILD

1) Robert Streatfeild of Chiddingstone, b. 1514, buried 1558. Married daughter of Richard Rivers of Chafford Place, Penshurst, sister of Sir John Rivers, Knt, Lord Mayor of London, and of Alice Woodgate of Penshurst.

   (a) Henry - of High Street House, Chiddingstone, bu. 1598

   (b) Richard of Chested

THE FAMILY OF STREATFEILD

1). Robert Streatfeild of Chiddingstone, b. 1514, buried 1558. Married daughter of Richard Rivers of Chafford Place, Penshurst, sister of Sir John Rivers; Knight Lord Mayor of London, and of Alice Woodgate of Penshurst.

a) Henry - of High Street House, Chiddingstone, bn. 1598
b) Richard of Chested

2). Henry of High Street House, Chiddingstone, bn. 1598. Married Alice, daughter of Henry Moodie, citizen of London.

a) Henry, died in infancy
b) John died in infancy
c) Elizabeth, married James Beecher of Penshurst
d) Richard, born 1561
e) Margerie, married John Hollamby
f) Anne
g) Agnes

3) Richard of High Street House, married Anne, daughter & co-heir of William Fremling of Kensing (who re-married William \Birsty of Chiddingstone) Died 1601.

a) Henry
b) Margaret, married Edward Moodie
c) Silvester, of the Inner Temple, filacer of Kent, Sussex & Surrey.
d) Thomas, of Shoreham, married Frances, daughter of John Reeve (she remarried John Seyliard of Salmons). They had issue:-

i. Francis, married daughter & heir of John Shatterden
ii Jane; married Edward Taylor
iii Dorothy, married Rev. Edward Powell, Rector of Chiddingstone.

4) Henry of High Street House, b 1586, married Susanna, daughter of Christopher Lamb; he died 1647, she died 1648.
a) Anne, died in infancy
b) Anne, married Thomas Slater, Citizen of London
c) Richard
d) Stephen, married Anne Sharp and had among others, Stephen of Somerden Green
e) William, b 1620, died unmarried
f) Thomas, b. 1629

5) Richard of High Street House, born 1611, married 1636 Anne, daughter of William Terry of Wadhurst and died 1676.

a) Susanna, died in infancy
b) Alice, married WILLIAM WOODGATE of STONEWALL, High Sheriff of Kent
c) Henry
d) Thomas, of Sevenoaks, b 1649, married Martha, daughter and heir of Thomas Godwin of Trottescliffe
e) Robert of London s.p.
f) John of Penshurst b. 1656 died 1726
g) William, of Hever Castle, b 1645 died 1728.

6. Henry Streatfeild - who rebuilt High Street House for the first time - born 1639, married Sarah, daughter of & heiress of John Ashdowne the younger, of Hever and Sarah his wife, who was the relict of John Woodgate of Stonewall. He died 1719.

a) Henry
b) William of Burghersh Court, Chiddingstone, born 1680, married first Elizabeth Cooper of London, second Elizabeth Rogers of Lenborough. He died 1724, having had one daughter Sarah,.who died in infancy.

7. Henry Streatfeild of High Street House, b 1679; married Elizabeth, only daughter & heiress of Richard Beard of Rottingdean. He died 1762.

a) Henry
b) Richard Beard Streatfeild of the Rocks Sussex. b 1709. died 1770 s.p.

8. Henry Streatfeild of High Street House, born 1706, married 1752 Anne Sidney, natural daughter of Jocelyn 7th Earl of Leicester. He died 1762, she in 1812.

a) Henry
b) Richard Thomas of the Rocks, High Sheriff of Sussex 1798
c) Sophia
d) Harriett, married Walter Bracebridge of Atherton Hall

9) Henry Streatfeild of High Street House, born 1757, High Sheriff of Kent 1792, married 1782 Elizabeth Catherine, daughter of the Dean Ogle of Westminster.

(a) Henry
(b) Thomas, Lieut-Col. in the Guards
(c) Sidney, private Secretary to Sir Robert Peel
(d) Richard of Hever, Commander R.N., married 1824, Anne daughter of Henry Woodgate of Riverhill
(e) William, Vicar of East Ham
(f) Charles Ogle Major-General R.E.
(g) Edward
(h) George Newton, died 1828 unmarried
(i) Anna, died at South Park 1830
(j) Sophia Catherine married 1822 Prebendary Whish of Wells
(k) Arabella, married 1831 Rev. Wilgress

(l) Jane Esther, married Major Scoones
(m) Frederick, died 1829
(n) Robert died 1824
(o) John, of the Home Office
(p) Francis Stanier
(q) Emily

10) Henry Streatfeild of High Street House, born 1784, married 1824, Maria, daughter of Magens Dorrien-Magens, relict of J. Pepper of Bigod's House. He died 1852
(a) Henry Dorrein
(b) Edward Ogle Captain 44th Regt.
(c) Newton William, married Flora, daughter of Rev. Hoskins, Rector of Chiddingstone
(d) Richard John of Chested, married Harriet, daughter of Colonel Henry Armytage
(e) Frances Charlotte, married Rev. Polhill

11) Henry Dorrien of High Street House, Capt. 1st Life Guards, born 1825, married Marion, daughter of Oswald Smith of Blendon Hall, and died 1889.
(a) Henry
(b) Sidney, married Lucy Jenney
(c) Gerald, married Ida Combe
(d) Oswald, married Hon. Geraldine Fitzgerald
(e) Eric, D.S.O., Capt. Gordon Highlanders
(f) Philip, M.V.O., Admiral - married Effie Carey
(g) Violet, married Lord Henry Neville
(h) Ruby, married Viscount Colville of Culross
(i) Ivy Marion, married F.G. Gunnis

12) Col. Sir Henry Streatfeild, G.C.V.O., &c. married Lady Florence Beatrice, daughter of the 2nd Earl of Lichfield.
(a) Henry Sidney John, Col. Grenadier Guards, married Dorothy, daughter of Sir Daniel Cooper, Bart.

The CHESTED Branch

Richard Streatfeild of Chested, younger son of Robert Streatfeild of Chiddingstone died 1584 leaving
Richard of Penshurst & Westerham, whose daughter & heiress Barbara married
Robert Streatfeild of Delaware.
The second wife of above Richard Streatfeild of Chested gave birth to:

ROBERT STREATFEILD of Chested, born 1571, married Susan Everest and died 1657

- (c) Richard of Chested died 1679 unmarried
- (e) Robert
- (f) Sarah, married JOHN WOODGATE of STONEWALL.

ROBERT STREATFEILD OF CRANSTED born 1608, married 1636 Sarah, daughter of WILLIAM WOODGATE of Stonewall. He died 1654, she in 1681.

- (a) Robert born 1640
- (b) Richard of Ford Place, ancestor of S's of Otford
- (c) Thomas of Vexour, ancestor of S's of Walters Green
- (d) Sarah, married Richard Goodhugh of Tonbridge
- (g) William of Delaware b. 1636 did 1676

Pedigree of Family of MEADE-WALDO

Edward Wakefield MEADE Esq., of New Bridge House, DAWLISH, Co. Devon.

Assumed by Royal Licence 8th June 1830, the additional surname and arms of WALDO.
He married 1826, Harriette Bloomfield, daughter of Colonel Gustavus ROCHFORT, M.P. for Rochfort, Co. Westmeath. He died 1858, leaving:

1) Edmund Waldo of Stonewall Park & Hever Castle
2) Gustavus Rochfort, who died 1863
3) Harriett Dorothea, married 1850 Rev. W.W. Battye, The Rector of Hever

----

Pedigree of the ALPHEW, READ & WILLOUGHBY Families

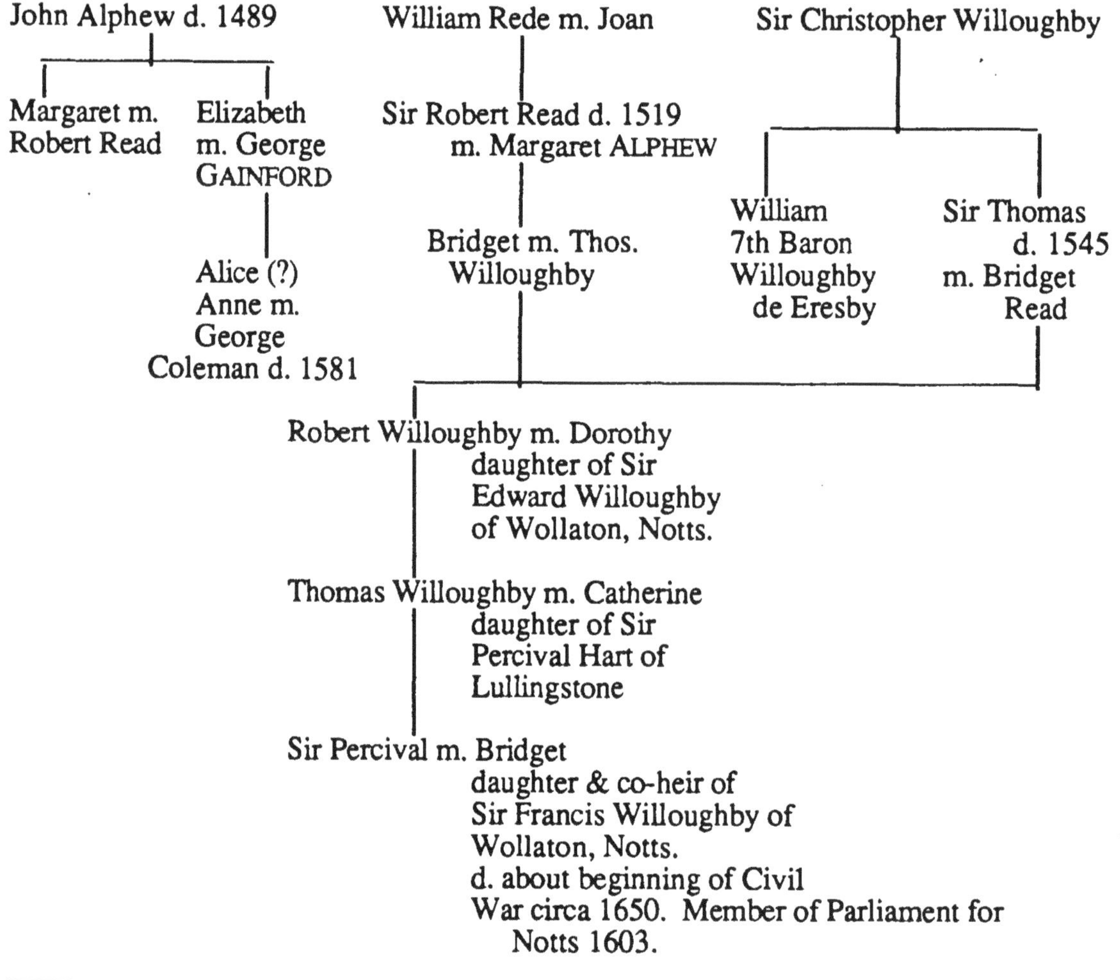

BORE PLACE (Family of Alphew)
Stow - Survey of London. Edtn 1618, p. 697

A Monument in the Parish Church of St Mary Magdalen.

George Colman, Gent, a Free-man of this Citie of London, was borne in Richmondshire, and after inhabited at CALLIS, in the time of the first surprise thereof by the French, Anno Domini 1558, where he lost all his lands and substance; and at the age of 95 years he died, the sixteenth of September, 1600, and lyeth interred on the north side of the Communion table. By him is buried Alice his wife, the only daughter of George Gainsford, Esquire, a younger sonne of Sir John Gainsford, of Crohurst, in the County of Surrey, knight and brother to the last Sir John Gainsford, of the same place, knight.

Which Anne (sic) was sole heir to her mother Elizabeth daughter and co-heir to John **Alphew**, of **Boare Place**, in the Countie of Kent, Esquire. She died the fourth of March, Anno Domini 1581.

Sir Robert Read of Bore Place
(Sir Robert Rede of Bore Place)

(Foss "Judges of England", Dict. - of Nat. Biog. The Black Book of Lincoln's Inn. Dugdale - Chronica Series)

SIR ROBERT READ (Rede) of Bore Place was of a family which originally came from Morpeth in Northumberland. His grandfather John, was a Serjeant -at-law in Hen. IV's reign, and was settled at Norwich, and his father's and mother's names were according to his will, and to a deed founding a fellowship at Jesus College Cambridge, William and Joan Rede. Robert was their third son, and was educated at Buckingham Hall, (afterwards Magdalen College) in Cambridge, and became a fellow of King's Hall (on the site of which part of Trinity College was built); he was placed at Lincoln's Inn:-

In 1468-9 Michaelmas Term: Governors...John Sulyard Master of the Revels Robert Rede.

1471/2	Governors............	John Sulyard
	Butler	Robert Reede
1472/3	Auditor	Robert Reed
1473/4	Governors	John Sulyard
	Pensioner	Robert Reed
1474/5	Pensioner	Robert Reede - and made Treasurer
1475/6	Treasurer	Robert Rede (till 1477/8)
1477/8	Marshall	Robert Rede
1480/1	Autumn Reader	Robert Rede
1481/2	Governors	Robert Rede (one of 4)
1483/4	Governor	Robert Rede
1485/6	Lent Reader	Robert Rede - & elected Serjeant-at-law in Lincoln's Inn

1503 Gave directions for the ceremony of washing the hands after the offertory, and before the second part of the service as to masses to be said in Waltham Abbey.

1508 Nov. 23rd Granted by the Governors and all the benchers to Robt Rede, Knight, Chief Justice of the Common Pleas, for the love that he has for the Inn, that whenever the office of Butler to the Inn shall become vacant the said Robert shall nominate whom he pleases to the said office.

1510 Order by Robert Reed, knight, C.J. of the King's Bench, and other judges concerning the keeping of vacations.

He was appointed King's serjeant on 8th April 1494, and was made a judge of the King's Bench on Nov. 24, 1495, when he was knighted. In Oct. 1506 he was raised to the Chief Justiceship of the Court of Common Pleas, for which advancement the judge was obliged to pay to the avaricious king the sum of 400 marks, as appears by an account rendered by the noted Edmund Dudley. King Henry VII named him as one of the Executors of his will.

Henry VIII retained him in his place which he retained till his death on Jan.. 8th 1519. He was buried in the chapel of St Katherine at the Charterhouse, where he founded a chantry of £8 a year for 30 years. He also left £100 to Jesus College to found a fellowship & brewery there, and established 3 public lectures at the University of Cambridge, called "Barnaby's Lectures", on humanity, logic and philosophy, which were, in 1858, consolidated into one lecture a year with the name of the founder.

By his marriage to Margaret, one of the daughters of John Alphew of Bore Place in Chiddingstone, Kent, he became possessed of considerable property in Kent. His will is in the London Registry, and he left a number of legacies to different religious houses, including the Austin, Grey and White Friars in London: Syon Monastery: and the Nunnery of Malling where Elizabeth, his daughter was a nun, later becoming abbess, and as she made known she would throw every obstacle in the way of Henry VIII suppressing it quietly in 1538, she was removed from post of abbess to make way for a tool of Cromwell.

He made bequests to King's College Cambridge: established a fellowship at Jesus College: and was also a liberal benefactor to both the universities and to the Abbey of Waltham.
Dugdale - Chronica Series. Servientium ad legem 1494 Rob. Rede - Serviens at legem T.R. apud Cantuar 8 Apr.

Justic. ad Plac. coram 1496 Rob. Read, constit. T.R.
Rege Apud. Westminster 24 Nov.
Justiciariorum de Banco 1507 Rob Rede, miles, Capitalis Justic.
" " " 1509 " " " " "

Sir Robert Read was elected a Member of Parliament which assembled 5 Feb. 1514.

The Family of Willoughby - Foss "Judges of England", the Black Book of Lincoln's Inn. Dugdale - Chronica Series.

THOMAS WILLOUGHBY was the fourth son of Christopher Willoughby, whose grandfather was the second son of William, the 5th Baron Willoughby de Eresby. William, the judge's eldest brother, succeeded to that title in 1508, as 7th Baron, on failure of the senior branch. Thomas, as was common with younger brothers, was destined to the Law: and preparing himself for this forensic career in Lincoln's Inn (of which he was admitted member on July 16th 1502), he was nominated:-

In 1505/6 Master of the Revels Willoughby Junior on his default is fined 26s8d.

1507/8	Auditor	Wyllughby	
1509/10	Butler	"	Auditor Wyllughby
1510/11	Auditor	"	
1512/13	"	"	Pensioner Wyllughby
1515/16	Marshall.	Thos. Willoughby	

1516 Thos. Willoughby is to answer for certain wastes & excessive expenses, not beneficial to the Community, at Christmas, and also for his contempt in not having a red gown when he was Marshal, according to the ancient custom & ordinance of the Inn.

1516/17 Autumn Reader: Willughby
1517/18 Governor & Lent Reader: Willoughby
1518/19 Governor & Treasurer

1519/20 Willoughby - newly-made serjeant.

Dugdale: Chronica Series: Justiciariorum de Banco. 1538. Thomas Willoughby, miles constitutus T.R. apud Westminster 9 Oct.

In 1521 he became a Serjeant-at-Law, and in 1530 was constituted King's Serjeant. While holding that dignity he and John Baldwin were made knights in 1534, being the first serjeant who had then ever accepted that distinction. He was raised to the bench as a judge of the Common Pleas on Oct. 9th 1537, and dying on Sept. 29. 1525, lies buried in the church of Chiddingstone, Kent. By his marriage with Bridget, daughter and co-heir of Chief Justice Sir Robert Read, he acquired the estate of Bore Place in Chiddingstone, which devolved on his son Robert, whose descendant Francis was made a baronet in 1677, and his successor, Thomas was, in 1712, created Lord Middleton of Middleton, Warwick, a title which still survives.

Thomas WILLOUGHBY - Christopher Rogers, Marriage Settlement - from Middleton MSS)
A.D. 1589. Elizabeth Willoughby, daughter of Thomas, was to marry Christopher Rogers of Sutton Valence, gent. One of the clauses was that "Thos. Willoughby should provide convenient and sufficient meat, drink and lodging, and convenient chambers and furniture thereunto" for Christopher Rogers & Elizabeth Willoughby, and for one man-servant and one maidservant "meete and convenient for their estates and degrees, with him the said Thos. Willoughby at BOARE PLACE or elsewhere at the dwelling house of Thos. Willoughby in Kent where he shall be resident, and also sufficient and convenient winter meat, summer meat, pasture and keep for two geldings of Christopher Rogers". Another clause was that if Thos. Willoughby died or **either side objects to their living together**, then £40 per annum is to be paid to Christopher & Elizabeth.
Thomas Willoughby was to pay Christopher £300 in three instalments, at Boare Place on the Nativity of St John in 1590, 1591 & 1592, £100 on each occasion. Thos. Willoughby was to convey to two trustees certain properties in Sundridge which he had purchased from his uncle Christopher Willoughby deceased, and also certain lands in Sundridge which bound the highway from Goldhill Cross to Chiddingstone. W, to lands of Thos. Willoughby late parcel of the tenement called BAYLYES (? Bayleaf) S & E, to the way from Goldhill Cross to Bowsell N. Thomas Willoughby was to continue to enjoy the use of this property as long as he paid the £300, otherwise the properties were to pass to Christopher Rogers. Now it seems that 5 months later Thos. Willoughby was unable to fulfil the above agreement regarding the £300 - for he mortgaged a block of his properties:-

Lands called Pollinlandes, Woodgatefielde, Stonye Crofte & Milbroke Meade, in all 60 acres. Bounds were- S. to land once Lord Burgh's called STONECROFT. S & W to land of heirs of Wm. Ware: S & E to BRODE EYE: E. to Polbrokemeade: W. to land of Thos. Willoughby Esq., formerly occupied by Richard Taylor, now by Thomas Taylor. N. to highway from Bowbeche to Pensherst: E to a certain lane there leading towards Chiddingstone.

1594 Thos. Willoughby raised a mortgage for £400 on above lands from Thomas Browne of Chiddingstone, IRONMASTER, and continued to occupy them at £30 per annum. 6 months later Thomas Browne sold these lands for £400.

Pedigree of the WOODGATE Family

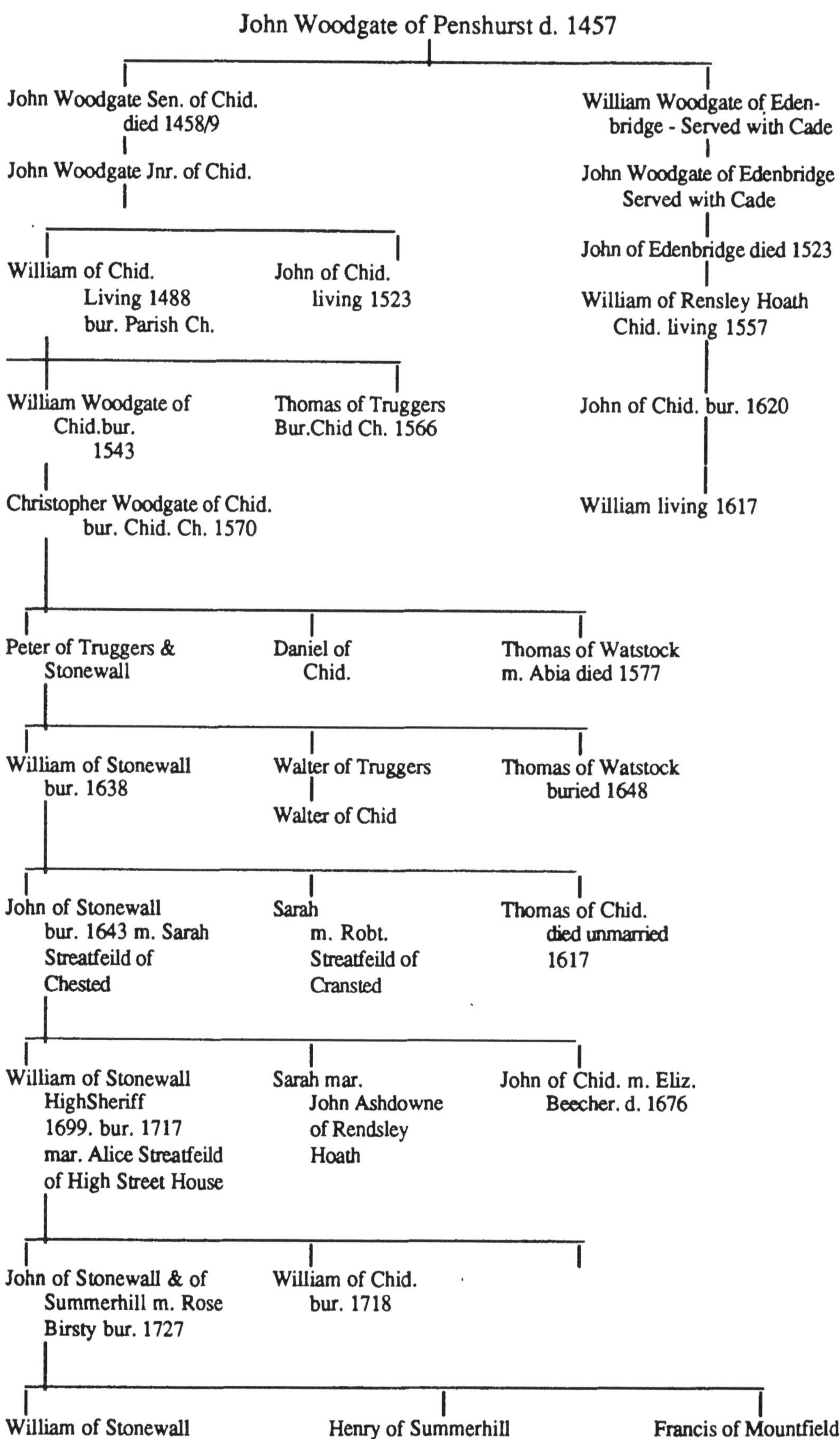

The Family of WOODGATE (Woodgate Family History)

Tradition on the Family states that WOODGATES are of Saxon ancestry. In 1271 there were Woodgates in Kent as well as in many other counties.

The origin of the name itself should inform us that those who bear it are likely to be numerous. Woodgates evidently dwelt by the gate or hatch leading into one of the numerous woods or deer forests. John-at-the Woodgate would be such a man's description, and when surnames crept in, Woodgate would be the one adopted.

The origin of the family was borne in mind when the arms were chosen. The squirrel - the denizen of the wood - the acorns outlined against the outline of the chevron, the blue sky: the livery colour, green, like that of the foliage: what could have been more appropriate?

The earlier history of the Kentish family is somewhat vague, though many documents exist to elucidate it. It is almost certain that with time at one's disposal a connected pedigree could be constructed almost as far back as the Conquest.

There was a Henry de Woodgate in a suit about Throwley (near Faversham) in 1281. And 100 years later in 1382 a John Woodgate was living. He settled in Penshurst, and founded a family which established itself in the south west corner of Kent in a neighbourhoos of which Chiddingstone may be termed the centre. No traces of Woodgates can be discovered in the chiddingstone area prior to the above-mentioned John Woodgate of Penshurst: he must have migrated there from some other locality, possibly from Throwley.

John Woodgate of Penshurst, in **1435**, hired lands called Hawden Mead and 60 acres of pasture. He is mentioned again as being feoffee, otherwise trustee, withRobert Darkynholl and John Dardynhall of Otford and John Reme of Tonbridge, of lands in Leigh, Tonbridge, Penshurst and Chiddingstone, under a deed dated 20th Jan. 1433.

He left two sons, John of Chiddingstone and William of Edenbridge. Both, together with their sons, took part in the great Kentish rising under Jack Cabe in 1450. The names of 4 Woodgates are found in the list of rebels.

John of Chiddingstone, the second son, married Thomasin Wickenden, and was ancestor of the Woodgates of Hever. Walter, of Penshurst, the 3rd son, (circa 1460-1540) was ancestor of the Woodgates of Penshurst, Sundridge, Hadlow, Brenchley, etc.

William, the eldest son, owned lands called BABEFIELD, held of the Manor of Chiddingstone Burghersh, in 1477. In 1490 he was owner of the Leas, Greffield, (otherwise Grottfield) and the Marle, all held of the same manor. William Woodgate was buried in the Parish church of Chiddingstone.

William was succeeded in Babefield in **1499** by his son **William Woodgate of Woodgate**, Chiddingstone; Thomas, the other son, appears to have had the Leas, Grottfield and the Marle as in 1629 they were vèsted in his descendant William Woodgate of Stonewall.

William, **the son**, was steward of the lands of the Duke of Buckingham, and keeper (i.e. land-agent) of the Manor & Parks at Penshurst.

In 1509 it was presented by the homage of the Manor on the part of FRENDEN that William Woodgate had encroached upon the highway at Westcroft 'in terr. de Curdehouse".

In 1512, on the death of John Alphew of Boar Place Chiddingstone, Lord of the Manors of Chiddingstone Burghersh and Smythestreet temp Edward IV, it was found that he was seised (that he owned) jointly with William Woodgate, John Ware and another (who survived) of 3 messuages and 100 acres arable, 26 acres meadow, 250 acres pasture and 30 acres woodland in Chiddingstone, Sundridge, Penshurst and Chevening...... He was also seised of a messuage called CHESTED, and 40 acres arable and $2^1/_2$ meadow in Penshurst.

William Woodgate's will dated Feb. 28th 1540 remains. He directs that he should be buried in Chiddingstone Parish Church next to his father, giving to the church for his burial there 6/8d. To be spend on his burial day 53/4d; and the same sum to the poor. For an honest priest to sing for his soul and his wife's soul, and for those he was found to pray for, for one year, £2.13.4 (Three score masses)...... To son Christopher, the house called Woodgates, and the lands thereto belonging in Chiddingstone & Penshurst, and all other lands &c. contained in a deed sealed 24th March 1538......Supervisor William Beecher, who was to have 3/4.

(signed) William Woodgate

Witnesses: Sir John Doggett, parish Priest, Thomas Bassett & others - proved at London 15th March 1540.

Christopher Woodgate was apparently unmarried. In 1540 it was presented by the homage on the part of Frendon that Christopher Woodgate complains of assault & battery committed on him by John Ellis. His brother John Woodgate who had been left lands in Cowden by their father, continued to occupy them until 1545, when he appears to have moved to Tonbridge.

There exists the will of John Woodgate of Edenbridge, the grandson of that William Woodgate who served under Jack Cade, and this was proved at Malling in 1523. A son of his, William, was living at Chiddingstone in 1557, when he attested a deed: he wa then at "Riversdale Heath" which must surely be Rendsley Heath, in the neighbourhood of Truggers & Stonewall.

His son, John Woodgate, lived at Rendsley Heath, and left a will dated 8th October 1617. "Being aged & sickly" he directs that he should be buried in the church or churchyard of Chiddingstone......Son William to have all the timber in the closes already felled, and the two boxes of title deeds......This William appears to have died childless, and so that branch of the family died out.

To revert to **Walter**, younger son of John Woodgate junior, who fought against Jack Cade. He appears on the Court Rolls frequently from 1480 onwards, and in 1509 owns land formerly belonging to Fynch. In 1515 he alienates to Henry Jessop[p and Thomas Skynner, lands etc., late of Alice Coleyn.

In 1518 (when Stretfield and Stretfyld begin to appear on the Court Rolls of the Honour of Otford, on the part of Somerden) he is a trustee of two properties; one, of house & 50 acres of John Alford, with John Goldsmith and Andrew Combridge. The other, Longmead & Kyngshell...... Walter Woodgate settled in Penshurst: he was there in 1513.... and left several sons.... of whom:-

Edward was living at Chiddingstone in 1543 and in Penshurst in 1544. In 1564 he and his wife Alice convey land in Penshurst to John Rivers of London. Alice seems to have been a daughter of Richard Rivers of Chafford Place, Penshurst, as was likewise her sister the wife of Robert Streatfeild of High Street House. Edward died in 1574 and his son:-

Thomas Woodgate settled first in Penshurst and then at Chiddingstone, dying at Hadlow in 1619.

To return to the last remaining branch of the Woodgates of this neighbourhood - that of Thomas Woodgate of **Truggers**, brother of Wiliam Woodgate of Woodgate, and ancestor of the Summerhill family.

In **1544** he purchased **Truggers**, a property at **Rendsley Heath**, consisting of about 50 acres of land, which continued in the family for many generations. Truggers belonged originally to John **Slighters**, afterwards to **John Pigott**, and then to Henry Pigott, who sold it to **Woodgate**. It was held of the Manor of Chiddingstone Burghersh. Woodgate also held various lands of the Keng in capite, and in the time of Henry VIII obtained the royal licence to alienate some 50 acres at Rendsley to Anne Bond, widow. Lands held in capite could only be alienated on payment of a fine, often arbitrary: and such fines continued to exist till the time of Charles II, when they were swept away, and an equivalent revenue granted to the crown. He seems also to have purchased the RYE, otherwise HOLMWELL, at Rendsley Heath, which in 1525 belonged to Henry Pigott and in 1557 to Thomas Woodgate. One year before he purchased Truggers, i.e. in 1543, Thomas Woodgate appears to have been one of the chief men of Chiddingstone (after the Willoughbys of Boar Place). There are about 80 names, and the following are the first nine:-

Thomas Willoughby, one of the justices of the King's Bench	Lands	£10
Humphry Walrond, Gent.	Lands	20/-
Thomas Woodgate	Goods	13/4
Stephen Pays	Goods	13/4
Richard Streatfeild	Goods	13/4
William Bassett	Goods	5/4
William Ashdowne	Goods	5/-
John Ashdowne	Goods	4/8
Radus Ashdowne	Goods	4/-

Two years later the order is as follows:- (1545)

Humphry Willoughby, Gent.	Lands	40/-
Christopher Willoughby, Gent.	Lands	40/-
Robert Stretfylde	Goods	32/-
Thomas Woodgate	Goods	16/-
William Ashedowne	Goods	13/-
William Pygot	Lands	12/-
Christopher Woodgate	Lands	10/-
Raff Ashdowne	Lands	10/-
John Bassett	Goods1	10/-
William Bassett	Goods	10/-
Bryget Willoughby, widow	Lands	9/-

About 1558, out of 55 names, the first three are:-

Richard Stretfelde	Goods	£22
Henry Stretfeld	Goods	£16
Thomas Woodgate	Goods	£12

The year before Thomas Woodgate's death, i.e. 1564, out of 52 names the first four are:-

Thomas Willoughby Esq.	Lands	£40
Richard Stretfelde	Goods	£20
Henry Stretfeld	Goods	£14
Thomas Woodgate	Goods	£12
9th comes Christopher Woodgate	Lands	£7
and Peter Woodgate	Lands	£5

Thomas Woodgate died in 1565. He left a will but it cannot be found in any of the Courts of Probate. We have learnt one or two particulars of it from a suit of chancery of 1595. The will was dated Jan. 1565. By it (amongst other things) he gave to William his third son a property at Rendsley Heath called CASDENNE, containing 24 acres, in tail male, with remainder to his second son, Thomas in tail male. **William** died unmarried soon after attaining his majority in 1570. **Thomas**, his brother died 7 years later (1577), but he had first mortgaged CASDENNE to Richard WATERS, of Chiddingstone, Miller, who, by directions contained in Thomas's will, sold CASDENNE to John & Francis COMBRIDGE of Penshurst, who entered into possession and settled it on ABIA, widow of Thomas Woodgate and then the wife of Francis COMBRIDGE. Both John & Francis died several years previously to 1595. The land was claimed by Andrew, John & Robert Combridge, as brothers and heirs of Francis: and also by Peter & Daniel Woodgate, the two remaining sons of Thomas the Elder, as heirs in gavelkind.

Of Daniel Woodgate, the youngest son, we know nothing, except that he was Churchwarden of Chiddingstone in 1578.

Thomas Woodgate, of the "Stooke" (or **Watstock**) the second son is described sometimes as "clothier". His marriage settlement was made in 1566, and he left no male issue surviving. He died in 1577 and devised **WATSTOCK** (The Stoke) to Abia his wife, for life, and after her death to his three nephews, Walter, Thomas & William Woodgate. The will was proved by Abia, who soon after married Francis Combridge, on whose death she married his cousin Anthony Combridge of Newhouse, Penshurst.

THOMAS, the second nephew, succeeded to Watstock under the entail, Walter having sold to him his interest under the will.

The eldest son of Thomas Woodgate of Truggers, was **Peter Woodgate**, who succeeded to that property. Once, in 1577, he is described in a deed as "Peter Woodgate, of Chiddingstone, clothier, son of Thomas Woodgate, late of Cranbrook deceased, clothier." If this deed is correct, then it can only be supposed that Thomas went off in early days to Cranbrook, at the same time probably as his brother Peter went to the adjoining town of Hawkhurst, (the two chief centres of the cloth manufacturing industry); that, Thomas while still there, purchased land at Chiddingstone under his description of "clothier", and eventually returned to Chiddingstone: and that when Peter sold the same land in 1575, it was deemed advisable by the attorney to identify Peter as the son of the purchaser.

Peter Woodgate married in 1562, Joan, daughter of John Bassett of Chiddingstone, whose family had been long settled in the parish. In the reign of Edward III (1373) Thomas Bassett appears as one of the chief men in Chiddingstone. About the time of Peter Woodgate, in 1558 and 1559, the Bassetts of Chiddingstone intermarried with the families

It is almost certain that **Peter Woodgate built** STONEWALL which was still in the family less than a century ago: the main part of the house has been pulled down and only a small remnant left. However, we are informed that the inscription **"W.W.1590"** is carved upon a beam in the remaining part of the old house. In 1590, Peter's son William was about 14 years old: what is more probable than some boyish instinct led him to climb up and carve his intials in his father's house? This shows at least that the place had been built, and was then inhabited by Peter. Again, two years previously, Peter Woodgate had settled **Truggers** in trust for his eldest son **Walter**: it seems that he left Truggers to reside at Stonewall. Peter Woodgate, who was living in 1605, died soon after; no entry of his burial and no will can be found.

Thomas, the second son of Peter, was of WATSTOCK.

Walter Woodgate of Truggers, eldest son of Peter Woodgate of Stonewall, owned Sealefeild, Rook's Hoath, and other lands. He was churchwarden from time to time, as in 1622. In 1625, on the occasion of his son William's marriage, he settled on him by deed dated 10th July:-

Truggers & 50 acres
Rook's Hoath in Chiddingstone & 24 acres.

William Woodgate of Truggers, the elder son, had a numerous famioly, and for the advancement on marriage of his son **Thomas**, by deed in 1655 settled on him:-

Truggers
Rook's Hoath
House & 8 acres at Rendsley Hoath purchased 1643 of John Care
16 acres of arable, pasture & woodland in Chiddingstone, purchased in 1626 of Henry Ashdowne.

By an indenture of 1664, John Sage of Speldhurst, in consideration of £305, conveyed to Thomas Woodgate of Chiddingstone, GEERES and its appurtenances containing 20 acres of land and 8 acres of wood, late in the occupation of John Sage of Sundridge.........
Thomas Woodgate's wife was Ann, daughter of Michael Bassett of Chiddingstone, Lord of the Manor of Stangrave in Edenbridge. In Michael Bassett's will, proved 1682, he mentions his daughter Ann Woodgate, widow, and her two children Anne and Thomas, both under age.
We have Thomas Woodgate's will of 1669, describing him as of Chiddingstone:-

> To wife Ann, life estate in Truggers and furniture
> Trustees to let Geeres, accumulate proceeds and hand them over to son Thomas at 21.
>
> All lands in Kent & Sussex to son William, including Sealefields: and son Thomas to release to William his right in ROBERT LANDS (Robertland consisting of 34 acres near Rendsley's Hoath was purchased in 1652 by Thomas Woodgate of Chiddingstone, of John Seyliard of Delaware for £310. In 1477 it belonged to John Ashdowne. (Rabbotteslande)

Thomas's elder son was William of Truggers who died 1714, leaving everything to his elder brother **Thomas**. This Thomas is described as "of Burwash, Sussex, gent:" in 1689. His will dated 1716 described him as of Chiddingstone, and after a few legacies he gave all his lands in Chiddingstone & elsewhere to John LONGLEY - will proved 1742.

STONEWALL PERIOD
1590 - 1718

William Woodgate of STONEWALL, third son of Peter Woodgate of Stonewall, married in 1602 Joanna, daughter & heiress of Andrew Combridge of Chiddingstone. The settlement was dated 1st September 1602, by which certain lands consisting of two houses in Penshurst, land called the EYLAND in Chiddingstone, and certain lands called BRAMSELL were by Andrew Combridge granted to John Turner of Cowden and John Ashdowne of Chiddingstone, in trust for the parties to the marriage and their issue, subject to the life interest of Andrew Combridge. At the same time John Combridge, brother of Andrew, settled on his niece a small property called KEYSDEN. Andrew Combridge died in 1624.

The **Combridges** were an ancient family of Penshurst, and in the 13th century held lands in Chiddingstone and other nearby villages. Coldharbour and Hawden were two of the ancient family estates in Penshurst.

William Woodgate continually signs the Chiddingstone Parish accounts in a clear well-formed hand, and for a number of years was churchwarden. He seems to have used sometimes for his seal the **acorn**, which perhaps is more properly the family crest than the squirrel. In October 1625 an assessment was made on the parish for repairing Chiddingstone Church which had been burnt down the 17th July previously at the rate of sixpence for every house and sixpence an acre. There is a list of 82 owners of property and their acreage, amounting to 2,851 acres (not including "outbounder" apparently, which would increase the total by many hundreds). The largest owners were:-

Bernard Hyde Esq.	200 acres
William Birsty	100 "
William Woodgate of Stonewall	100 "
Henry Streatfeild	100 "
Samuel Godden	100 "
John Piggott	100 "
Thomas Walter	100 "
William Hawkins' wo.	89 "
William Woodgate Jr of Truggers	70 "
Thomas Brett	70 "
Richard Hollamby	70 "
Walter Tye	70 "
William Everist	70 "
Widow Combridge (of Andrew)	65 "

The outbounders included:-

William Everist senr	90 "
Matthew Ashdowne	80 "
Robert Streatfeild	70 "

William Woodgate's land is stated to consist of 10 acres meadow, 70 acres pasture, and 20 acres wood. This is not altogether satisfactory; for there is no **arable** land mentioned. Bejsides which Stonewall comprised 200 acres, and William owned considerable property besides, which was worth altogether £200 a year.

He died at Stonewall on 24th August 1638, and was buried at Chiddingstone. On his death an Inquisition post mortem was held, to ascertain what lands were held of his of the King in capite: the jury returned that the only lands held in capite consisted of a house and 100 acres occupied by John Bassett, two houses in Chiddingstone, one of which was occupied by Thomas Ledett, and the capital messuage in which he himself dwelt.

His WILL (the first extant will of the Stonewall branch) dated 1638, begins in the quaint style of the period:-

> "I bequeath my soule to Almightie God (who gave it mee) and to Jesus Christe my onlie saviourе and redeemer by whose death and passion I fullie trust to have all my sinnes freelie forgiven and to attain to the joyfull resurrection of eternall life committing my bodie to the earth from whence it was taken to be buried in the Church of Chiddingstone aforesaid"......

He gives...... his grey colt and all his goods in FRENDEN House to his son Thomas: his piebald mare and other goods to his daughter Sarah Streatfeild: and the residue to his son **John**. As to his lands he gives to his second son **Thomas** a house and land called KNIGHTS in Penshurst, the lands called Great MUDDINGS, KEYSDEN, the EYLAND near Chafford Bridge, and a small house and garden at Penshurst. To his son Andrew he gives a house and land called SKIPREED, lands called OLD REEDES, YEOMAN LANDS, BARNE MEAD, CLOUDS MEADE and the house in Penshurst occupied by Thomas Leddall.

As he had already settled Stonewall, containing 200 acres upon John, the eldest son, he only gave him the house occupied by Thomas Levett. Will proved October 1638.

It must be remembered that in 1638 money was very much more valuable than it is today. One pound in the time of Henry VIII was equal to £6 in the reign of Queen Anne, and £10 in the reign of George III. By this standard, William Woodgate's personal property consisted of £20,000 and he had land worth £2,000 a year.

On William's death, John succeeded to Stonewall, and two suits in Chancery began. In the first, Thomas Woodgate, as plaintiff filed his bill in 1639 against his brother John. Thomas alleged that the settlement of Stonewall was made on condition that John would release certain rights under the Combridge marriage settlement; John in his reply denied this. It does not appear that friendly relations between the two brothers were interrupted.

In the second suit, John Woodgate as plaintiff filed his bill in October 1639 against his sister Sarah Streatfeild and Robert Streatfeild, her husband. He complains that the Streatfeilds and "Thomas Woodgate, one of the sons of the testator, all or some of them being allwayes dwelling in the house of the said testator untill and at the time of his decease", entered all or most of the rooms and chamber, chests, trunks and presses, and took possesion of various securities. John, being married and keeping house by himself, was a stranger to the estate of his father. He believed that Thomas was indebted to his father. The personal estate should have amounted to £2,000, which Thomas admitted, but he said in reply that he only borrowed £10 or £11. Sarah Streatfeild said she had only taken an old taffeta apron which used to belong to her mother, and which had been promised to her. All parties wrote good handwriting.

John Woodgate had married during his father's lifetime Sarah, daughter of Robert Streatfeild of Chested, Penshurst, sister of the above mentioned Robert. William Woodgate, desiring to advance his son in marriage, by deed dated 1637, conveyed Stonewall and the appurtenances (some 200 acres) to Robert Streatfeild and William Wallis in trust for himself for life, and after his death for John Woodgate absolutely. During his father's lifetime, John lived at FRENDEN HOUSE, but on the death of his father removed to Stonewall.

John Woodgate came in for the troublous scenes of the Civil War. Kent declared strongly for the Parliament, but the Woodgates appear to have been divided in their sympathies. There is an absurd tradition in the family that the Woodgates fought for the King and were punished for their loyalty by the loss of their motto! It is said that the motto was: "Spe, Diligentia, Numine", but that no motto was used until the last century when it was revived. Chiddingstone was mulcted successively in tax, fine, voluntary contributions, ticket, excise and sequestration. In 1643, for instance, the following sums were raised:-

	£	s.	d.
"Collected by Robert Goodhue (Goodhugh) and Thomas Birsty, a tax for the raising of volunteers otherwise called the proportion made by the sub-committee..........	93.	11.	0
Collected by Walter Tickner and John Woodgate, a shilling Tax paid to Col. Boothby..........	104.	11.	3
Collected by Michael Bassett and Clement Basden, shilling Tax paid to Mr Whitting..........	110.	6.	6
Collected by Thomas Bassett & Robert Streatfeild, paid to Mr Whitting, two shillings tax..........	220.	19.	8
Collected by Thomas Rodgers and William Woodgate (of Truggers) paid to Mr Whitting, the 5th & 20 parts..........	348.	0.	0
Collected by Edward Beecher & John Norris paid to Col. Boothby, a tax for 13 weeks..........	69.	8.	11
	£946.	17.	4

Even modern taxation is made by comparison to appear inconsiderable!

The parson of Chiddingstone, the Rev. Edward Powell, (imprisoned in Leeds Castle 1643-1647) a staunch Royalist, was sequestered from the living in Nov. 1643, by Thomas Birsty and Robert Goodhugh: and the Rev. Thomas Seyliard M.A. put into possession, allowing Powell 1/5th of the income. The Seyliards of Delaware were the principal people in the neighbourhood at this time. The parishioners, however, who were mostly royalists, refused to pay him tithes, and the unfortunate minister was reduced to dire straits.

The Hydes were particularly active in the Parliamentary cause. Bernard Hyde of Bore Place, one of the Commissioners of Customs, raised large sums in Chiddingstone for the Parliament, in which he was assisted by his brother John. He died in 1655, and his son was created a Baronet by Charles II soon after his accession.

The Woodgates of Stonewall appear to have been Royalists though one of the family, Captain Woodgate, commanded a troop of horse under the Parliament. This troop and other like it, plundered the inhabitants without much discrimination, certainly not exempting the Woodgates and their relatives from their attentions.

The following is a list of those who lent money to the state, i.e. Parliament, upon "ticket" about 1642:-

John Seyliard Esq	£30.	0.	0	
Henry Streatfeild, Gent.	30.	0.	0	
More to the Commity, at Westerham	35.	0.	0	
" " " " at Aylesford	40.	0.	0	
William Reeve, Gent.	25.	0.	0	(£20 in original)?
William Woodgate (of Truggers)	5.	0.	0	
Robert Goodhue	20.	0.	0	
Robert Ashdowne	10.	0.	0	
Michael Bassett	3.	0.	0	
William Everest junior	10.	0.	0	
Thomas Woodgate (younger brother of John Woodgate of Stonewall)	20.	0.	0	
Robert Streatfeild	5.	0.	0	
Richard Streatfeild, Gent.	10.	0.	0	
	£243.	0.	0	

With this must be read the list of those who paid a fine to Col. Boothby amounting to £253.

		£	s.	d.
Amongst whom are:-	Henry Streatfeild	5.	0.	0
	William Woodgatt	10.	0.	0
	Robert Goughue	30.	0.	0
	Robert Ashdowne	20.	0.	0
	Thomas Bassett	15.	0.	0
	William Everest junior	10.	0.	0
	Thomas Woodgatt	30.	0.	0
	Robert Streatfeild	30.	0.	0
	Walter Woodgate	10.	0.	0

Observe that there is no Seyliard or Hyde, and that Henry Streatfeild escapes with £5 only. John Woodgate of Stonewall neither lends money, nor pays fine!

Then there is a list of those plundered in 1643:-	£	s.	d.
From Walter Woodgate	7	19	8
Thomas Woodgate in money	40	0	0
William Wallis	13	6	8
Robert Streatfeild in money	22	0	0
" " more for redeeming 2 horses	5	0	0
" " more in linen & goods to the value of	10	0	0
" ' one mare stagg, the which the said Robt. Streatfeild was offered for	10	0	0
(all the above were plundered by Capt. Bonnett)			
From Robert Streatfeild one mare more worth	5	0	0
(plundered by Capt. Westroo, under Sir Mill Lusse)			
From John Woodgate one sword		12	0
William Everest one horse	8	0	0
(both above plundered by Capt. Woodgatt)			
From Thomas Backett (Bassett?) one sword & belt		10	0
(plundered by a sergeant of Capt. Woodgatt)			
From Mr Powell one mare	10	0	0
(plundered by Capt. Woodgatt)			
Walter Tickner charged upon free quarter with man & horse by Capt. Woodgatt himself	1	0	0
	£133.	**8.**	**4**

One thousand Volunteers, and also such troops of horse as should be subscribed for, were to be raised in Kent, according to a declaration of 30th May 1643. None were to be of the trained bands. The Lord Lieutenant was to nominate a Major General and to give battle gainst all forces raised without the consent of Parliament. These forces were not to go out of the County without special leave. Tonbridge Castle was seized for the Parliament and fortified; £6.10.0 of the expense was charge dupon the inhabitants of Chiddingstone. In 1646 the Committee at Maidstone (of which John Ribers and Thomas Seyliard were two) had the fortifications dismantled.

Other items of interest are the disbursements of Henry Streatfeild, which include "a horse taken from him by order of the committy, delivered to Capt. Woodgate's lieutenant £12"; John Seyliard's disbursements; and Mr Hyde's contributions, amounting to about £600. The latter include:-

Freely given to the Committee at Knowle..........................	£200.	0.	0
Lent to Deputy Leiutenant at Westerham for finding a horse.....	20.	0.	0
A black horse & arms sent out under Major Welden. The arms were lost & the horse not worth £5 at his return.			
More for one volunteer to Mr Whitting..............................	3.	0.	0
For the bringing in of our brethren the Scots......................	40.	0.	0

A number of persons joined in finding arms "after £3 and arms for the raising of volunteers" John Seyliard, Richard treatfeild, Robert Goodhugh, Thomas Woodgatt, William Wallis and Michael Winter, Widow Woodgatt, and others each paid £3. William Walter and John Woodgate and others paid less.

Andrew Woodgate, youngest brother of John Woodgate of Stonewall, died in Sept. 1641, aged 22, and was buried at Westerham. **John Woodgate** of Stonewall also died in his prime, and was buried at Chiddingstone in 1643, aged 41. Whether either of them was killed in an affray we do not know, but apparently no property of the Woodgates was forfeited in any way. We do not know who the Capt. Woodgatt was: he may have been one of the Woodgates of Penshurst. One Edward Woodgate was very active in the Parliamentary cause, and was instrumental in discovering a Royalist plot.

No will of John Woodgate can be found; but in the parochial books, Richard Streatfeild, his brother-in-law and Thomas Woodgate his brother are assessed on behalf of the heirs of John Woodgate, so there must have been some testamentary instrument. Sarah Woodgate, the widow, remarried in 1647, John **Ashdowne** the Younger of Hever, son of John Ashdowne of Hever and Chiddingstone. The marriage articles were dated 3rd March 1647, and Sarah's brother, Richard Streatfeild was trustee. By these John Ashdowne granted his wife an annual rent charge of £15 a year out of Larkins, Jemmetfield, Lorkinshope, Chiddingstone Cross and 28 acres in Penshurst; and by a deed dated the next day John Ashdowne the father, in consideration of the marriage, settled the above-mentioned lands, together with a house in Chiddingstone, occupied by Richard Streatfeild, Kitchen Croft, Martin's Field (10a) and Hallfield (14a) on his son subject to his own life-interest in part of the lands.

John Ashdowne the younger died intestate in 1654, and his widow took out letters of administration on Oct. 20th. His personal estate exceeded £500 in value; and from the inventory of effects we note the names of the rooms of his house at Hever - namely the hall, parlour, old parlour, drink buttery and room adjoining, brew house, chamber over

brew-house, chamber over entry, chamber over hall, milkhouse, and chamber over, chamber over parlour, and chamber and garret over old parlour.
Sarah Ashdowne died in 1686 and was buried at Hever. The only surviving child of her second marriage, Sarah Ashdowne, married Henry Streatfeild of High Street House who descendants, the Streatfeilds of Chiddingstone, are entitled to quarter the Ashdowne arms.

To return to the Woodgates of Stonewall. William the eldest son, who was only 4 years old at his father's death, was brought up at Hever, and eventually married Alice, only surviving daughter of Richard Streatfeild of High Street House (with whom he had a handsome portion) and sister of Henry, who maried Sarah Ashdowne as already mentioned. The marriage licence was dated 2nd June 1663, and authorised the wedding to be at St Pancras Soper Lane London.

WILLIAM WOODGATE inherited Stonewall and the family estates, subject to his mother's dower; and by his careful conduct very considerably increased their extent. William's uncle Thomas had died when William was about 22, leaving him considerable benefits; but he took more largely under the will of his uncle Richard Streatfeild of Chested, who died in 1679. It is somewhat curious that, of his two rich bachelor uncles, his uncle Woodgate should have left so much to the Streatfeilds, and that his uncle Streatfeild should have left most of his property to the Woodgates.

Thomas Woodgate, by his will in 1656, being then "very sick and weak" appointed his uncle William Wallis and Michael Basset his executors. As to his lands he left SKIPREED, FRENDEN and other property to his sister Sarah Streatfeild for life, and after her death SKIPREED was to go to her son Robert Streatfeild, and FRENDEN to his godson and nephew John WOODGATE. He left to William Woodgate, his nephew, Knights, Muddings (in occupation of William Wallis) and half the lands which had descended to him from his brother Andrew - the other half to his nephew John Woodgate. The will was proved in 1660.
Richard Streatfeild, the other uncle, left all his personal estate to his nephew William Woodgate and made him sole executor. He left £100 to his kinsman Richard Streatfeild of High Street House. As to lands, Chested in Penshurst, Gillridge, Buckhurst in the occupation of William Woodgate, Seedrobs and divers other lands in Chiddingstone, Penshurst, Langton Green, in Kent and Sussex, to William Woodgate for life and after that to his son **Richard** Woodgate. His will was a bitter disappointment to the 3 Streatfeild nephews, - William of Delaware, Richard of Ford Place, Chiddingstone, and Thomas of Vexour, Penshurst, who were induced to contest the will but without success.

(There is an old counterpart of lease dated 1769, whereby the Rev. Francis Woodgate of Mountfield, demised upon Richard Delves of Tunbridge Wells, butcher, for 11 years at an annual rent of £48 the messuage and farm called Gillridge with buildings, etc., and 80 acres in Chiddingstone, etc.)

William Woodgate's eldest son was JOHN: he married Rose **Birsty** the "fair Rose of Kent", and was the first Woodgate of Summerhill, Tonbridge. William Woodgate's second son was William of Chiddingstone, married Hannah Coney of Sevenoaks, but died without issue at a comparatively early age. William Woodgate's third son, **Henry**, was the first attorney in the family and settled at Goudhurst. He had six children who were apparently brought up at STONEWALL by their grandfather, who refers in his will to the "chest of linen brought from Goudhurst". There is in existence an old book of Stonewall days marked with some of their names: "Wm. Woodgate", "Lydia Woodgate", "Seth Palmer", "Mrs Ann Streatfeild". Henry seems to have been a man of considerable fortune. He died at Goudhurst 1714 aged 46. Henry's duaghter Sarah appears to have inherited the Chiddingstone portion of her father's property, for in her will of 1759 she leaves "NEWTYE" in Chiddingstone & Hever (some 100 acres), LOW BUCKHURST in Chiddingstone & Hever, and NESPRIDGES in Hever to her sister Lydia Woodgate for life, and then to her three nephews Henry & John Woodgate and James Fremling.

William Woodgate's 4th son, **Thomas**, was a citizen & "Ironmonger" of London, that is, he was free of the Ironmongers' Company. He died at an early age and was buried at Chiddingstone 4th October. 1706. A stone near the altar rail marks the spot:-

> "Here lyeth the body of Thomas Woodgate, late Citizen & Ironmonger of London, son of William Woodgate of this parish, gent, who departed this life ye 30th of September 1706 in ye 34th year of his age.
> He married Susanna the daughter of Thomas Seyliard of Penshurst, (Salmans) Esqr, by whom he had 2 sons and 4 daughters".

(This inscription is wrong as he had 2 sons and 2 daughters only)

William Woodgate's 5th son was **Richard**, the devisee in remainder under the will of his great uncle Richard Streatfeild of Chested. During his parents' lifetime he lived with them at Stonewall: we know, from a will, that his room there was known as "the milk house chamber". At their death, he removed to Chested, where he died in 1724, unmarried, and was buried at Chiddingstone on 29th March. In his will dated 1723, he gave to his brother Stephen, his sole executor, (William's 6th son).... the house and lands called Chested & Seed Cubbs in Chiddingstone... Guildrigge and house and lands called Buckhurst in Hever and Chiddingstone, all in his own occupation.... also a house in the "town" of Chiddingstone occupied by William Pope and Thomas Eagleton, and all other lands in Chiddingstone & Penshurst.

William Woodgate's 6th son, **Stephen** of Sevenoaks Weald, was also a bachelor: his niece Sarah Woodgate (daughter of Henry) and his nephew Robert Durrant lived with him. He died in 1754 and left a number of legacies charged on Frenden and Tophill. He left to his nephew **Rev. Francis Woodgate of Mountfield** (Robertsbridge):-

FRENDEN in Chiddingstone containing 100 acres occupied by John Head.

Silcocks Meads in Chiddingstone containing 17 acres & all other lands in occupation of Robert Head.

Tophill in Chiddingstone containing 60 acres, in occupation of Thomas Butcher.

Meadow land in Chiddingstone near Chafford Bridge called EELPANS all other lands in occupation of Butcher.

Chested & Seedrops occupied by Samuel Waite.

House & 10 acres in Chiddingstone occupied by Thomas Wallis.

Cottage & gardden in Chiddingstone occupied by Robert Hollamby and all other lands occupied by Wallis or Hollamby.

GILDREDGE in Chiddingstone containing 80 acres, occupied by himself, subject to 10 years enjoyment thereof by nephew Robert Durrant.

He gave to his niece Sarah, daughter of brother Henry:-

NEW TYE in Chiddingstone & Hever containing 100 acres, occupied by John Fuller

Low Buckhurst containing 50 acres in Hever & Chiddingstone

12 acres called Nespridges **adjoining**, all occupied by James Knight.

William Woodgate of Stonewall became High Sheriff of Kent in 1699. He died in 1717 and was buried "in linen". His will of 1714 directs that he should be buried in the Parish Church... to his dear & loving wife Alice... tables & chairs in the parlour at Stonewall......To John, his son, three silver salts... To son Richard, bedstead "in the milk house chamber where he lyeth".... To son Stephen... his silver hilted sword..... To daughter Sarah Durrant.... sheets etc., and to her son William Durrant £5 at 21.... To grandson William Woodgate, son ofThomas deceased, £5.... To grandson William Woodgate, son of John, a silver cup. Sarah, Anne, & Lydia Woodgate, daughters of son Henry decd. "chest of linen which was brought from Goudhurst". To grandson William Woodgate, son of John:-

House and lands at Chiddingstone, called HILDERS, purchased from William Kent.

House opposite the church occupied by Fortunatus Terry to wife Alice for life then to son Richard.

To son Richard, all the goods that wer in the house at Chested and were left by his Uncle Richard Streatfeild.

To son Stephen, capital messuage called "LAWRENCE'S and 73 acres in Sevenoaks, in occupation of Stephen. Also part of the lands called ROTHERDEN, next Hale Oak Green......

From the death of William Woodgate in 1717, SUMMERHILL in Tonbridge became the chief family seat: though Stonewall was for some years deemed of almost equal consequence.

John Woodgate, the eldest son of William Woodgate of Stonewall, (the High Sheriff) married "the fair Rose of Kent", the beautiful and wealthy heiress of the Birsty's of Hever. Rose's grand uncle was Charles Polhill, a Commissioner of Excise, who had married Martha Streatfeild of Chiddingstone, John Woodgate's aunt.
The settlement made on the marriage included Stonewall but subject to William Woodgate's life-interest. John Woodgate therefore started his married life at Chested, which had been left by his great-uncle Richard Streatfeild. In 1712 JohnWoodgate purchased Summerhill in Tonbridge and soon after removed there. John Woodgate died in 1728, and was buried "in woolen" the 21st Aug. at Chiddingstone, where a marble tablet on the north wall perpetuates his memory:-

"Sacred to the memory of John Woodgate Esqre of Summer Hill and Rose his wife whose ashes are deposited near this place.
He died August 17th 1728, aged 68: She Sept. 22nd 1744 aged 71. John Woodgate Esqre, was the eldest son of William Woodgate of Stonewall Park, The High Sheriff for the County in the year 1700, and of Alice his wife.
The filial piety of Francis Woodgate, M.A., late REctor of Watlington and Vicar of Mountfield Sussex directed by will this monument to be erected as his last token of sincere respect for his honoured parents".

His will dated 1727 he left to eldest son:- William - All lands in Chiddingstone & Penshurst...... Stonewall, the ancient family seat, thus fell to William the eldest son; Henry, the second son, had to be content with Summerhill; Francis the third son, Howgreen, and all lands in Hever & Brasted: John the fourth son, the Moat Farm, Cowden and lands at Withyham, etc..... WILLIAM died intestate and unmarried in 1743. **John** who had been living with William at Stonewall, remained there. He signs the Chiddingstone registers in a firm, clear, well educated hand, and was there certainly as late as 1766 (when Churchwarden) and 1769 (Overseer), and died in 1770 intestate and unmarried. He was buried at Tonbridge. On his death, there was a deed of partition between HENRY & FRANCIS, by which the latter obtained amongst other things, the Moat Cowden.
ALICE Woodgate, John's second daughter, married Arthur CHILDREN of Riverhill, and by her will in 1768 she left to her dear sisters Rose Swayne and Anne Woodgate, HALE OAK in Chiddingstone and Sevenoaks, occupied by Richard Saunders.
HENRY Woodgate died in 1787 and was buried at Tonbridge. In his will in 1782 he devises to brother FRANCIS his moiety of the Stonewall Estate in Chiddingstone and Penshurst.
FRANCIS Woodgate died in 1790 aged 84 and was buried at Tonbridge. By his will in 1789 he gave:-
.... To son **Henry**, house and lands called Isele Dale in Sevenoaks, Leigh and Chiddingstone (? includes Hale Oak) occupied by Richard Saunders: and Howgreen in Hever and Brasted, occupied by John Humphry......
.... To son **Stephen**, Chested and Seedrups in Chiddingstone, and Penshurst, occupied by Page; cottage in Chiddingstone, occupied by Hollamby; farm called Gildredge in Chiddingstone occupied by Richard Delves; farm called Frinden in Chiddingstone, and two pieces of land there called Sibords Meads. (? Silcocks Meads), - "the plain of lands" and woodlands purchased by him of.... Thorpe Esq in Chiddingstone; also the farm called Tophill in Chiddingstone, occupied by the widow of John Streatfeild gent.,... subject to erecting in Chiddingstone Church a monument to his (testator's) uncle Stephen Woodgate, gent. Executor to erect monument to Francis' father and mother in the parish church of Chiddingstone.

Taken from the book "The Woodgate Family History"
p.185. On 1st June 1811, **Stephen** Woodgate died at his house at FAWKE, in Seal, after a lingering illness, aged 66. He was by profession a lawyer, having been sworn and enrolled an Attorney of the Queen's Bench on 30th April 1768. In 1781, Stephen Woodgate and William Norton (his clerk) attest the will of Mary BOAKES of Chiddingstone. In a letter from Mrs Humphry:-.... We do not know at present what

property Stephen Woodgate left nor what became of it; his father had left to him Chested, Seedrups, Gilredge, Frinden, Tophill, and other lands in Chiddingstone & Penshurst....

p.371. **William Woodgate** began to decline in 1809 and his life was evidently despaired of for some time before his death. He died 29th May 1809, aged 65, and was buried 3rd June. His will is dated 1805:-
.... To son John Woodgate, Stonewall with house, cottages and lands and the Nunnery Wood & Pookden Wood, all in Chiddingstone and Penshurst, and lately occupied by George Kiddar but then by himself.... To son Stephen Woodgate £500 in cash payable by John out of Stonewall....

Soon after his father's death, John Woodgate took up his residence at STONEWALL with his sister Maria as housekeeper. Stonewall consisted of about 1,400 acres. **He pulled down** the house, which had been inhabited by successive generations of Woodgates since 1590, if not before, and built a large red-brick Georgian house which is substantially the present building. The road now runs over the site of the old mansion, which is entirely destroyed except for a portion that has been made into the principal entrance lodge, probably the old servants' wing. The beautiful old timber work and plaster in front has been concealed by red tiles, but may still be seen from the rear, just as it originally was.
It seems that John Woodgate was involved in the same fate as Major Woodgate of Summerhill over the failure of the Tonbridge Bank. In 1813 he put up for sale some of his outlying property.... In 1815 and 1816 John Woodgate was Churchwarden of Chiddingstone, and signs the accounts in a good hand. In 1814 he was seriously ill. We read of him staying at Pembury in 1818 and acting as Steward of a Ball in 1819, and about this time **he sold Stonewall.** (1817) He then went out to India as a Major on the Staff and died at Hastings in 1842.

THE WARE HOUSE AND THE GATE HOUSE

(These lay between the Castle Inn and the Castle, about where the Castle Lake now is - and of course on the building line of the street)

A.D.

1527 The Gate House was part of the Ware House. Thos. Ware leaves to Gilbert Ware all his housing except GATE House. Thos. Ware leaves to son Drewe, the GATE HOUSE and a yarde of grounde "ye said Drewe shall have half a rod of ground as he cometh in at the gate and so to go up along within ye pale over the Street till he have a yard of ground".

1369 Robert the Ware of Chiddingstone: has lands of Mathilda, relict of John de Chydingston

1561 Thos. Ware leaves to Drewe Ware the house "neare the Gate House".

1565 Thos. Ware sells to John Ware the tenement in occupation of Drewe Ware,

1573 John Ware sells to Henry Streatfeild, messuage late in tenure Drewe Ware, except the Gatehouse and a yard of land as it lyeth along the street side in Chedyngstone.

1580 Henry Streatfeild sells to Henry Ashdowne (? mortgage) messuage in Chiddingstone Street in occupation widow of Drewe Ware and 2 parcels adjoining - bounds, to lands of Henry Ashdowne E, John Ashdowne S, Spatman's Lane W, highway leading to Chiddingstone Street N, and adjoining the Gatehouse somtime Thos. A Wares. In all 10 acres. (? the 10 acres which was Targatefield).

1585 Ashdowne reconveys to Henry Streatfeild

1586 Henry Streatfeild purchased of Gilbert Ware's sons some years before 1586

1601 (Possibly this is house where Richard Streatfeild died)

1666 J. Ashdowne is west bounder of Rockhouse

1683 Henry Streatfeild is west bounder of Rockhouse

1737 " " " "

1740 On a map of this date a house is shown to west of the Castle Inn, (is it this house?)

1724 Pew Plan of Chiddingstone Church records:- "A house in the Towne" owned by Stephen Woodgate and tenants were Wm. Pope & Thos. Egleton. - but more likely this Ware House was that of Thomas Streatfeild which he owned and lived in at this date, whilst Stephen Woodgate's house would then have been the "Atte Wode" house at the other end of the Street.

1760 Ware House was presumably pulled down when the present Castle was built and the lake dammed up.

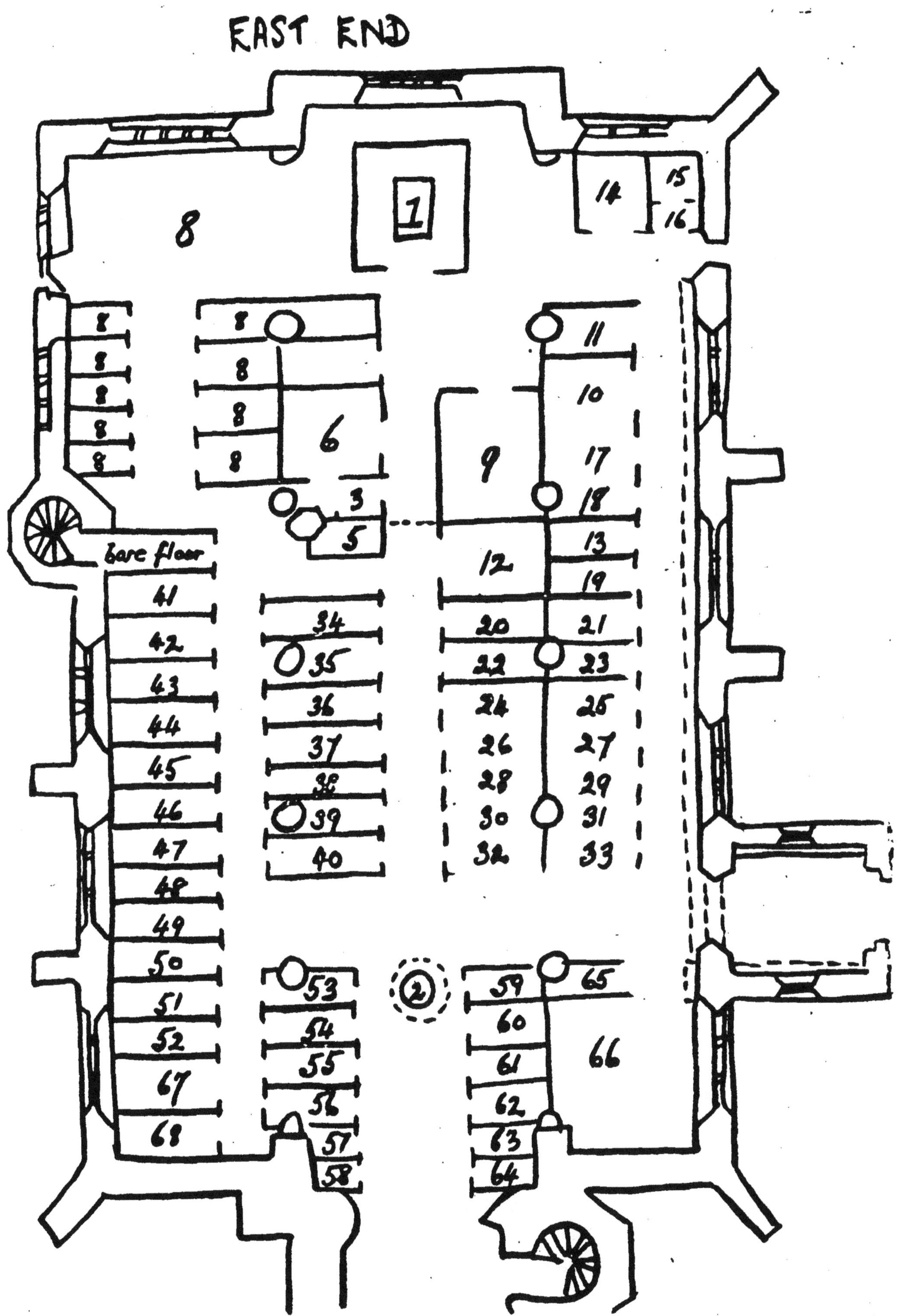
EAST END
8
1
14
15
16
8
8
8
8
8
8
8
8
8
11
10
6
9
17
3
18
5
13
bare floor
12
19
41
34
20
21
42
35
22
23
43
36
24
25
44
37
26
27
45
38
28
29
46
39
30
31
47
40
32
33
48
49
50
53
2
59
65
51
54
60
52
55
66
61
67
56
62
68
57
63
58
64

WATERSLIP HOUSE - alias Rock House - Now Castle Inn

1420 William Chellesfeld for his messuage next WATSHIP (? Watership) at terms 12d.
1499 John Pygot for his messuage next **Watership** once Wm. Clerke at 2 terms ... 12d & for same messuage at Xmas 1 hen.
1639 Richard Beecher has aliened to John Ashdowne, a messuage & garden "in vico de Chidd:", near "Le Waterslipp", held of the Manor of Chiddingstone. Burghersh in fee farm @ 12d and 1 hen

A.D. Rock House alias Castle Inn

1666 John Ashdowne of Hever, conveys to Thos. Wakelyn of Chiddingstone, butcher, for £180 - "messuage with barn & called **Rockhouse**, late in occupation Thos. Wakelyn - bounds, to lands of John Seyliard E & S, lands of J. Ashdowne W., Chiddingstone Town N.
1683 Wm. Wakelyn, occupier - bounds, Sir J. Seyliard E., Henry Streatfeild, W.
1695 Wm. Wakelyn sells to John Ashdowne for £100
1712 J. Ashdowne sells to Thos. Weller of Chiddingstone; taylor: bounds, to Henry Streatfeild E & S: occupied by Eliz. Terry widow and Daniel Nicoll, butcher (a party to the deed) for £120
1713 Thos. Weller occupier
1732 Henry Streatfeild records that he holds **Rockhouse**, now the **Castle** @ 1s.10d of Chiddingstone Burghersh Manor. Ware House was presumably pulled down
1737 T. Weller sells to Henry Streatfeild for £160: occupied by Thos. & George Weller: bounds, to Henry Streatfeild W.: Sidney Streatfeild E & S. (endorsed Castle Inn - but Rockhouse in body of deed)
1752 **Castle Inn** occupied by Henry Wapham @ £14 per ann. from Henry Streatfeild.
1764 Manor Courts "adjourned to H. Whapham's".
1724 Pew Plan of Chiddingstone Church records:-
The Rock House (a later date correction calls it THE FIVE BELLS).
Landlord - Thos. Weller - tenant, himself

Manor House of Chiddingstone Cobham

1572 Henry Streatfeild is tenant of Chiddingstone Cobham, but nothing is presented until 1600 when he dies. (?Did he live in this house)
1600 Henry Streatfeild held a house and garden in Chiddingstone @ 6 1/2d. Is dead. Richard is son & heir.
1601 Will of Richard Streatfeild: To wife Ann for life - house of Thomas Huggin in Chiddingstone Street - remainder to son Thomas.
1663 Two daughters of Thomas Streatfeild convey to Thos. Wakelin of Chiddingstone: "messuage in Chiddingstone Street in occupation Stephen Arnold. South end of outhouse belonging to heirs of George Beecher deceased: to pay part of 61/2d quit rent.

1673 3rd daughter releases her share: Thos. Wakelin is a butcher.

1695 April 8th. Benjamin, son of Thos. Wakelin deceased, conveys to Anne Woodgate of Chiddingstone, widow for £150. Bounds, to Sir Thos. Seyliard's close W & S, to house and backside wherein Thos. Farmer dwells E. (On house plaster is A. 1695 W).

1702 Will of Anne Woodgate: the "hall chamber" mentioned

1717 Now in two - Anne Woodgate dead - occupied by widow Ashdowne & John Luckhurst @ 6½d

1723 Henry Streatfeild pays @ 6½d for "messuage in two, bought of Ann Leggat in Chiddingstone Town".

1727 court of Chiddingstone Cobham held at "usual & accustomed place, i.e. house in occupation William Cronk and John Longhurst.

1727 Anne Woodgate's death presented, Richard Leggatt, husband of her daughter Anne, pays @ 6½d. (but record of Court is wrong).

1737 Estimate for repairs.

1737 Daughter of Anne Woodgate converys to Henry Streatfeild for £200. It is "messuage now in two, occupied Daniel Longhurst, glazier, and William Cronke, Carpenter. (Endorsed **Chiddingstone Cobham Court House**).

1746 Same occupants as in 1727. Owners are "heirs of Anne Leggatt".

1752 Occupied by Richard Bevan and Daniel Longhurst.

1764 "We went next into Edward Bevan's kitchen & called the Court of Chiddingstone Cobham".

1724 The Pew plan of Chiddingstone Church records:- Cobham\ Manor House:- Landlord Richard Leggatt Tenants - John Longherst & William Cronke.

Chiddingstone Shop @ 3d

1572 James Beecher & Richard Beecher of Vexour - Edward Beecher & Richard Beecher Junr. are tenants - William Walter tenant.

1575 Edward Beecher sells 3 acres called Lowerhill @ 2d & ½ a hen to Henry Ashdowne.

1595 William Waters held a house & 18 acres @ 4d, and sold to Edward Beecher. The latter died in 1618.

1604 Edward Beecher to son Edward of Kingston-on-Thames:- "A messuage in Chiddingstone Town with half of barn and seven parcels, 20 acres. Occupied by Mathye Walters & purchased in 1592 from Wm. Walters of Item (Ightham) Kent. Thomas Walters tenant in 1584.

1608/9 Richard, son of Richard Beecher, tenant of Chiddingstone Burghersh, is under age.

1621 Richard Beecher sells to James Beecher of Chiddingstone: his brother, tenant as in 1604.

1622 Edward Beecher held "a house and ½ a garden, barn, close etc." and 18 acres @ 4d. Gave same to sons Richard, James & Andrew. Andrew sold his share to James: James and Richard divided and James had the house and 3 parcels, and 1 acre mead @ 3p: Richard had 3 parcels in Chiddingstone @ 1p.

1636 James Beecher sells to George Beecher of Chiddingstone, mercer, "messuage wherein George Beecher dwells over against Church, with half a barn etc. £200.

1638 House in Street has over fireplace G.I.B. 1638.

1661 George Beecher barn garden etc. @ 3p. Daughters Susan & Elizabeth are under age, heirs.

1667 Lease. Richard Hayward (who married a daugher of George Beecher) to Thos, Harrison, Mercer, messuage, half a barn etc. in occupation Thos. Harrison.

1699 Heirs of George Beecher sell to Henry Streatfeild for £306 - messuage wherein Robert Farmer dwells with half barn etc. as before.
(endorsed Chiddingstone Shop - abstract says Nicholas Pigott in occupation).

1700 Lease - Henry Streatfeild to Nicholas Pigott of Chiddingstone, mercer, - messuage late in occupation R. Farmer over against the church gate.

1712 Same to same (Endorsed Chiddingstone Shop).

1725 Occupied by widow Piggot @ 3d of Chiddingstone Cobham, Owner Henry Streatfeild.

1727 Henry Streatfeild, Lord of Chiddingstone Cobham - @ 3p, Chiddingstone Shop, half a barn etc.

1746 Same in occupation of self. Henry Falconer, & Henry Whapham (Steward's note ? should be Castle & others).

1752 Messuage & mercer's shop, in occupation Nicholas Pigott, but now if William Martin

1764 "Thence into Mrs. Pigott's Hall, and called the Court of Chiddingstone Burghersh".

1724 Pew Plan of Chiddingstone Church records:-
Landlord, Henry Streatfeild: Tenant Thos. Smith. A pew was alotted for women servants in this house, but a correction of later date seems to annul this.

LONGHOUSE ALIAS HUNTS ALIAS BURGHERSH COURT

A.D.

1453 Trustees of Anne Chaloner (which family gave name to Chantler's Farm) deceased, grant **Longhouse** to **Wm. Hunte** - bounds, to land of Thos. Willott E, to Cattfields, messuage of Roger Atte Wode E, and opposite Chiddingstone Churchyard N.

1485 Will of Wm. Honte - house goes to wife Alice, remainder to son John.

1517 It would seem that **Sir Thos. Boleyn** purchased from William son of John Hunt, and sold to Richard Hamond.

1537 Richard Hamond to John Seyliard - Longhouse, bounds, to lands of Thos. Willoughby, Knight, W. to land of John Wodde E., to Highway N.

1546/8 Curious agreement between John Seÿlerde and Thomas Deye, giving Deye in certain circumstances right of entry on "tenement of John Selyerde in Chiddingstone Street now in occupation of John Pollynger, late Hunts.

1580 William Seyliard of Brasted suffers a recovery of Hunts, occupied by John Pullinger.

1598 William Seyliard dead, holding Hunts @ 6p of Chiddingstone Cobham. Heir Thomas, aged 14.

1615 Thos. Seyliard of Delaware, leases to Thomas Waters, yeoman, a mansion all together with 84 acres in Chiddingstone in occupation said Sir John Seyliard. (But manor house is never otherwise mentioned and apparently was **HUNTS**, though it may be that Chiddingstone Shop was used as the Manor, although part of old **LONGHOUSE**).

1653 Thomas Seyliard dead, devised **HUNTS** @ 6d to son John.

1669 Sir Thomas Seyliard holds Hunts @ 6d

1700 Sir Thomas Seyliard Bart. dead. Left **HUNTS** @ 6d to son Thomas, who has aliened to Henry Streatfeild Lord of Manor.

1717 Henry Streatfeild dead. **HUNTS** in occupation Richard Chapamn. son William Streatfeild inherits.

1727 William Streatfeild dead. Hunts in occupation Richard Chapman. Devised to nephew Sidney Streatfeild (not of age).

1727 Chiddingstone Burghersh Court held at accustomed place, viz:- **BURGHERSH COURT**, in the town of Chiddingstone.

1739 Sydney Streatfeild sells part of orchard of Burgherst Court to Henry Streatfeild. It abuts to garden of Rock House N.

1724 Pew Plan of Chiddingstone Church records that Burgherst Court and Hunts were separated. William Streatfeild was landlord of both and lived in former, Richard Chapman in latter. Burtghersh Court had a pew for women servants.

LONGHOUSE --- BURGHERSH COURT (in 17th and 18th Centuries)

NOW POST OFFICE

1383 Richard Chapman had **Tenacres & Berefield**, 5 acres.

1420 William Hunt pays Manor of Rendeslegh for **Herefeld, Le Mote**, and half **Court Green** 20 sh. Roger atte Wode has **Cattesfeld** at 10 sh.

1453 **Longhouse** with a garden in Villlage of Chiddingstone. J. Sleghter & J. Bassett to Henry Sleghter & Wm. Hunt: endorsed "Hunts": once Anne Chaloners.

1453 William Durkynghole, son & heir of William Durkynghole and Joane his wife, who was relative and heir of Anne Chaloner of Chedyngstone deceased - to H. Sleghter & Wm. Hunte - a messuage called Longhouse with a garden in the village of Chedyngstone, bounding **Cattefield** to the south, & opposite the churchyard of Chedyngston towards north "which came to me with other lands on the death of my mother Joane."

1485 Will of William Hunt. (Wm. Honte of Chedyngston). My son **John** - "my tenement in Chedyngston" ... My son **Thomas** ' "My messuage with 2 gardens & 2 crofts at **HYLDEHOTH** ..."

1470 William Ware & Wm. Durkynghole de Chedyngstone grant to Wm. Hunte of Chedyngstone & Alice his wife (a) A Messuage called **LONGHOUS** with a barn & garden in Chedyngstone. (b) A field called **Thenacres**, a croft called **Berecroft**, 2 pieces of land called **Waterlond & Hamme** in Chedyngstone.

1537 Richard Hamond of Chedyngstone sells to John Selyard & Henry Asshedowne:- (a) **LONGHOUSE** in Chedyngston - upt to ... lands of Thos. Willoughby, knight west: to Highway north to land of John Wodde east.

1546 John Selyerde enfeoffed Thos. Deye of Chedyngston in a messuage, barn & 20 acres, 2 acres mead & 4 acres wood in Chedyngston & Hever, which late were John Slytters (Sleghter's) John Selyard agrees that if Thos. Deye "be putte from the lawful possession" ..." of the same by the heirs of John Slytter" ... "soe that it be not by crafte collusion or deceyte of the said Thos. Deye"... that then Thos Deye may enter a tenement of John Selyard in Chedyngston strette now in occupation of John Pollynger, late Hunts to hold to him for ever.

1579 Wm. Sulyard of Brasted gent owns "Huntes tenement alias Longhouse, occupied by John Pullynger."

1592 Edward Beecher, of Eastfarleighe, yeoman, purchased from Wm. Walters of Item (Ightham) Kent, "one messuage of tenement in Chiddingstone Towne with the moiety of a barne, houses & belonging, one garden, one close & seven parcels". (20 acres).

1604 Last-mentioned Edward Beecher makes above property over to his son Edward Becher, of Kingston-on-Thames, husbandman. It was then in occupation of Mathye Walters.

1608 Richard Beecher is under 21 years of age.

1621 Richard Becher of Chiddingstone, yeoman, surrenders all claim to above property to his brother James Becher

1636 James Beecher of Chiddingstone, Yeoman sells for £200 to George Beecher of Chiddingstone, mercer, that messuage wherein George now dwells in Chiddingstone Streete over against the Churchyard & church there with half of a barne & the staule, edifices etc., and way leading to the said barne.

1638 Initials G.I.B. are now over fireplace with date 1638 in Chiddingstone Post-Office. There was a George Beecher here in 1661, - Richard Beecher in 1634.

1699 Richard, son of Richard Hayward, who married Susan, daughter of George Beecher, sells to Henry Streatfeild. Robert Farm is in occupation.

BURGHERST COURT

1383 Richard Chapman leases various lands plus the site of the manor with the FORELESE (? Old manor house with Mote)

1383 The Court of Dartford is paid 8 1/4d for half the forlese before the gate of the Court.

1615 Thomas Seyliard of Delaware leases it to Thos. Waters "In Chidd. Street".

1727 Court held at accustomed place - viz Burghurst Court in town of Chiddingstone

1724 Monument to Wm. Streatfeild gent, late of Burgherst Court, in Chiddingstone Church.

THE "ATTE WODE" HOUSE

No Date Thomas Willot holds a messuage & croft adjacent, @ 20 sh. of Chiddingstone Burghersh.

1453 Land of Thos. Willot & messuage of Roger atte Wode are E. boundary of Longhouse

No date Roger atte Wode holds CATTESFELDE of Rendsley Manor @ 10sh.

1458 Roger atte Wode a witness in Chiddingstone Street

1537 John Wodde's land is E. boundary of **LONGHOUSE**

1724 Pew Plan of Chiddingstone Church records:-
"A house in the Towne" - owned and lived in by Thomas **STREATFEILD** - 3 pews allotted to this house one for the "quality" - and one each for men and women servants - same allowance as for Henry Streatfeild 's High Street House.
(?? is "A house in the towne" the Atte Wode house??)
But it is more likely that this house was:-
"A house in the Towne" which belonged to Stephen Woodgate, and the tenants in 1724 were William Pope and Thomas Egleton - Thomas Streatfeild's large house was probably Ware House, lying westward of Castle Inn where lake was made in 1760, and house presumably destroyed.

"HOUSE AT THE CHURCHYARD GATE"
(Where Lych Gate now is, but on road side of it)

A.D.

1593 Henry Streatfeild leases to John Moodye, taylor, "all that dwelling house being at the Church yard gate of Cheddyngstone" with a shop being part of it, for 19 years @ 28sh. per annum.

1601 Richard Streatfeild leaves "the little house at the Church Gate" to the parish on condition that the inmate keeps the clock in repair.

1690 27th march 1690. The widdow Goldsmith & Eliz. Everest at ye Church Gate for halfe a hundred of faggots 3sh.

1703 Shown on estate map

1724 Shown on plan of Church boundaries and upkeep marks. Entered as "owner" Parish and described as "a tenement belong to the Parish" - no name of occupier.

1843 Amongst Henry Streatfeild's enfranchisements is:- "tenement at Church Gate now part of the highway" @ 1d.

GILWYNS IN CHIDDINGSTONE

AD

1363 John de Chidyngston to Wm. Partrish & his sons:- House & Garden formerly Gyleweynes, bounds - to road **BOUEBECHE-CHIDD**: Church W.land of John **FIXOR** (?Vexour) E.

1389 Thos. Partrych buys adjacent lands

1400 Thos. Partrych lives at **GYLWAYNES**

1405 Thos. Partrych sells to John Chaloner - Gylleweynes

1417 John Chaloner sells to Richard Whysle certain lands

1422 Emma, relict of John Chaloner, releases all claim in messuage called **GYLEWEYNES** to Richard **WHISLE**, taillour

1524 Richard Wyschley mortgages it

1527 Richard Whysler (called Taylour) releases all right to Richard Scorier et AL but keeps lease of Gilwynes & some lands - (another mortgage)

A.D.

1537 Richard Whysler, (otherwise Taylour), finally releases all right to Richard Scoryer.

1579 Wm. Sulyard of Brasted owns **GILWYNES**, in occupation of Rauffe (Ralph) **WELLES.**

1580 The same in marriage settlement

15809 A recovery of same.

1662 Lease. Samuel Seyliard, clerk, to William **Wickenden**, of Chiddingstone **GILLWYNS** & 30 acres for 21 years @ £20, payable at now dwelling-house of Sir John Seyliard Bart in Chiddingstone.

1666 In marriage settlement. **GILLWYNES** in occupation of Wm. Wickenden.

1697 Lease - Sir. Thos. Seyliard to John Cronke.

1718 The **Four Acre Mead** late parcel of a farm called **Gilwyns**, in occupation John Cronke. Thos. Streatfeild grants to Henry Streatfeild, rights over a carrying way from same.

1733 Assessment for outside of Chiddingstone Church, **Gilwyns,** owner Henry Streatfeild, pays 3s. 9d.

1772 Ann Streatfeild, guardian of Henry Streatfeild, leases to John Iggelsden that part of **Gilwyns** West of Chiddingstone-Bowbeach Road.

1724 Pew Plan of Chiddingstone Church:-**Gilwins** - (spelling corrected at some later date to **Gillwyns**), owner Henry Streatfeild, tenant William Halcomb - two pews allotted this house, one for men and one for women, but none for servants.

TYEHAW (See Sketch))

1603 A son of Thos. Hayward of Chiddingstone sells to Thos. Willoughbye 1/5th of a messuage at **TIGHGREENE** with a garden adjoining called**TIGHAWE**, and a croft adjoining called **BENGELAND**, 3 acres occupied by Owyne Parker.

1606 Another son executes similar deed

1612 William Birstie for a messuage called Tyhawe @ 8d of Tyhurst Manor.

1656 Anthony **COMBRIDGE** for **TYHAWE** @ 8d

1656 Anthony has it for life - remainder to son Francis - bounds, "to highway there E."

1657 A daughter and heir of **BIRSTYE** makes a fine of messuage and 3 ares in Chiddingstone, once Richard **TYE**, now George Waters, to Francis Combridge, who is heir of the other daughter and coheir.

1685 Francis Combridge leaves to daughter Mary the tenement where George Weller, blacksmith, dwells near Tye Green, now in occupation George Weller & George Children.

1686 Francis Combridge holds @ 8d and does fealty.

1691 Mary Combridge leases to Rev. Richard **NURSE**, 3 acres next to tenement where George Weller dwells.

1697 Philip Seale of Tonbridge & Mary his wife, lease to George Weller the messuage tenement and Inne wherein George Weller dwells, called the **THREE HORSESHOES**,with the forge etc.

1698 Philip Seale and Thomas Eldridge's deed to uses - they married co-heirs of Francis Combridge. The property is (a) House where Gilbert Kipps lately dwelt,

(b) House where John Ingram dwells, 3 acres, (Endorsed **TYHAW** and **BENGELAND**)

1699 Lease. Henry Streatfeild to Thomas Weller, taylor, all that part wherein Thos. Weller dwelleth of a tenement formerly in two in Chiddingstone Towne, other part occupied by Stephen Arnold, with barn. (Inventory of fixtures attached).

1700 Philip Seale to Henry Streatfeild. Messuage wherein George Weller,blacksmith, deceased, dwelt and Margaret his widow now dwells, with forge etc. and 3 acres mead ajoining, near **TYHURST GREEN** in Chiddingstone now in occupation Richard Nurse. (Endorsed **TYHAW** and **BENGELAND**)

1700 Manor Rolls give descent from Francis Combridge to Henry Streatfeild. Messuage called **TYEHAW** in occupation Margaret Weller.

1717 Henry Streatfeild has devised to Henry Streatfeild, **TYHAW** in occupation George Chapman, with Bengeland adjoining in occupation Henry Streatfeild @ 8d.

1752 Henry Streatfeild owns - Messuage and land in Chiddingstone Towne 3 acres, once Samuel Weston, no John Leigh, called **TYHAW** and **BENGELANDS**.

1764 "We went under the **POUND OAK**, on this side o't which is nearest to J. Leigh's and called the Manor of Tyhurst Court". (Note:- in 1752 J. Leigh held **Tyhawe**).

1724 In Pew Plan of Church there were 2 pews allotted to Tyhaw, one for men residents and one for women. The landlord was Henry Streatfeild, the tenenat, George Chapman.

1930 William Brigden lives at **TYEHAW**, a blacksmith but now too old to work

CHIDDINGSTONE SHOP FARM (see sketch)

A.D.

1604 The Farmhouse apparently in the town and not on the 20 acres opposite.

1605 Beecher interest of 1604 derived from William Waters who sold house and 18 acres held at 4d of Chiddingstone Cobham to Edward Beecher.

1622 The transfer recited in Court Rolls of Chiddingstone Cobham.

1636 Only 9 acres of this plus the farmhouse "over against the churchyard & Church is sold to George Beecher, mercer. The 9 acres seem to be those on left of pond.

1664-1707 The land not in Beecher hands is sold in 1664 by Michael Knight of Westerham to Thomas Wakelyn of Chiddingstone, butcher, and the Streatfeilds seem to have got in by mortgage.

1677 The house and 10 acres leased to Harrison, mercer by Hayward.

1699 The whole now in Henry Streatfeild's hands, he having previously acquired the 11 acres.

1700 House & 10 acres leased to Piggott, mercer, by Streatfeild. Renewed in 1712 with only 3 1/2 acres

1724 Belongs to Henry Streatfeild. In occupation Thomas Smith

ALMERY MEAD(see Sketch)

1470 (about) Clynton Lands: 1 acre in Awmereye and 4 acres in ditto - both "held of the barony".

1589 The same as last, now 7 acres in Cransted and a mead called Le **AMERIE**.

1619 A mead called **LITTLE AMRYE** goes with Cransted Mills - it is not Mill Mead.

1673 **LITTLE AMRYE** still attached to mills.

1668 Richard Streatfeild leaves to son Henry as a separate item - "1 acres in **ALMEREMEADE** in Chiddingstone, lying at the upper end between the brook and Sir Charles Wallgrove's land". Also the 7 acres above mentioned.

1708 Richard Peerless titched on 2 acres in the **EMMERY**.

SOMERDEN MEAD (see Sketch)

about 1470. 6 acres in **SOMERDENNESMEDE**, part Clinton lands held of Sundridge Manor @ 12s

1598 4 acres in Somerden Meade in Chiddingstone belong to Mowses in Edenbridge.

1609 2 acres in Somerden Meade go with Somerden Farm. (Somerden Green Farm)

1608 Ware sells to Theobald above farm with the 2 acres called **HITHER HOPE** & **FARTHER HOPE**

1673 Whitaker to Petley - **SOMERDEN MEADE ALIAS CHIDDINGSTONE MEADE** "being heretofore part of a greate Meaddowe called **SOMERDEN MEADE**" - 8 acres in Chiddingstone, to lands of Mitchell & Somerden Green - north, Clapper from Somerden Green to Chiddingstone Church - east, lands of Seyliard - south, lands of Hyde - west. Half of this 8 acres was purchased from Thomas Studley, and half from Robert Steel.

1708 Robert Peerless pays tithe on Somerden Mead 1 acre and the **HOPE** just above Webb's Mill 1 1/2 acres.

1723 The Right of Way (see Map of "Somerden Mead") crosses Somerden **MEADE**.

BROAD HEY

1589 Willoughby to Tunstall: 2 1/2 acres in Chiddingstone called **BRODEHEY** and **POLBROOKS** mead, to **BRODEHEY** east south & west, to river east & west, to Thomas Willoughby's land in Pollbrookes mead west & north, mead of James Goldsmith - east.

1596 Hollamby to Crowmer - as above

1598 William Crowmer held a mead called **BRODLEY** of Manor of Sundridge Weald.

1616 Heirs of George Berisford Esq owe 18s for mead **BRODAYE** to same manor. (Note - a mead called **BRADNEY** is near Frienden - the names are confused).

MALLING MEAD

1668 Manor of Tyehurst includes **WAREMEADE** alias Malling Meade (in demesne?)

1695 3 1/2 acres

1708 Robert Picknell tithes in Malling mead 3 1/2 acres.

MILLBROOK MEAD

1362 Manor of **MELBROK** includes "6 acres water meadow flooded in wet weather and a water mill let to Robert Tannere at 8/- per annum.

1589/94 Willoughby has Pollinlands, Woodgatefield, Stony Croft & **MILBROKE MEADE**, in all 60 acres in Chiddingstone, bounding south to Stone Croft, S & W to late William **WARE**, S & E to **BRODEYE**, East to **POLBROKEMEADE**, west to Willoughby, north to Bowbeech-Penshurst road, East to a lane leading to Chiddingstone.

1716 William Streatfeild has 3 yards in **MILLBROOKE MEAD** in Chiddingstone.

SOMERDEN FARM (See Sketch)

1608 William Ware, son of William Ware, late of Somerden, to Steven Theobald - messuage called **SOMERDEN**, near **SOMERDEN GREEN**, with field next house - Upper Field Hither Ware Field, Further Ware Field, Pease alias Stony Croft, Lower Leaze, Hammell, the Impe Gardine, Calves Leaze, Beare Croft, 2 acres in Somerden Meade, Little Hope & Further Hope. 30 acres.

1609 Admeasurement of same. No fields named. Areas given on plots described by position.

1617 Will of Steven Theobald. Leaves above to occupier - his nephew John Godden, at £6 per ann. with reversion to Edward & John Mitchell, sons of daughter Katherine & Edward Mitchell Esq.

1724 Somerden Green owned by Henry Streatfeild - occupied by George Beaven.

CLAPPER MEAD

1708 Thomas **BOAKES** pays tithe from the Clapper Mead 2 acres.

1746 John, son of Thomas Boakes, holds above 2 acres with Fowks, alias **Sharp's Place.**

1809 Above still with Sharp's Place

GANGRIDGE MEAD (see sketch)

1312 Roger, son of Master Roger de Sevenak, to Master Jordan Moraunt, all claims in 1 1/2 acres in Chiddingstone next to **GANGBREGG**, in length between mead of heir of Lawrence de Polle and **MEDEWAYHAM**.

1318 3 acres in **GANGBREGGEMEDE**, part of demesnes of Chiddingstone Burghersh.

1429 Lease of same by the Lord of Chiddingstone Burghersh @ 6/8d per ann.

1499 Half of Gangebriggemede leased to Edward Lytyll & 6/8d.

1596 Lady Burgh to Richard Streatfeild **GANGRIDGE** Meade $4^{1/2}$ acres & 1 rood.

1703 Endorsed on map - "the two parts of this mead changeable yearly with the owner of Larkins & Penshurst lands". There is no trace of this in Larkins very full records.

HOBBS HILL

1482 **HOBBYSHELLYS**

1488 William Woodgate for above

1556 Richard Saxpes, formerly of Cowden died owning a messuage & 4 parcels in Chedyngston called **HOBBESHILL**, Kent filde & Kent meade, formerly Water Woodgate, 20 acres, @ 17d to Sundridge Manor: John is heir & son.

1586 John Saxpies held messuage **HOBBES HILL** and lands called **BRIDGWELL** @ 12d of Chiddingstone Cobham. George Saxpies, aged 34 is son & heir.

1591 George Saxpies a very negligent "bedle" of manor of Chiddingstone Cobham.

1603 No Saxpie is mentioned in Manor Court Rolls.

1632 George Saxpie is dead @ 12d: George & John are co-heirs but homage does not know if they inherit.

1662 George Saxpie sold Bridgwell to Michael Bassett, except a parcel @ 1s. (? Hobbs Hill)

1708 Widow Ellen Everest has 23 acres there.

Spring Field	1 acre
Gate	1 acre
Marlpit	2 acres
House	3 acres
Wilmots	4 acres
Top	2 1/2 acres
Church	2 acres
Tory Mead	3 acres
Grimsbridge Mead	3 1/2

1724 Matthew Everest owns and occupies.

PILBEAMS

1708 Edmund Medhurst has 30 acres there:-

Pond Mead	4 1/2 acres
Kitchen Mead	3 acres
Hog Croft	3 acres
Cowlows	6 acres
West Croft	2 3/4 acres
Lay lower field	2 1/2 acres
Lower Bullfinch	3 acres
Hilly Field	5 acres
Stack Plot	1/2 acre

1724 Edmund Medhurst owns and occupies.

PRINKHAM

1708 Widow Everest has about 42 acres - her name is Ellen.

Pitfield	3 acres
Middle Field	2 acres
Penstock	2 acres
Penstock	4 acres
Moory Plot	1 acre
Middle Field	3 acres
Hobs Hill Mead	3 acres
Mill Mead	3 acres
Bridge Mead	3 acres
Little Field	2 acres
Long Field	3 acres
East Field	9 acres
Spring Field	3 acres
Wenners Croft	2 acres

1724 Belongs to Michael Bassett. Henry Piggott occupies.

HORSESHOE LAND (IN PENSHURST PARISH - YOKE (SKETCH OF CHESTED)

1615 James Salmon of Penshurst - paylemaker - to William **BIRSTYE**: messuage wherein I live barn, close, 2 gardens, 1 acre 1 yard - in Penshurst. South to - Penshurst-Bowbeech road and to a cottage of James Salmon, to Hollamby lands - west, to other lands of James Salmon called Droveden, east & north.

1651 Judith, daughter of James Salmon, marries Robert Stanford, who sells to Richard Wallis of Penshurst, blacksmith - messuage, orchard, and one parcel 1 acre in Penshurst:- Hollambie west - road, south - Widdow Morant N & E - in occupation of Richard Wallis.

1732 John Cronk of Bowbeech wills to wife one little messuage in Penshurst in occupation Samuel Ovenden.

1753 William Cronk conveys to Samuel Ovenden, victualler, of Penshurst: a messuage long in S.O's occupation - N to John Wallis, S to road from Somerden Cross to **DROVEDEN** Green in Penshurst: E & W to Wallis and to same road.

1762 Same is now called the **THREE HORSESHOES** in Penshurst near Somerden Cross.

1768 Wallis heirs mortgage to George Lock: messuage with 1 1/2 acres. Ann Streatfeild buys it.

1779 It is now untenanted.

1813 Sold to Henry Streatfeild.

1907 Called "The Horseshoes" on 6 inch map.

CHIDDINGSTONE SHOP FARM

NAME IN BOLD PRINT FROM SEVENOAKS LIBRARY

GANGRIDGE MEAD NORTH (GANGRIDGE MED N)

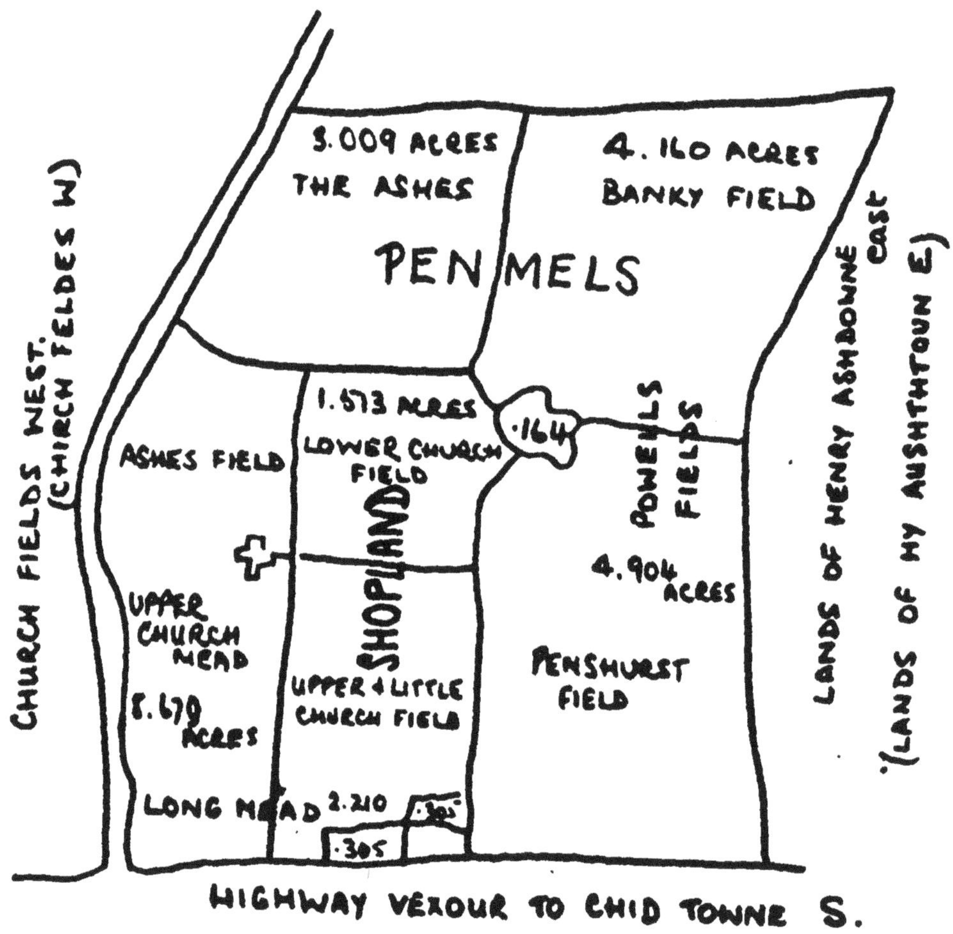

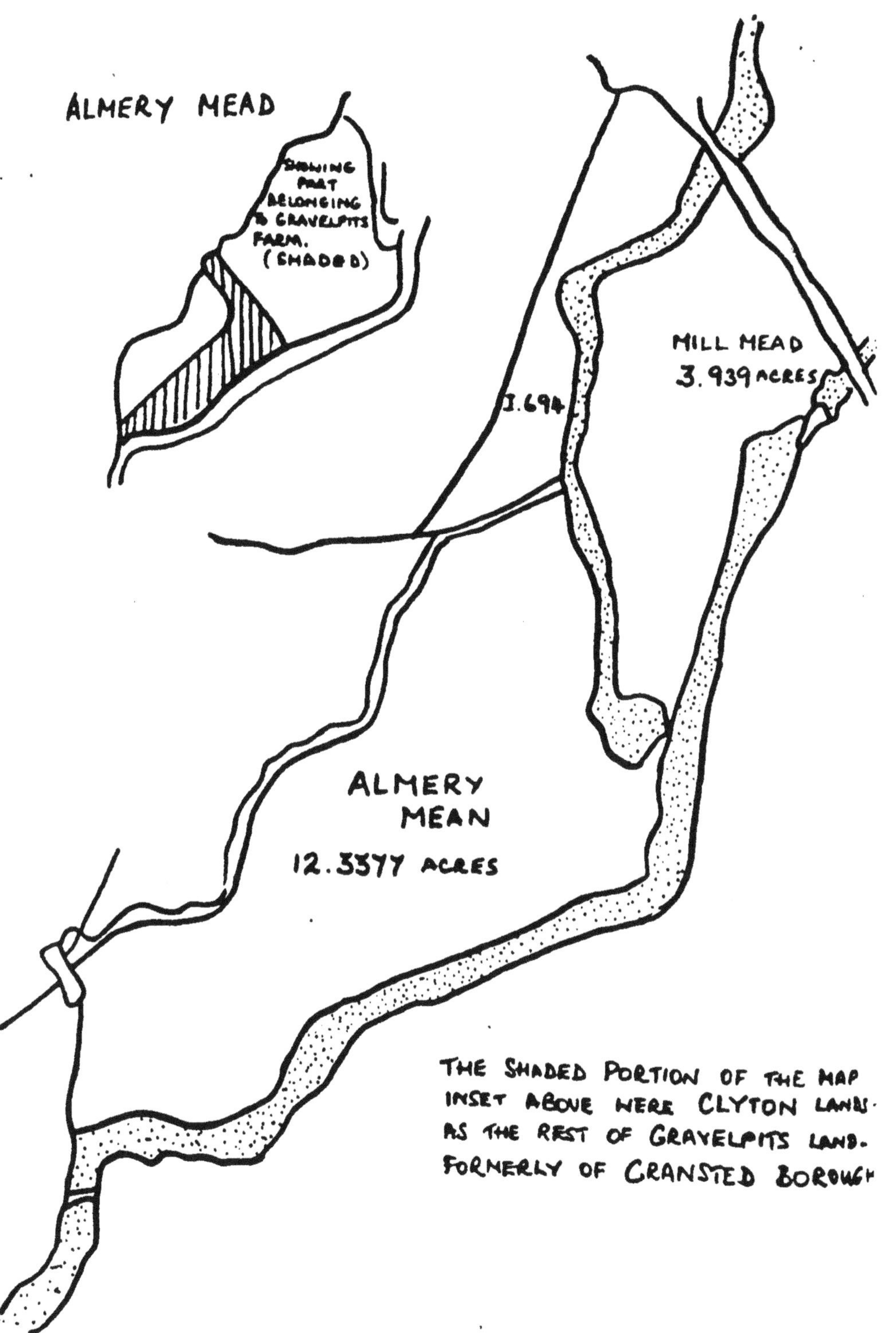
ALMERY MEAD
SHOWING PART BELONGING TO GRAVELPITS FARM. (SHADED)
MILL MEAD
3.939 ACRES
J.694
ALMERY MEAN
12.3377 ACRES
THE SHADED PORTION OF THE MAP
INSET ABOVE WERE CLYTON LANDS.
AS THE REST OF GRAVELPITS LAND.
FORMERLY OF CRANSTED BOROUGH

WEST MEAD

1668. MANOR OF TYEHURST HAS WEST MEAD—BELONGS TO RICHARD STRE

1708. ROBT PICKNEL TITHED FOR WEST MEAD — 3½ ACRES

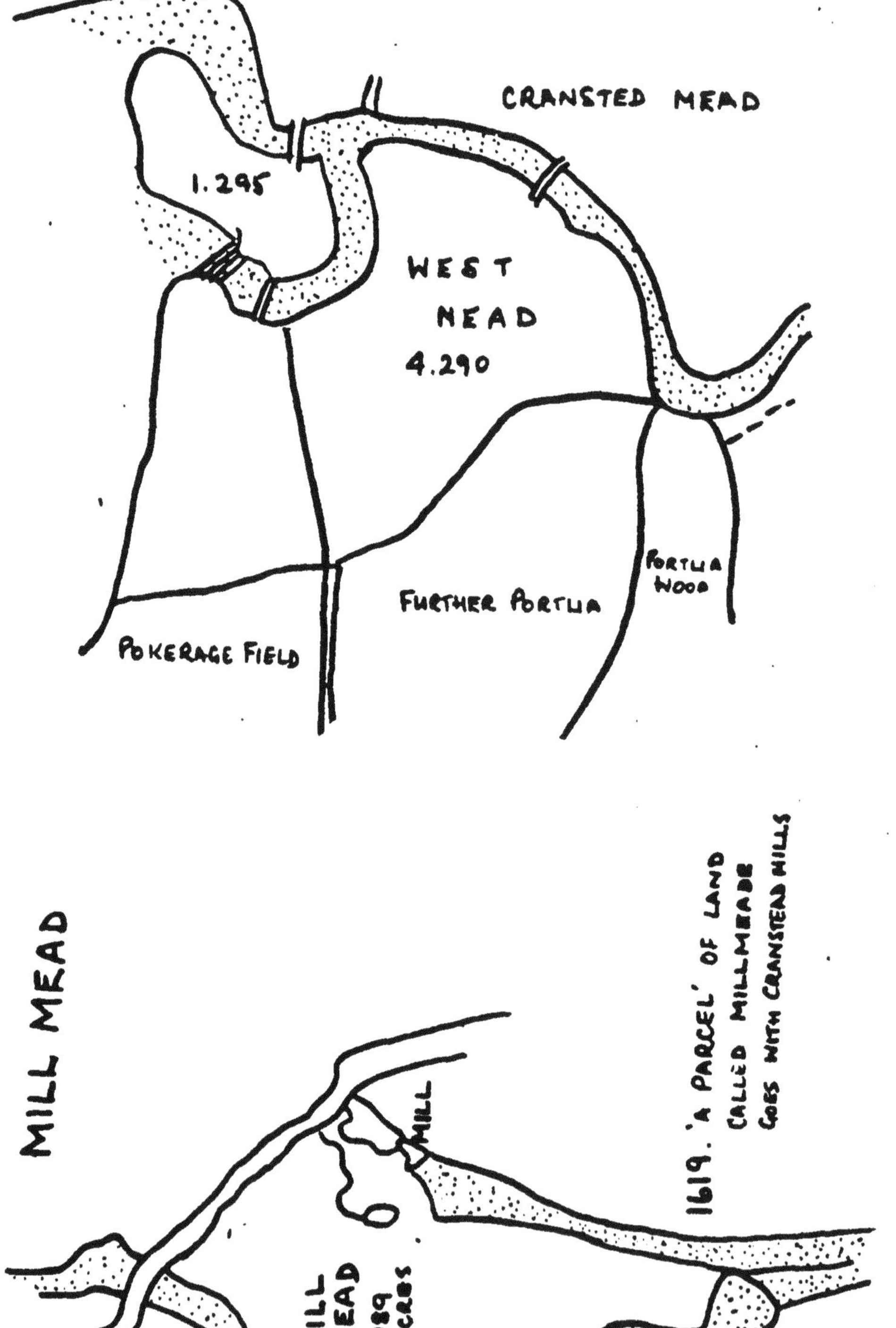

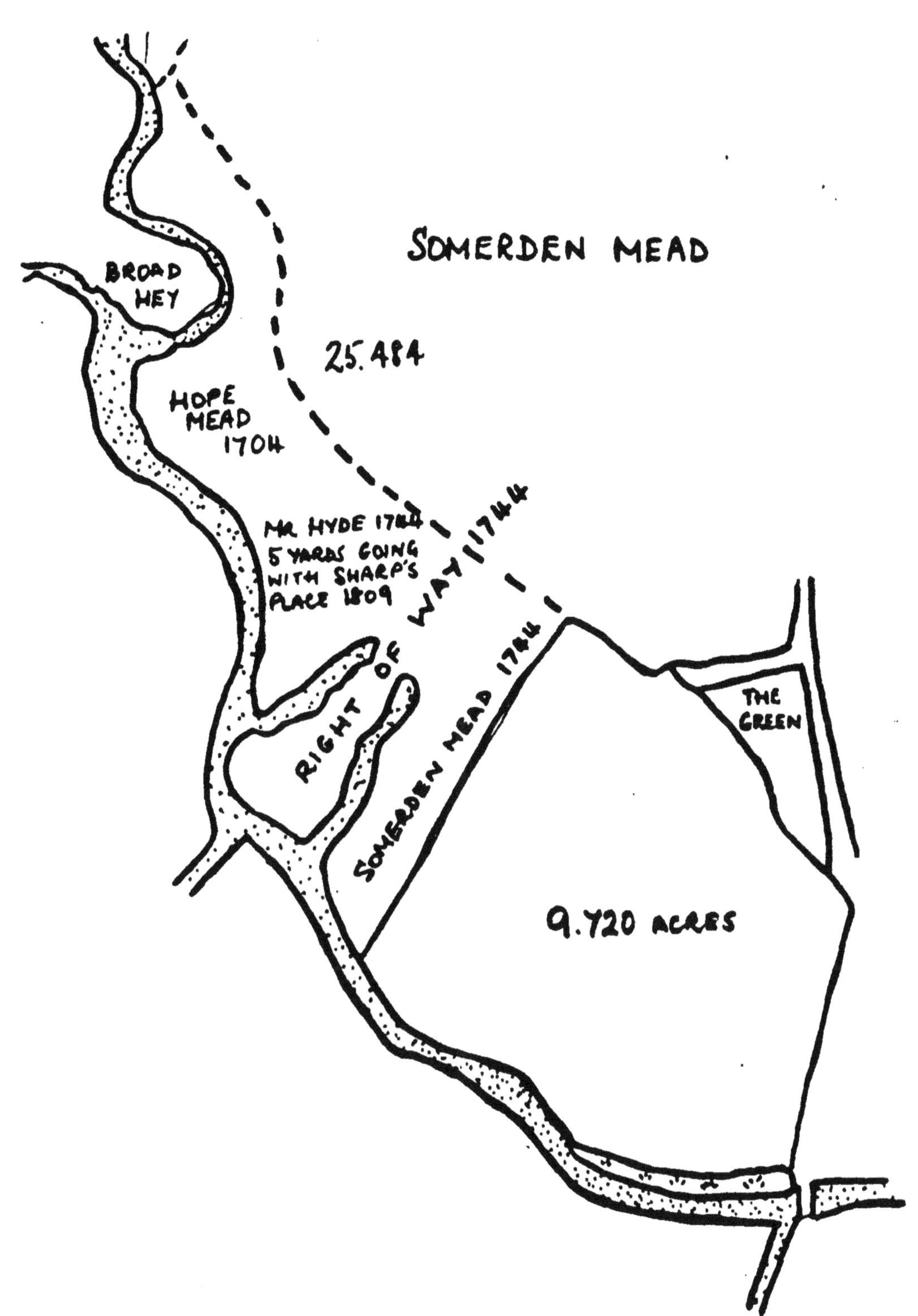
SOMERDEN MEAD
BROAD HEY
25.484
HOPE MEAD 1704
MR HYDE 1744
5 YARDS GOING WITH SHARP'S PLACE 1809
RIGHT OF WAY 1744
SOMERDEN MEAD 1744
THE GREEN
9.720 ACRES

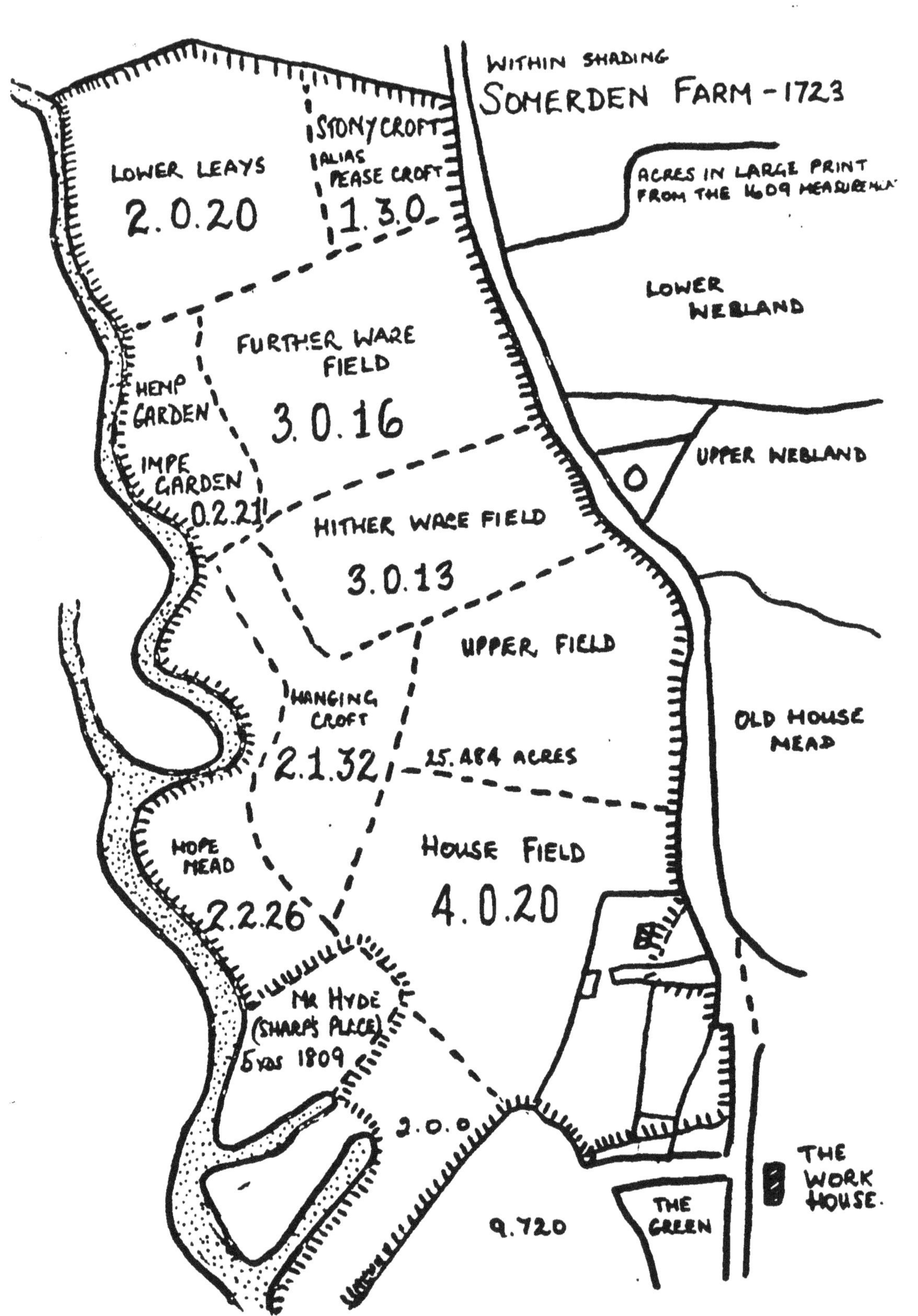
WITHIN SHADING
SOMERDEN FARM - 1723
ACRES IN LARGE PRINT
FROM THE 1609 MEASUREMENT
LOWER LEAYS
2.0.20
STONY CROFT
ALIAS
PEASE CROFT
1.3.0
LOWER
WEBLAND
FURTHER WARE
FIELD
3.0.16
HEMP
GARDEN
IMPE
GARDEN
0.2.21
UPPER WEBLAND
HITHER WARE FIELD
3.0.13
UPPER FIELD
HANGING
CROFT
2.1.32
25.484 ACRES
OLD HOUSE
MEAD
HOPE
MEAD
2.2.26
HOUSE FIELD
4.0.20
MR HYDE
(SHARP'S PLACE)
5 YDS 1809
2.0.0
9.720
THE
GREEN
THE
WORK
HOUSE

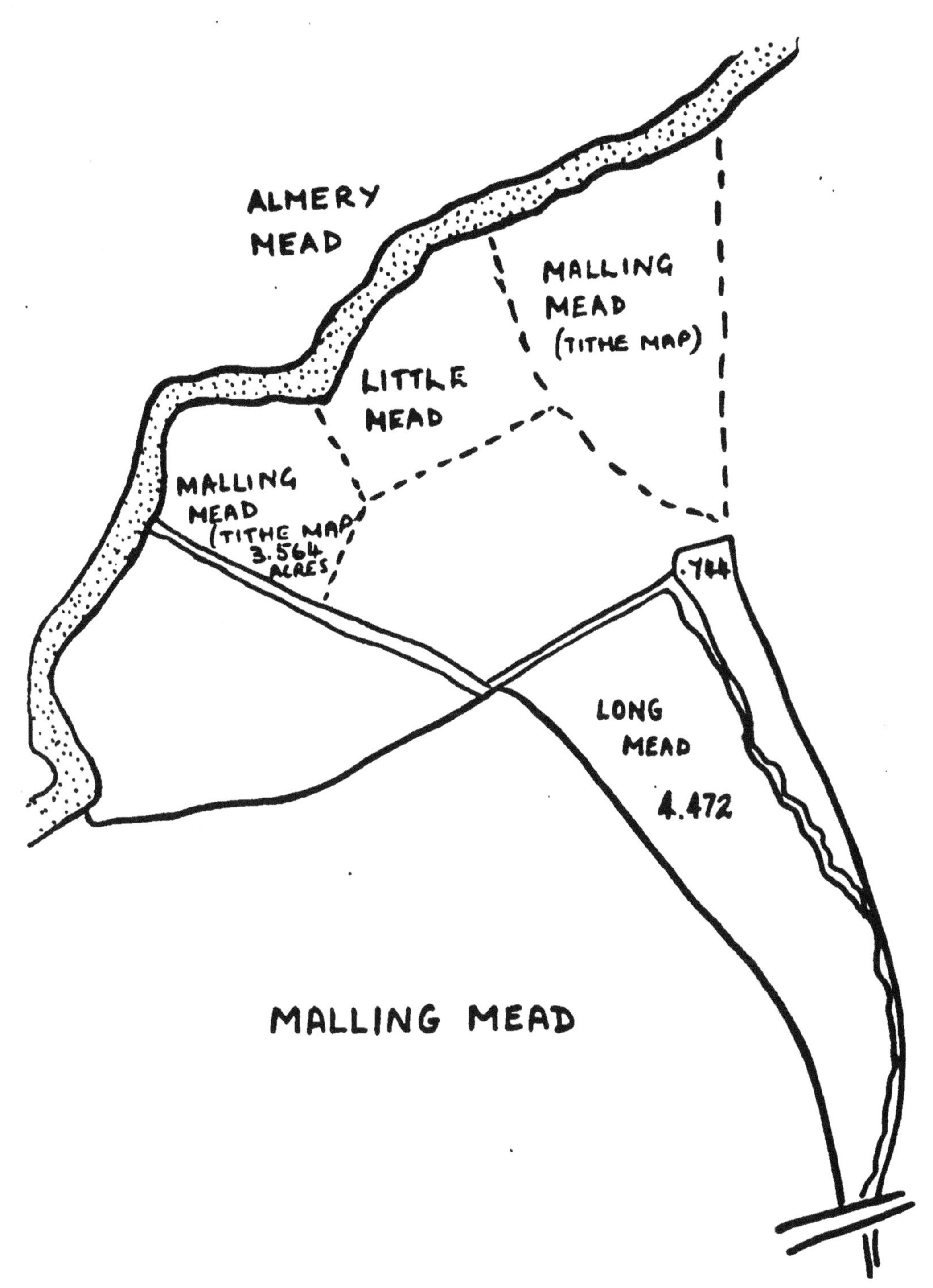
ALMERY
MEAD
MALLING
MEAD
(TITHE MAP)
LITTLE
MEAD
MALLING
MEAD
(TITHE MAP
3.564
ACRES
744
LONG
MEAD
4.472
MALLING MEAD

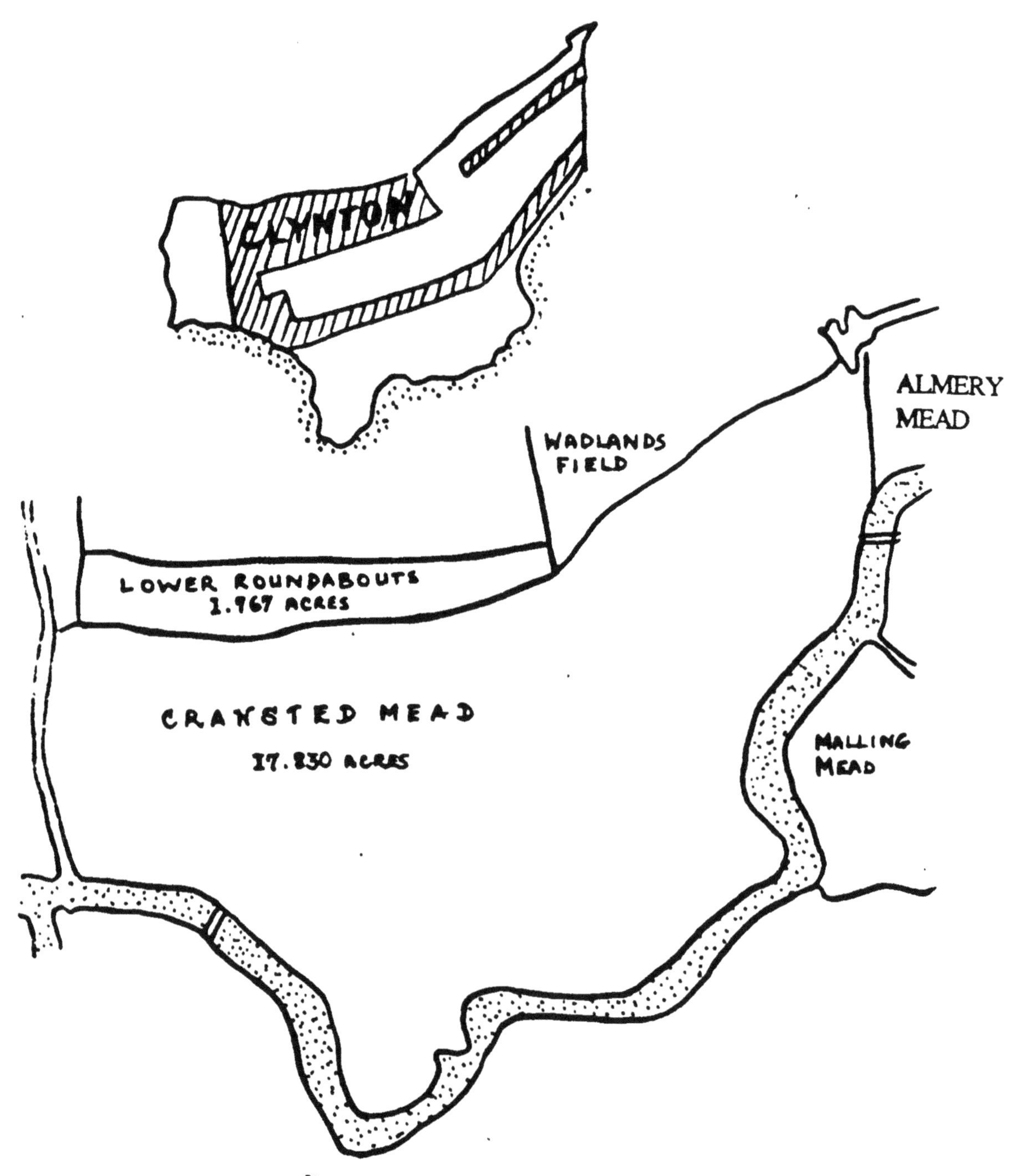
ALMERY
MEAD
WADLANDS
FIELD
LOWER ROUNDABOUTS
1.967 ACRES
CRANSTED MEAD
17.830 ACRES
MALLING
MEAD

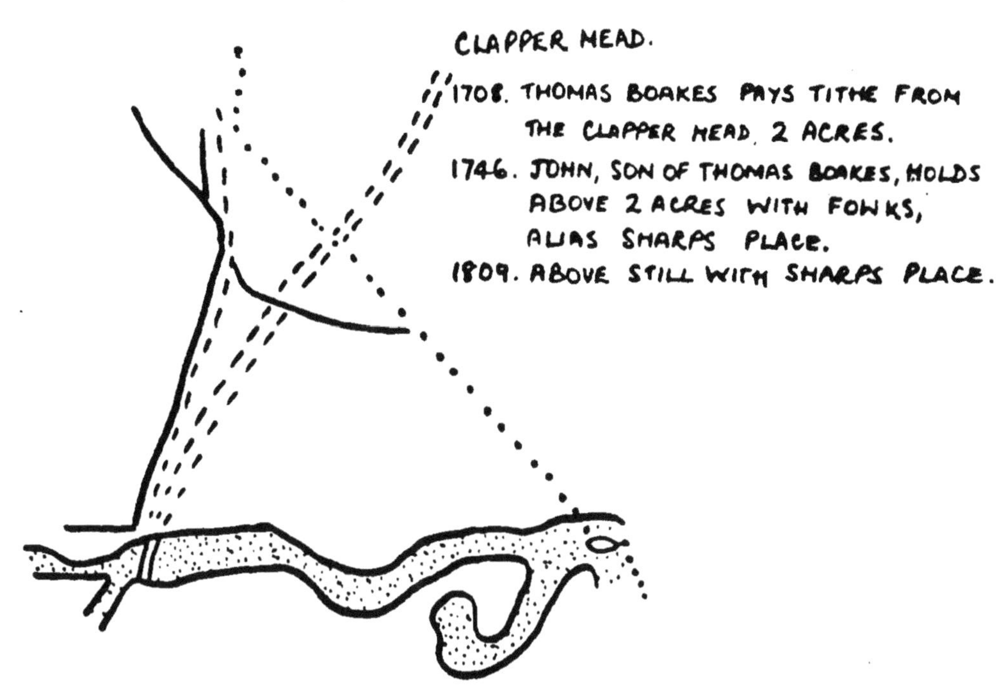

GANGRIDGE MEAD

ROGER, SON OF MASTER ROGER DE SEVENAK, TO MASTER JOHN MORAUNT,
1312. ALL CLAIMS IN 1½ ACRES IN CHIDD: NEXT TO GANGBREGG, IN LENGTH
BETWEEN MEAD OF HEIR OF LAWRENCE DE POLLE AND MEDEWAYHAM.
1318. 3 ACRES IN GANGBREGGEMEDE, PART OF DEMESNES OF CHIDD. BURGHERSH
1429. LEASE OF SAME BY THE LORD OF CHIDD. BURGHERSH @ 6/8 PER. AN.,
1499. HALF OF GANGEBRIGGEMEDE LEASED TO EDW. LYTYLL @ 6/8.

1596. LADY BURGH TO RICHARD STREATFIELD GANGRIDGE MEADE
4½ ACRES ½ 1 ROOD

1703. ENDORSED ON MAP - THE TWO PARTS OF THIS MEAD CHANGEABLE
YEARLY WITH THE OWNER OF LARKINS AND PENSHURST LANDS.
THERE IS NO TRACE OF THIS IN LARKINS VERY FULL RECORD.

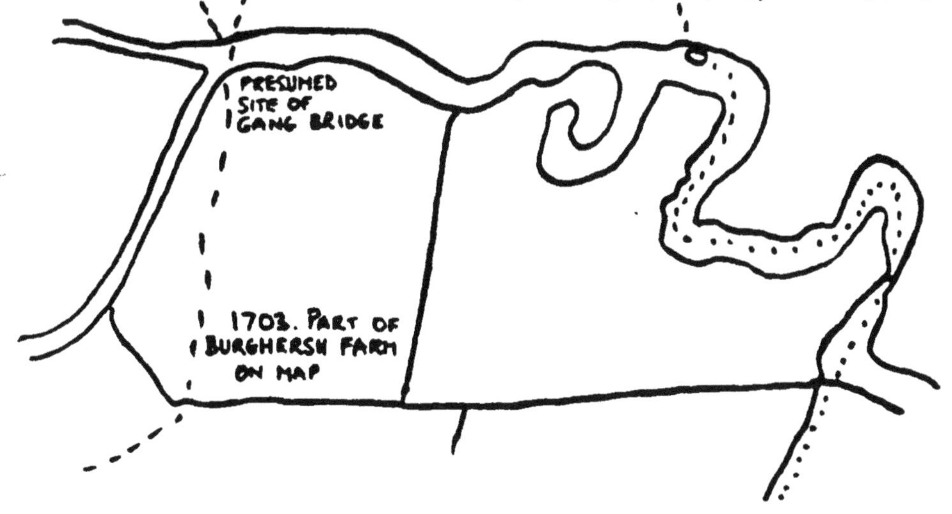

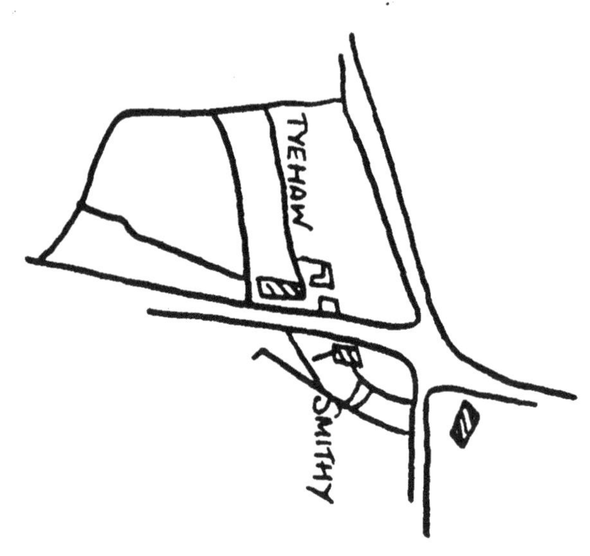
TYEHOW
SMITHY

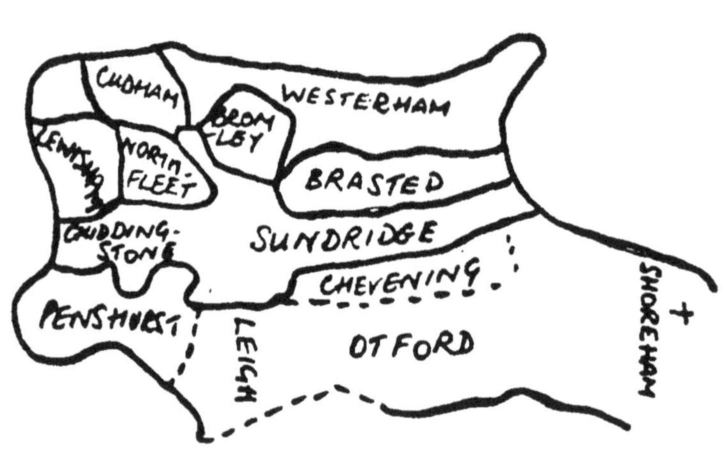
CUDHAM
WESTERHAM
BROM-LEY
NORTH-FLEET
BRASTED
CHIDDING-STONE
SUNDRIDGE
CHEVENING
PENSHURST
LEIGH
OTFORD
SHOREHAM

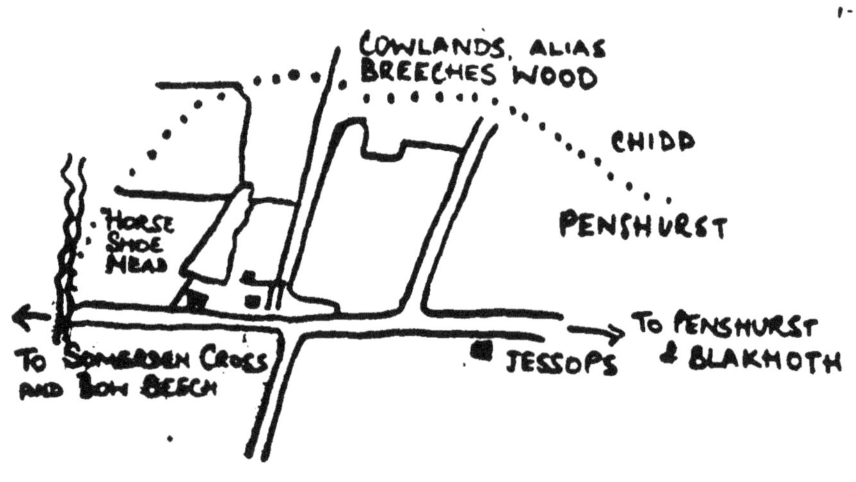
COWLANDS, ALIAS
BREECHES WOOD
CHIDD
PENSHURST
HORSE
SHOE
MEAD
TO SOMERDEN CROSS
AND BOW BEECH
JESSOPS
TO PENSHURST
& BLAKMOTH

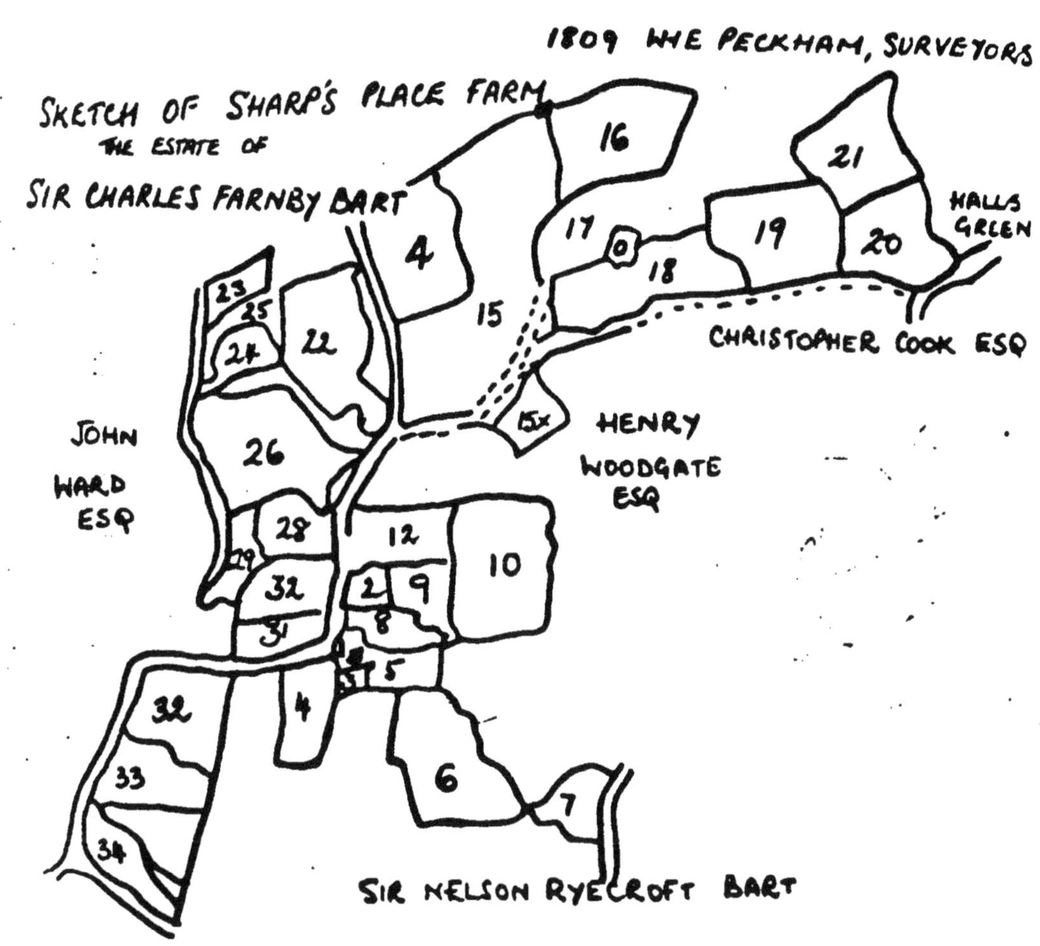
1809 WHE PECKHAM, SURVEYORS
SKETCH OF SHARP'S PLACE FARM
THE ESTATE OF
SIR CHARLES FARNBY BART
HALLS GREEN
CHRISTOPHER COOK ESQ
HENRY WOODGATE ESQ
JOHN WARD ESQ
SIR NELSON RYECROFT BART

THE FIELD OF SHARPS PLACE FARM - 1809

Map No.	Description	Acreage		
1	Site of the Buildings	1	1	15
2	Orchard		3	24
3	Orchard		3.	20
4	High field	3	3	13
5	Hill Orchard	2	3	0
6	Hale Field	10	0	0
7	Little Hale Field	2	2	30
8	Forestal or Green	1	2	14
9	Barn Field	2	0	26
10	Haystack Field	8	0	58
11	Shaw	1	0	8
12	Coneybury Field	5	3	57
13	Five Acres	6	1	0
14	Eight Acres	8	3	10
15	Black Pits & Bushes Wood	17	3	30
15 X	Spurs	2	2	0
16	Coles Field	8	2	0
17	Apple Tree Field	9	3	12
18	Peartree Field	9	0	0
19	Eight Acre Wood	8	0	28
20	Halls Green Five Acres (Sevenoaks)	6	0	24
21	Inner five acres (Sevenoaks)	5	3	36
22	Kiln Field	10	0	17
23	Little Field	2	2	25
24	Little Field	2	1	6
25	Shaw	1	2	22
26	Peg Hole Meadow	11	0	20
27	Shaws	2	1	4
28	Little Peg Hole	4	0	10
29	Little Hop Garden Field	2	0	20
30	Great Hop Garden Field	3	1	17
31	Hop Garden	2	3	26
32	Cut Field	7	2	0
33	Middle Cut Field	6	3	22
34	Further Cut Field	5	0	32
35	Bear Croft	2	1	35
36	Three yards	1	0	9
37	Five yards	1	1	1
38	Clapper Meadow	2	3	0
39	Lady Hope	1	0	10
	Half part of the Broad Acre & the two Doles	1	3	8
	Par of West Chested Mead changeable yearly	8	0	0
	Land	205	0	9
	Highways	2	2	28
		207	**2**	**37**

ZONE 1 MAP

To. OAKENDEN
WORK FIELD
STONEWALL WOOD
ALLENS
MALLS
ALLENS
BROOKERS FARM
CLIPPERS HEAD
UPPER KESDEN
THE WOODGATE
BATFIELD
LEES
To. PENSHURST
HARRIS FIELD
MUDINGS ALIAS MURINGS
WELLERS CROFT
KESDEN FIELDS
MARLPIT F
KNIGHTS
HARRIS CROFT
WELL CROFT
BAB HOUSE
BRANSELL FIELD
BLACKSMITHS ARMS
PARISH BOUNDARY
HILL FIELD
GREAT OAK
To. SMARTS HILL
FRIENDEN
PRINKHAM
HOBBSHILL
KENT WARTER
To. WALTERS GREEN
To. BLACKHAM
KENT WARTER

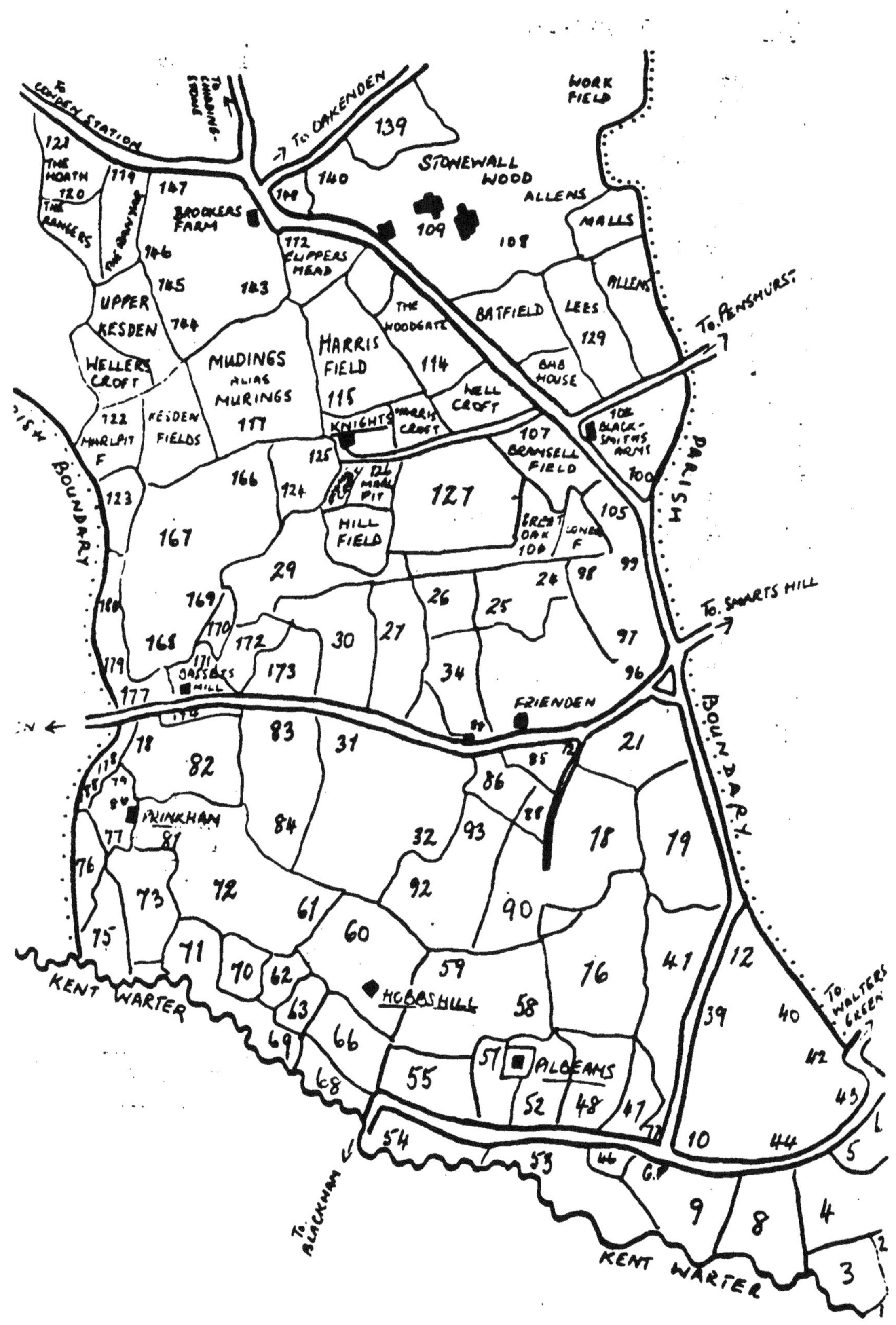

FIELD-NAMES Zone 1. From 1841 Tithe Map

1. Eel pan mead
2. Lower Selcox
3. Upper Selcox
4. Great Saxby Field
5. Little Saxby Field
6. Pt.Cobweb Mead
7. Cott.
8. Barn Plat
9. Bradley Mead
10. Hammer field
11. Acre Coppice
12. tophill Field
13. Old road (part)
14. Barn Wood
15. Hammer Field
16. Hollow field
17. Gravel Pit
18. Tench field
19. Middle Barn fields
20. Barn & Yard
21. Crossway field
22. Clay Corner
23. Doctors Wood
24. Farther Doctorsfield
25. Hither Docktorsfield
26. Old Hop Garden
27. Pit Field
28. Gill (Part)
29. Mill Pond Wood
30. Pond field
31. Hobbshill field
32. Upper & Lower Frienden
33. Three corner orchard
34. Curd Field
35 Orchard
36 Young Orchard
37. Frienden Farm
38. Frontage
39. Upper bullfinches
40. Lower Bullfinches
41. Bullfinches Wood
42. New Barn Field
43. Kings Farm
44. Bradley Plat
45. Parks Mead
46. Forge Field
47. Farther Cowlees
48. Hither Cowlees
49. Barn & Yard
50. Barn & Plat Mead
51. Pilbeams House
52. Well Mead
53 Pond Mead

54. 4 acre mead
55. Corner field
56 Shaw
57 Garden
58 Hilly field
59. Eight acre field
60. House Field
61. Wilmots Field
62. Wells field further
63. Wells field hither
64. Orchard field
65. Homestead Hobbeshill & Pilbeams Farms
66. Barn field
67. Pitt field
68. Tory Mead
69. Wen mead
70. Three acre field
71. Brook field
72. Ten acre field
73. Six acre field
74. Pitt
75. Prinkham mead
76 Bridge mead
77. House field
78. Shaw
79 Prinkham farm
80 Barns & yards
81. Two acre field
82. Seven acre field
83. Spring field
84. Eight acre field
85. Corner field
86. Three acre field
87. Barn & &Yard
88 Barnfield
89. Square field
90. Hobbshill field
91. Road wood
92 Pit field
93. Five acre field
94. Cott.
95. Cott.
96. Whitepost wood
97. Seamans field
98 Doctors field
99. Bannisters Field
100. Marlpit field pt.
101 Old road pt.
102 House
103. House
104 House
105 Brick field

106. Brick field mead
107 Cott.
108 Stonewall House
109 Kitchen garden
110 Garden field
111 Cott
112 Barn field
113 Yards & barn
114 West lawn
115 Knights Orchard
116 Knights Orchard
117.The Laying
118 Rangers Shaw
119 Hither Rangers
120 Rangers Wood
121 Further rangers
122 Laying Wood
123 Keysden wood
124 Knights field, part
125. Knights field, part
126 Little mead
127. Hoth laying
128. Plantation
129 East Lawn
130 Rough Wood
139 Parkers field
140 Springfield
141 Stonewall & Brookers Farm

142 Garden
143 Coney burrow field
144 Lower 3 acre field
145 Upper 3 acre field
146 Pit
147 Johns land
148 Capens pen mead
166 Eight acre field
167 Six acre field
168 Hilly field
169 Quarry field
170 Upper Mill Pond
171. Lower Mill Pond
172. Robins Meadow
173. Frienden field
174. Upper Plats
175 -
177 Oast field
178 Brook Mead
179 Shaw
180 Old Mill Pond pt.
188 House field pt.

ZONE 2 MAP

WILKINS GILL
504
LOCK SKINNERS
503
482
THE CLUMPS
484
497
496
505
DYEHURST BRIDGE
PARISH BOUNDARY
STOCK WOOD
487
241
244
240
235
238
236
NEWTYE
230
231
232
TRUGGERS GILL
257
258
255
260
259
268
267
272
TRUGGERS
269
266
274
492
NEWTYE HURST
219
220
221
222
229
228
BUCK-HURST
217
218
223
224
264
265
275
TO COWDEN STATION
216
214
211
226
202
209
191
227
201
192
200
197
199
189
193
198
195
190
187
PARISH BOUNDARY
186
188
183
182
ZONE 2

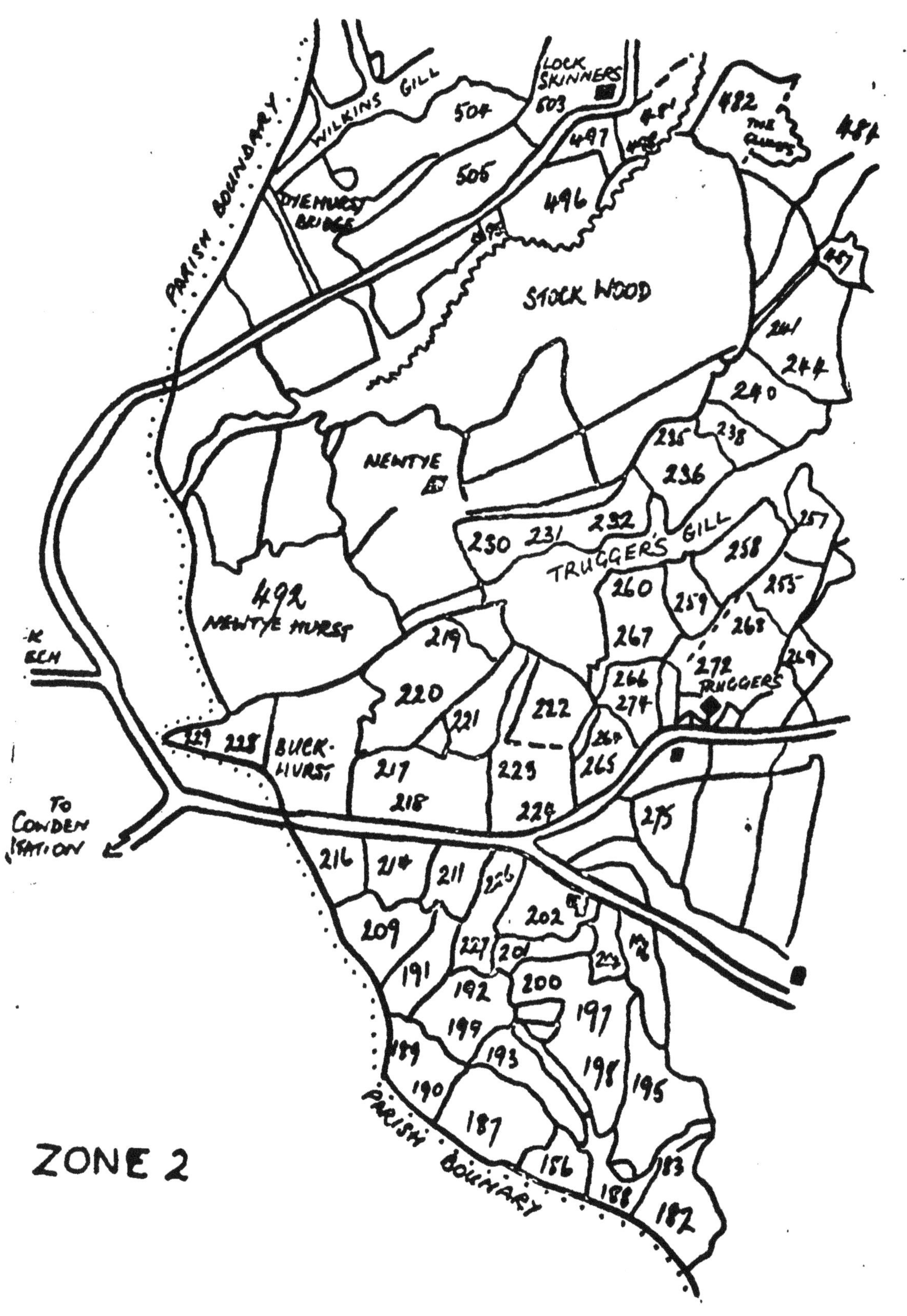

FIELD NAMES ZONE 2 FROM 1841 TITHE MAP

182. Pit Field
183 Old Furze field
186 eight acre field
187. seven acre field
188. House field (pt)
189 Broad Biltons (pt)
190 Long Biltons (pt)
191. Long Croft Field
192 New Mead1
193 Tough Coat Field
194 Rangers Field
195 Lower Cow field
196 Upper Cow field
197 Great Mead
198 Heart Mead
199 Grove Mead
200 Gove Mead
201 Tory Field
202 Orchard Field
203 Gt. Batts & Walnut Tree Cross Farm
204 Malt House garden
206 Carters Field
207 Beech field
209 Tare Grattan
211 Barn field
212 Homestead
214 four acre field
216 Buckhurst field
217 Wet Field

218. Fatten Pen Field
219 Three corner field
220 Eight acre field
221 Longfield
222 Grubfield
223 Alder Plat
224 Dry field
226. High field (pt)
227 High Field (pt)
228 Lower Slade Field
229 Upper Sale Field
230 Upper Geers
231 " " 5 acres
232 Gt. Marlpit Field
233 Upper Truggers Field
234 Lower Truggers Field
235 Lower Geers 5 acres
236 Upper Geers Mead
238 Lower Geers Mead
240 Geers seven acres
241 Healer Mead
242 Great Riddens
243 Little Riddens
244 Pit field

255 Shoals Field
256 Mudfield Shaw
257 Mud Field
258 Old Garden
259 Lower Mead

260. Minty field
264 Culver Croft (pt)
265 Culver Cróft (p6)
266 Hurdle field
267. Rushetts field
268 Shoals Mead
269 Tanyard Mead
270 Orchard
272 Malthouse Mead
273 Great Truggers Farm
274 Garden
275 Wainhouse Hothe
276 Great Hoth
277 Wood Hoth

481 Stoney Field
482 Coney Burrow field
483 Warren field
484 Great High Field
487 Barn
492 Great Wood (pt)

495 Shaw
496 Iron Field
497 Stoney Field
498 Shaw
503 Barn Mead
504 Inner Kicks Field
505 Lower Kicks Field

ZONE 3 MAP

VILLAGE
LARKINS
CASTLE
SCHOOL
GREAT OATFIELD
FOUR ACRES
SAND FIELD MEAD
GREAT SAND-FIELD MEAD
ELEVEN ACRES
HARE FIELD
GREAT STONY CROFT
LONG PARK
FIVE ACRES
TWO ACRES
FOUR ACRES
MORT MEAD
THE MORTS
LOWER GREEN FIELD
ISCARS FIELD
THE FORLESE
LITTLE GREEN F.
THE SLIPS
THE CLUMP
LEW CROSS
BRIDLE ROAD
TO PENSHURST
ROBINS LAND
PARISH BOUNDARY
PIT
SKINNERS LANE
HORTH CORNER
OAKENDEN
FORESA SCHOOL
ZONE 3
434
446
448
468
470
481
494
486
424
305
425
487
243
241
246
306
307
310
309
244
245
240
235
236
303
304
301
302
339
340
355
356
355A
421
300
258
259
255
254
257
253
269
293
289
252
420
314-17
324
275
276
277
252
251
328
325
318
329
330
334
133
131
160
156
151
149
157

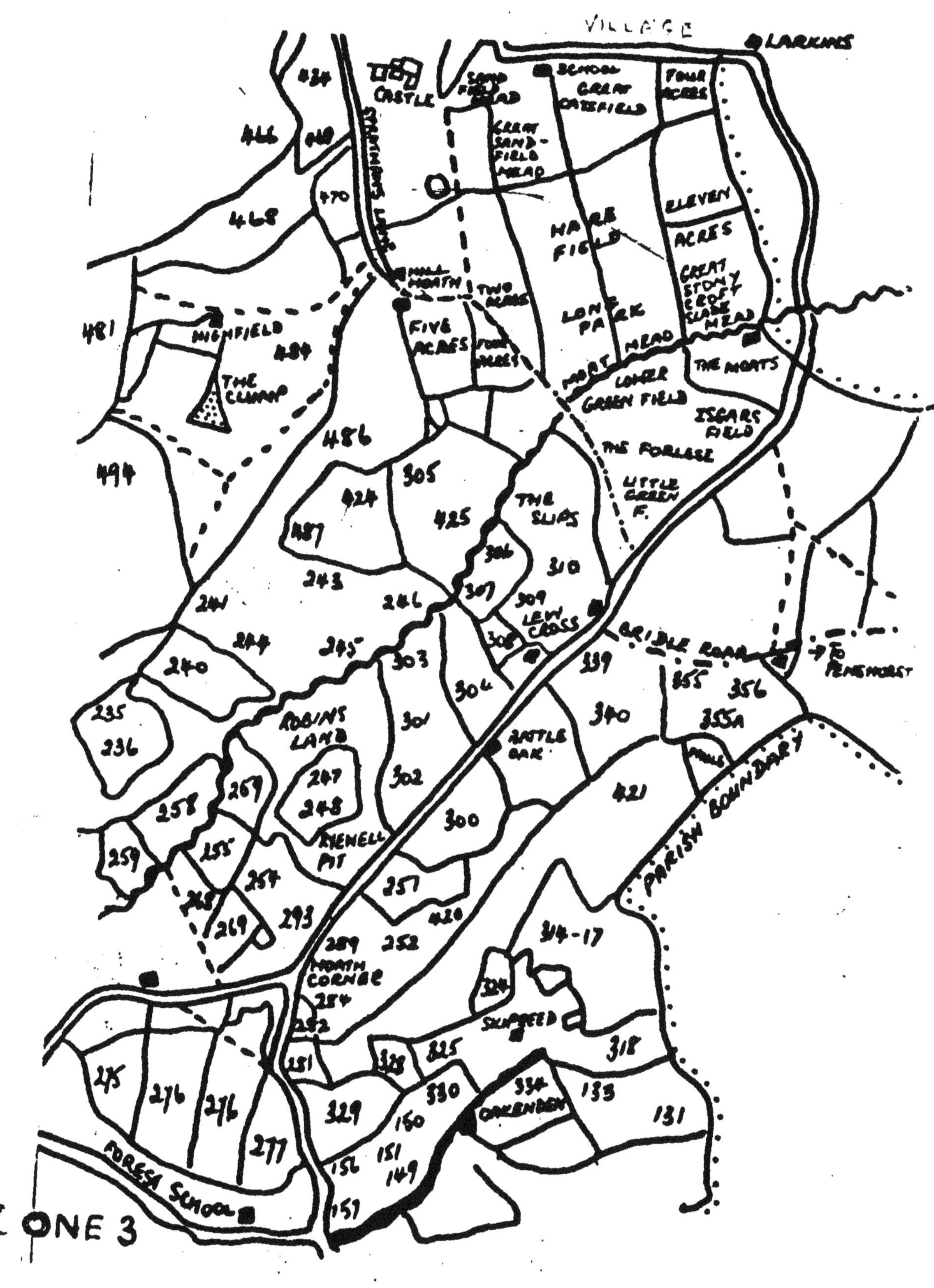

Field Names Zone 3 - From 1841 Tithe Map

131 Lower Pond field
133 Long Pond F. shaw
135 Long Pond Field
137 Cottage
139 Parkers Farm
148 Capens Pen Mead
149 Orchard
150 Hop Garden (pt)
151 " "
156 Cottage
157 Cottage
235 Lower Geers 5 acres
236 Upper Geers Mead
238 Lower Geers Mead
240 Geers seven acres
241 Healer Mead
243 Little Riddens
244 Pit Field
245 Upper Bridge Field
246 Lower Bridge Field
247 Kiln Field
248 Pond Field
251 Upper Ryes
252 Ryewell Orchard
254 Barn field
255 Shoals Field
257 Mudfield
258 Old Garden
259 Lower Mead
268 Shoals Mead
269 Tanyards Mead
275 Wainhouse Hothe
276 Great Hothe

277 Wood Hoth
279 Broockers Hoth
281 Hollow Field
282 Puckden Mead
284 Orchard
285 Little Truggers Farm
289 Further Meadow
293 Cottage
300 Lower Ryes Field
301 Upper Robert Land
302 Lower Robert land
303 Shaw
304 Battle Oak field
305 Long Slip Mead
306 Great Banky Field
307 Little Banky Field
308 Orchard
309 Barn Field
310 Shifting Croft
313 Banks Field
314 Four acre Field
315 Shaw Field
316 Long Shaw
317 Six acre field
318 Long Mead
321 Pit Mead
324 Old Hop Garden
325 House Mead
327 Little Mead
328 Hop Garden Field
330 Cottage Field
329 Skipreed field
333 Oakenden Mead
334 Lodge Mead

338 Farther Scotlands
339 Hither Scotlands
340 Shaw
342 Iron Cross Field
343/4 Pitts
345 Green Field
346 Church Field
351 Lodge & Yard
352 Stall Field
353 Pitt Field
354 Yard Field
355 Banks Field (pt)
356 Forestall

420 Puckden Wood
421 Russells Coppic (pt)

424 Great Marls Field
425 Little Marls Field
434 Kitchen garden

466 Mill Pond Mead
468 Moor Wood
469 Pond Field
470 Sharpers Croft

481 Stoney Field
482 Coney Burrow Field
484 Great High Field
486 A field
487 Barn

494 Stock Wood

FIELD NAMES ZONE 4: From 1841 Tithe Map

346 Church Field
347 Lodge Field
348 Moyces Field
349 South Field
350 Old Garden
351 Lodge & Yard
358 Marl Pit Field
360 West Field
362 Yard
363 Gore
364 Wych Field
366 Little Honey Mead
367 Great Honey Mead

368 Clapper Mead
369 Shaw & Frontage
370 Little WEN (?Weir) Field
371 Dunstans Field
373 Shaw
374 Great Hartridge Field
376 Upper Gillridge Field
377 Shaw
379 Shaw
380 Marshope Mead
381 Great WEN (or Weir) Mead
382 Road

383 Nursery Field
389 Gate Field
390 Lower Spring Field
391 Stack Field
392 New Mead
393 Great Alder Mead
394 Bourn Mead
395 Clove Mead
396 Gillridge Mead
397 Barn Field
398 Toll Field
399 Marshope Mead (pt)
400 Marshope Mead (pt)

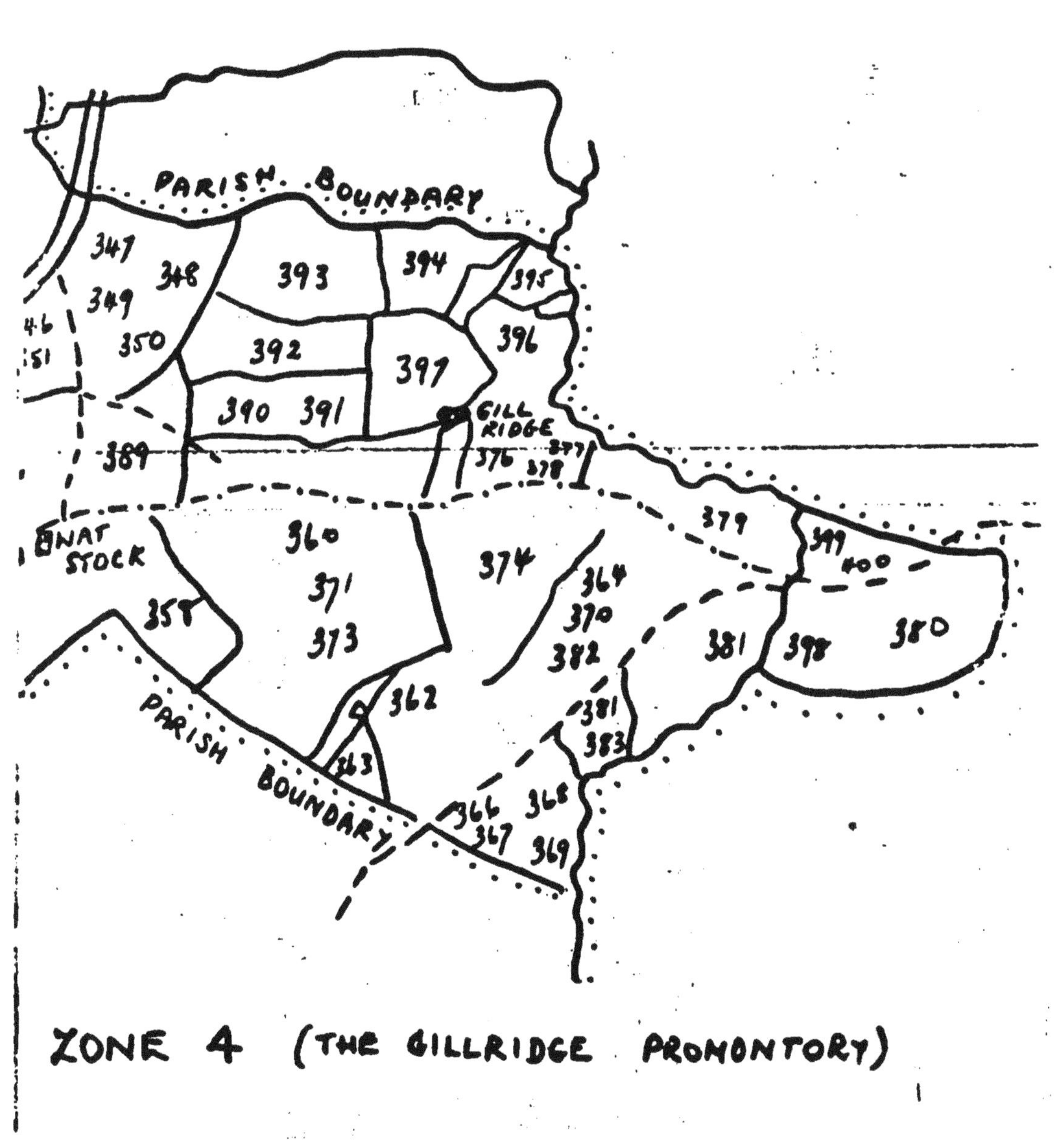

ZONE 4 (THE GILLRIDGE PROMONTORY)

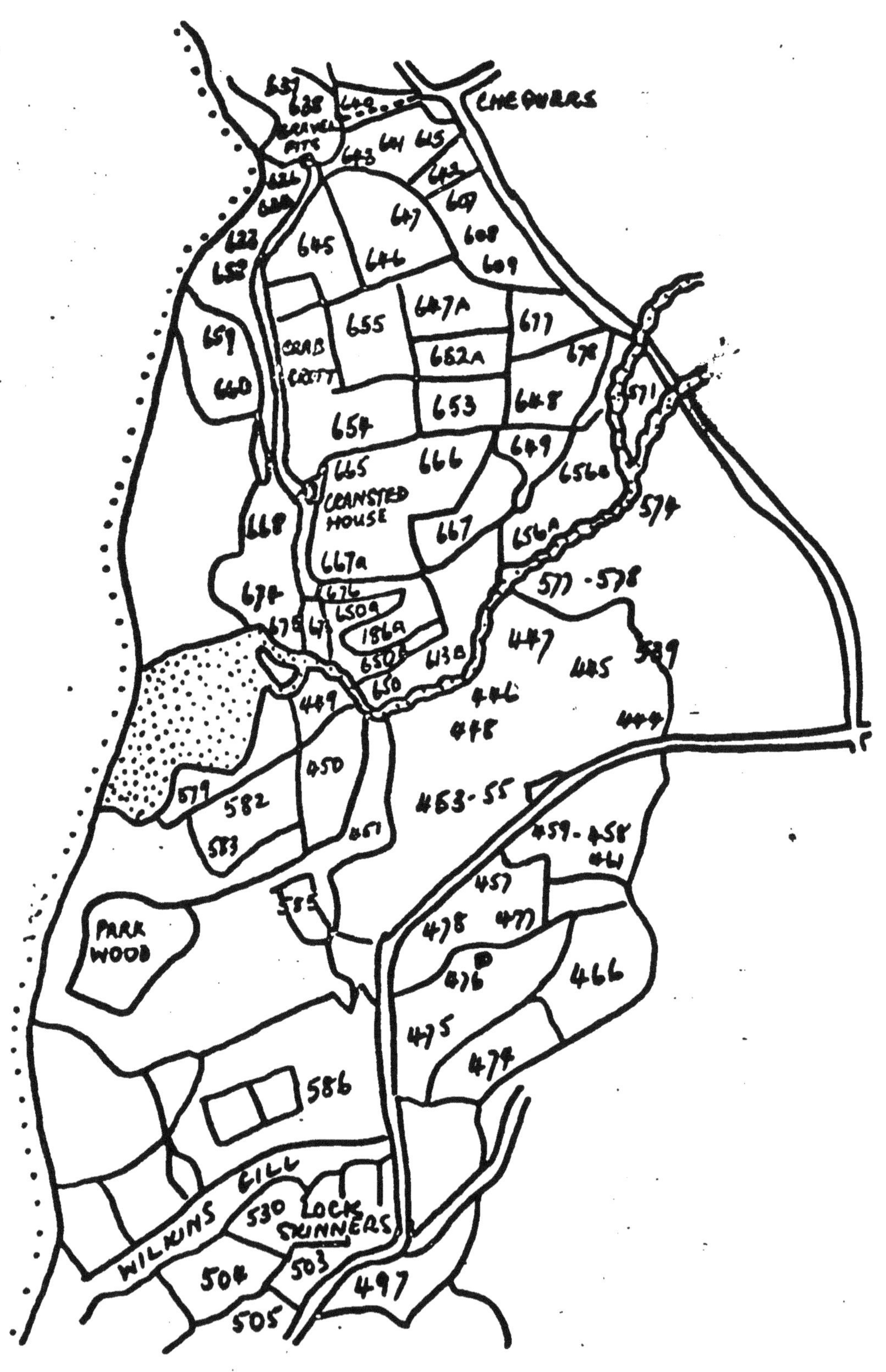
CHEQUERS
GRAVEL PITS
645
646
647
655
647A
677
CRAB CROFT
682A
653
648
659
660
654
666
665
649
CRANSTED HOUSE
668
667
574
667a
571-578
674
186A
447
445
444
449
448
450
453-55
579
582
583
451
457
585
478
477
PARK WOOD
476
466
475
474
586
WILKINS GILL
530 LOCK
SKINNERS
504
503
497
505
ZONE 5

FIELD NAMES ZONE 5 From 1841 Tithe Map

South of River Eden

444 Great Wen Field
445 Infward Wen Field
446 Outward Wen Field
447 Malling Mead
448 Log Field
449 West Mead
450 Further Portlia
451 Portlia Wood
453 Great Broad Field
454 Long Park Field
455 Dencher Field
457 Inland Road
458 Yard
459 Forestall
461 Little Culver Croft
464 Tighurst Field
466 Mill Pond Mead

473 Mud Field
474 Moor Mead
475 Well Field
476 Barn
477 Sugens Field
478 Little Broad Field
479 Mud Field Shaw
480 Chequers Field
497 Stoney Field
503 Barn Mead
504 Inner Kicks Field
505 Lower Kicks Field
530 Lower Wilkins
539 Long Mead
571 Mill Mead
574 Shaw
577 Malling Mead
578 Little Mead
579 Old Pokerage Mead
582 Pokerage Field
583 Shaw
585 Little Wisdoms
586 Farther Thrashers Field (pt)

North of River Eden

607 Oak Field
608 Middle Field
609 Tao acre Field
615 Chequers House
623 Further Field
624 Middle Field
626 Pasture Field
637 Near Gravel Pit Field
638 Further Gravel Pit Field
640 Cottage
641 Gravelpit Field
642 Jups Field
643 Yard & Buildings
646 Old Hop Garden
647 Broomy Field
647a Broad Whorps Field
648 River Field
649 Hamread Field
650 Cransted Mead
653 Broad Field
654 Sorrelly Field
658 Great Pond Field
659 Second Pond Field
660 Third Pond Field
652 Old Hop Garden
656 Crab Croft
656a Weir Mead
656b Great Hamreed Field
656c Little Hamreed Field
656d Almery Mead
665 Little High Field
666 Little Lodge Field
667 Wadlands Field
668 Dry Mead
673 Wood Field
675 Pipers Grove (pt)
674 Lower Four acres
677 Upper Roundabouts
678 Bridge Mead

ZONE 6

561
562
568
569
570a
HOPGARDEN FIELD
EQUERS
604-06
558
560
RUSHY MEAD
RIDGY FIELD
GREAT RIVER FIELD
559
BROADHEY
LOWER LAYS
FURTHER WARE
UPPER WARE
HEAP GARDEN
570
572
573
579
575
578
571
MILL
576
440
441
575
574
577/8
LITTLE KINGS
GREAT KINGS
457
HOPE MEAD
HOUSE FIELD
SOMERDEN GREEN
CLAPPER MEAD
539
442
548
GILWYNS
568
542
LOWER CHURCH FIELD
567
552
553
565
551
556
564
RECTORY
CHURCH
ZONE 6

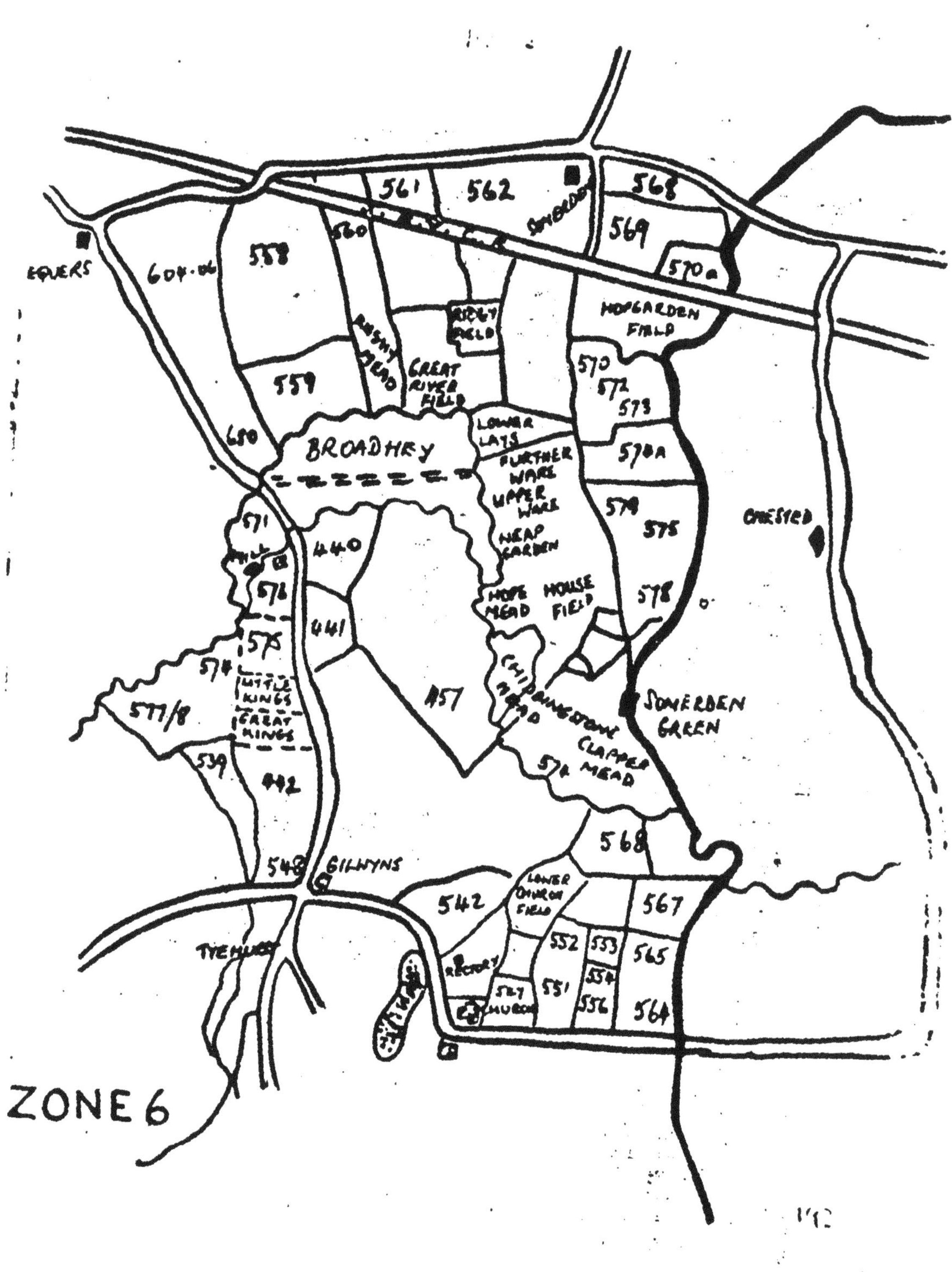

FIELD NAMES -ZONE 6 FROM 1841 TITHE MAP

South of River Eden

440 Mill Hop Garden
441 Chestnut Wood
442 Forest Field
539 Long Mead
542 Parsonage
547 Cottage
548 Lower Church Field

551 Upper Church Mead
552 Ashes Field
553 Lower Church Field
554 Upper Church Field
556 Little Field
564 Penshurst Field
565 Orchard
567 Banky Field
568 Gangridge Mead
571 Mill Mead
573 Chiddingstone Mill Farm
574 Shaw
575 Little Kings Field
576 Great Kings Field
577 Farther Thrashers Field
578 Hither Thrashers Field

North of River Eden

558 Sixteen acre Field
559 Then acre Field
560 Long Field
561 Ox Pasture
562 Riddy Field

565 Upper Pollands (Potlands or Pollinlands)
568 Orchard
569 Cock Oak
570 Hurdle Field
572 Upper Bears Croft
573 Lower Bears Croft
574 Workhouse Mead
574a Lower Webland Field
575 Upper Webland Field
576 Bushey Mead (pt)
577 Brissleden Field
578 Old House Mead
604 Waterlake Field
605 Well Field
606 Clouts Field
607 Oak Field
608 Middle Field
609 Two acre Field
610 Mount Field
611 Flat Field (pt)
612 Bridge Field
680 Frontage to Clouts Farm

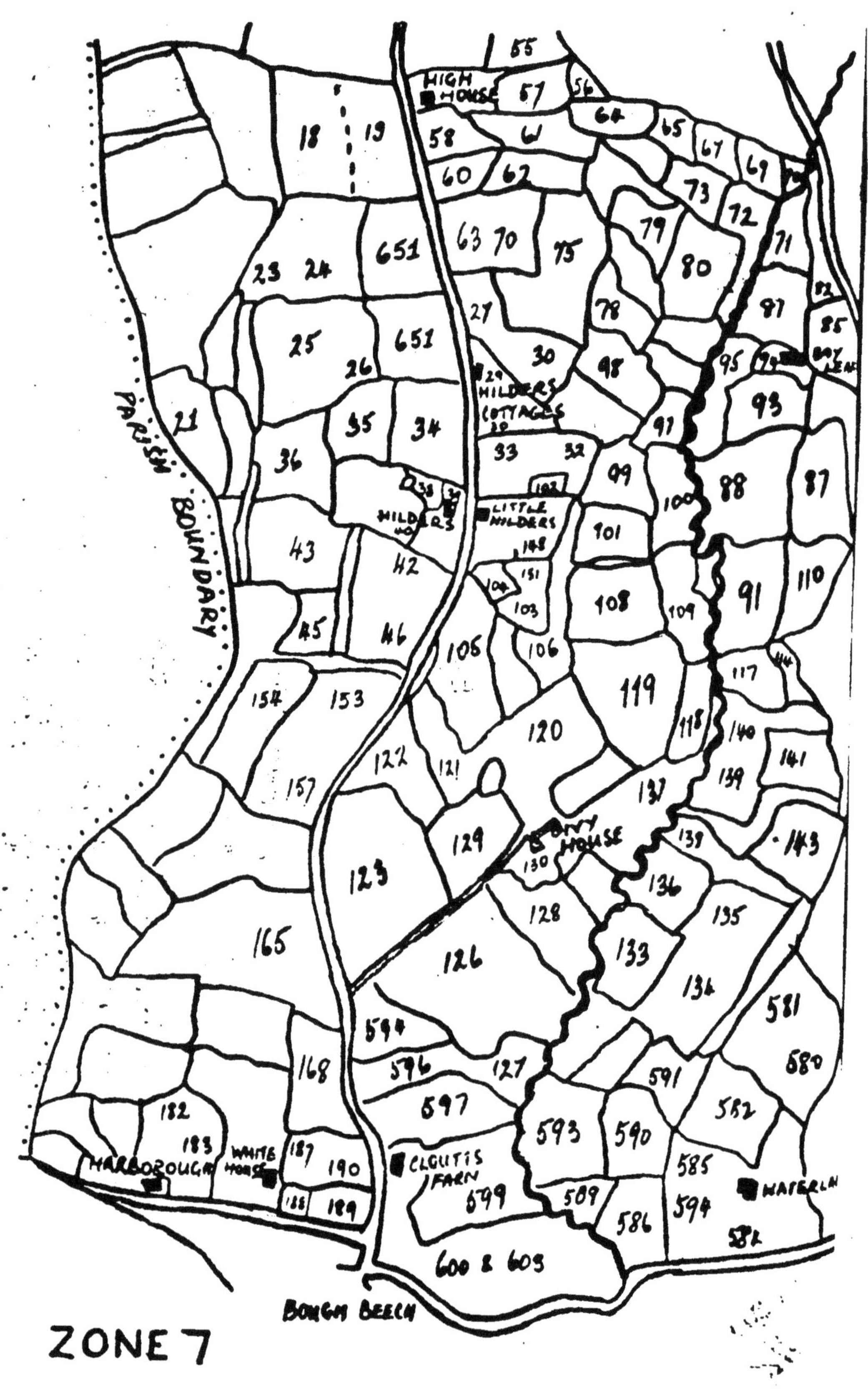

FIELD NAMES - ZONE 7 From 1841 TITHE MAP

18	Marls Croft	75	Dane Field	133	Lower Dencher Field
19	Horn Field	77	Butteries Field	134	Upper Dencher Field
21	Perry Field	78	Shaw	135	Cowfield
23	Two acre Mead	79	Square Broom Field	136	Brook Field
24	White Field	80	Six acre Field	137	Barn Mead
25	Nine Acre Field	81	House Mead	138	Stony Plat
26	Furze Field	82	Shaw	139	Further 2 acres
27	Old Hop Garden			140	Mill Wood
29	Hilders Cottage	85	Nine acres	141	Five Acre Wood Field
30	Magpye Field	91	Weir Field	143	Square Field
31	Old House Mead	93	Oast Field	148	Great Mead
32	Little Banks Field	94	Ivyhouse & Bailey Farms	151	Shaw
33	Great Banks Field			153	Lettendens Field
34	Groveden Field	95	Mill Pond	154	Old Kiln Field
35	Rushett's Field	97	Bridgers Field	157	Half Mile Field
36	Hop Garden Mead	98	Great Hook Lands	165	Ten acre Field
37	Kiln Field	99	Little Hook Lands	168	Furnace Mead
38	Forestall	100	Lower Mill Pond	182	Stack Field
39	Salmonds Farm (Hilders)	101	Bushey Croft	183	Barn Field
		102	Half acre Plat	187	Mead
40	Home Pasture	103	Crooked Croft	188	Farther Field
42	Lower Church Field	104	Coles Acre	189	Near Field
43	Ray Field	87	Upper Houletts	190	Barlow Pasture
45	Marlpit Field	88	Lower Houletts	580	Further 6 acre
46	Upper Church Field	105	Kiln Field	581	Near 6 acre
55	Three Corner Field	106	Kiln two acres	582	Square Field
56	Great Mead Pitt Field	108	Little Mill Farm	583	Great Snidland
57	Four acre Field	109	Shaw	584	Little Snidland
58	(High) House Field	110	Clems Acre	585	Hollow Field
59	High House Farm	114	Upper Wood Farm	589	Three acre Mead
60	Barn Field	117	Lower Wood Farm	586	Yard Field
61	Four acres	118	Mill Hop Garden	590	Upper Barn Field
62	Dane Field	119	Great Mill Farm	591	Faress Field
63	Brick Field	120	Fourteen acre Field	593	Sourers Field
64	Upper Field	121	Long Field	594	Poor Croft
65	Middle Field	122	Bettys Plat	596	Wood
67	Upper Mead	123	Street Field	598	Clouts Farm
69	Long mead (pt)	126	Maple Shaw Field	599	Great Mead
70	Old House Mead	127	Maple Wood	600	Rail Mead
71	Old House Mead	128	Sawpit Field	603	Six acre Mead
72	Stip Mead	129	Pond Field		
73	Long Brooms	130	Ivy House		

ZONE 8

WINKHURST WOOD
BORE PLACE
BLUE LANE
CHIDDINGHURST
COLES FARM
POLEBROOK FARM
SONERDEN CROSS
ZONE 8

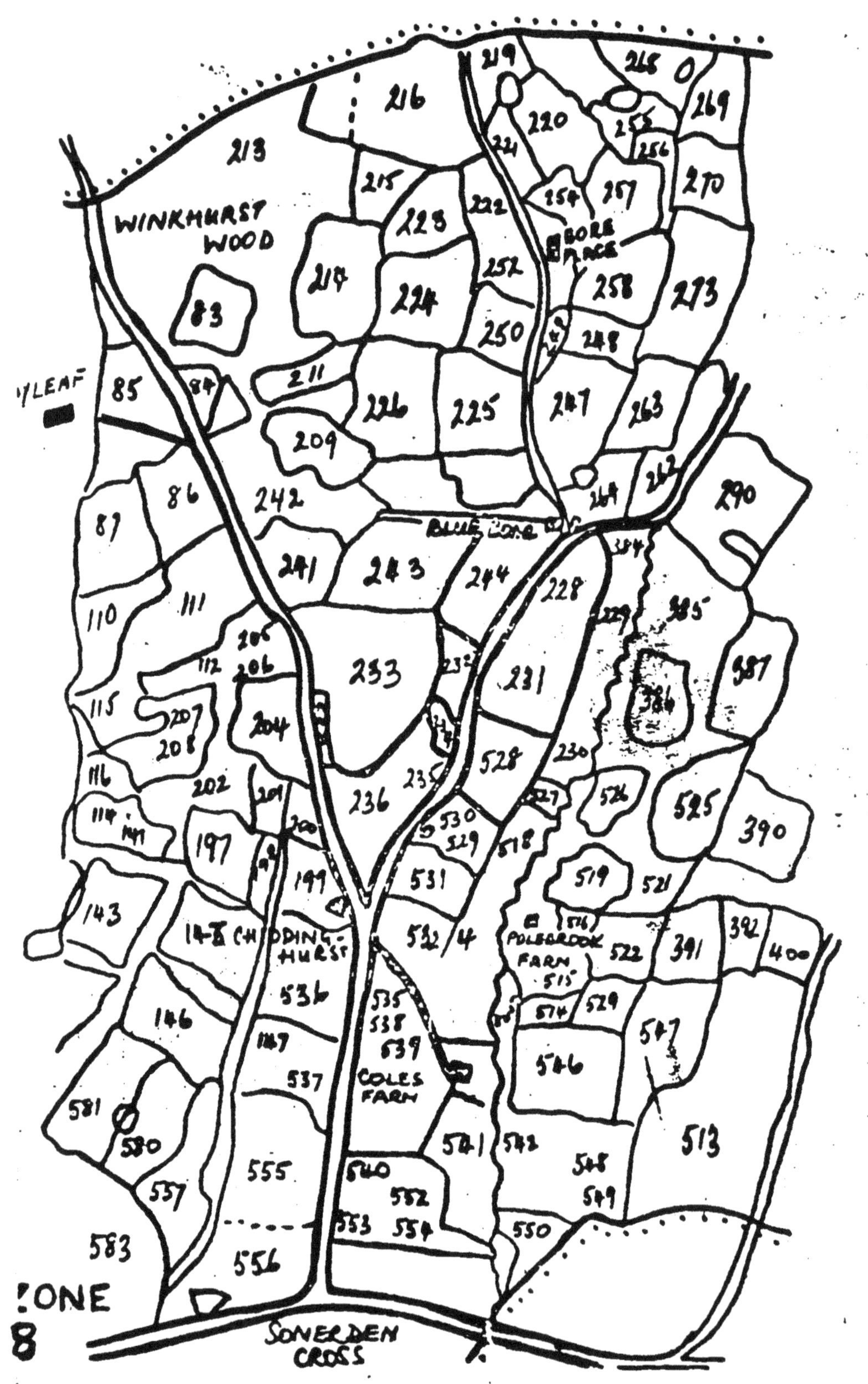

FIELD NAMES - ZONE 8 FROM 1841 TITHE MAP

83 Brick Field
84 Kiln Pasture
85 Nine Acre Field
86 Little Pit Field
87 Upper Houletts Field
110 Clems Acre
111 Eleven Acre Field
112 Shaw
114 Upper Wood Field
115 Middle Wood Field
116 Shaw
141 Five Acre Wood Field
143 Square Field
145 Eight Acre Bakehurst
146 Seven Acre Bakehurst
147 Five Acre Bakehurst
197 Upper Kiln Field
198 Middle Kiln Field
199 Lower Kiln Field
200 Shaw
201 Wood Field
202 Wood
204 Kiln Mead
205 Russett
206 Kiln House Farm
207 Fore Plat
208 Brick Plat
209 Five Acre Batfold
211 Hopyard Field
213 Winkhurst Wood
214 Wood Field
215 Claves Plot
216 Great London Field
217 Sevenoaks Field
219 Little Marlpit Field
220 Great Marlpit Field
221 Cold Heath Mead
222 Orchard
223 Oast House Field
224 Orchard Field
225 Seven Acre Batfold
226 Great Batfold
227 Little Batfold Field
232 Sevenoaks Field
233 Two Acres
234 Pond
235 Beech Land Field
236 Dentons Grave Field
228 Near Riddens Field
229 Near Riddens Mead
230 Far Riddens Mead
231 Far Riddens Field
237 Lower Three Acres
241 Kiln Field
242 Kiln Wood
243 Eleven Acres
244 Eight Acres
245 Shaw
246 Batfold Field
247 Eight Acres
248 Little Warren Field
249 Walk Mead
250 Beggar House Mead
252 Old Orchard
253 Homestead (Bore Place)
254 Kitchen Mead
255 Mount Field
256 Shaw
257 Great Warren Field
258 Middle Warren Field
262 Lower Donalds Field
263 Six Acres
264 Forge Pasture
266 House (Blue Boar)
268 Daisey Field
269 Nine Acre Field
270 Ladderstaves Field
273 Ten Acre Field
290 Great Cut Field
384 House & Garden
385 Bushey Field
387 Upper Six Acres
390 Near Six Acres
391 Birch Hurst Field
392 Two Acres
400 Mead
513 Beeches Wood
514 Little Field
515 Barn Field
516 Upper Mead
519 Dean Field
518 Brook Mead
521 Shoulder of Mutton Field
522 Church Field
525 childrens Field
526 Daisey Field
527 Lime Kiln Plat
528 Ridings Field
529 Higgens Mead
530 Cottage (Hickens)
531 Hither Rough Field
534 Rye Grain Field
535 Dung Croft
539 Church Field
540 Lower Crutch
541 Great Mead
542 Two Acre Mead
545 Long Mead
546 New Land
547 Seven Acre Field
548 Smithershaw Field
549 Strawberry Field
550 Lodge Field
552 Medhurst Field
553 Corner Crutch Field
554 Upper Crutch Field
555 Twelve Acre Field
556 Marlpit Field
536 Highlands
537 Beggars Oak Shaw

ZONE 9 MAP

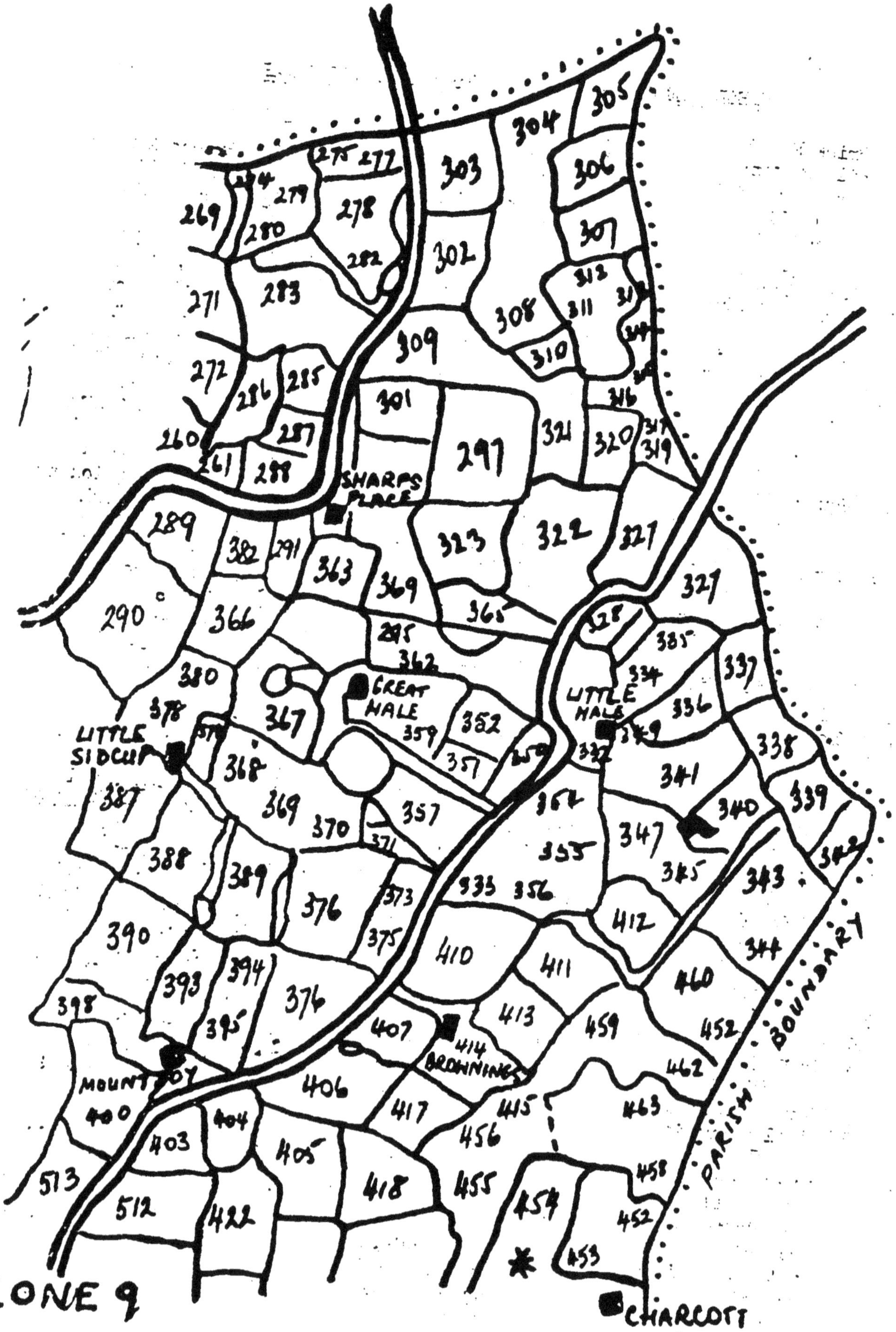

SHARPS PLACE
GREAT HALE
LITTLE HALE
LITTLE SIDCUP
MOUNTJOY
BROWNINGS
PARISH BOUNDARY
CHARCOTT
ZONE 9

FIELD NAMES - ZONE 9 FROM 1841 TITHE MAP

260 Shaw
261 Little Donalds Field
269 Nine Acre Field
271 Upper Donalds Field
272 Lower Donalds Field
274 Grove Wood
275 House Mead
277 Hop Garden
278 Kiln Field
279 Further Little Field
280 Hither Little Field
282 Shaw
283 Great Peghole
285 Little Pegshole
286 Bridge Mead
287 Hop Garden Mead
288 Old Hop Garden
289 Little Cut Field
290 Great Cut Field
291 High Field
293 Forestall
295 Hale Road
299 Barn Field
297 Haystack Field
300 Orchard
301 Coney Burrow Field
302 Five acre Field
303 Eight acre Field (pt)
304 Eight acre wood
305 Coles Field (pt)
306 Apple Tree Field (pt)
307 Pear Tree Field (pt)
308 Spurs Field
310 Little Spurs Field
311 Beechy Field
312 Shaw
313 Furze Field
314 Old Orchard
315 Young Orchard
316 Forestall
319 House Mead
320 Little Cowlees
321 Great Cowlees
322 Great King's Field
323 Banky Field

327 Hale Field
328 Second newlands
332 Hale Farm
333 Nagshope Field
334 Sawpit Field
335 Snails Croft Field
336 Old Mead
337 White Field
338 Broad Field
339 Thisley Field
340 Seriousberry Field
341 Banky Field
342 Chiddingstone Croft
343 Upper South Field
344 Lower South Field
345 Upper Females Field

347 Lower Females Field
349 Little Hale Farm
350 Grove Mead
351 Grove Orchard
352 Shawfield
353 Goldfinches Field
354 Near Brook Field
355 Further Brook Field
356 Little Brook Field
357 Upper Lane Field
359 Pasture Mead
362 Acre Plat
363 Sharps Field
365 Mares Field
366 Cut Field
367 Railey Field
368 Marlpit Field
369 Lower Marlpit Field
370 Little Pond Field
371 Little Wood Field
373 House Mead
375 Shaw
376 Little Pond Field

378 Barn Field
379 House Mead
380 Plough Field
382 Gate Field
387 Upper Six Acres
388 Gate Field
389 Five Acre Field
390 Near Six Acres
393 Four Acre Field
394 Upper Spring Field
395 Lower Spring Field
398 Barn Plat
400 Mead
403 Two Field
404 Carrotty Field
405 Kiln Field
406 Great Church Field
407 Little Church Field
409 Brownings Farm
410 Barn Field
411 North Field
412 Shaw
413 House Mead
414 House Field
415 Shaw
417 Barn Pasture
418 Upper Yew Tree Field
422 Upper Bridge Field
452 Orchard
453 House Mead
454 Banky Field
455 Bushy Field
456 Wood
458 Six Acre Field
459 Furze Field
460 Great North Field
461 Little North Field
462 Half Field
463 Great Daisey Field
512 Upper Breeches Field
513 Breeches Wood

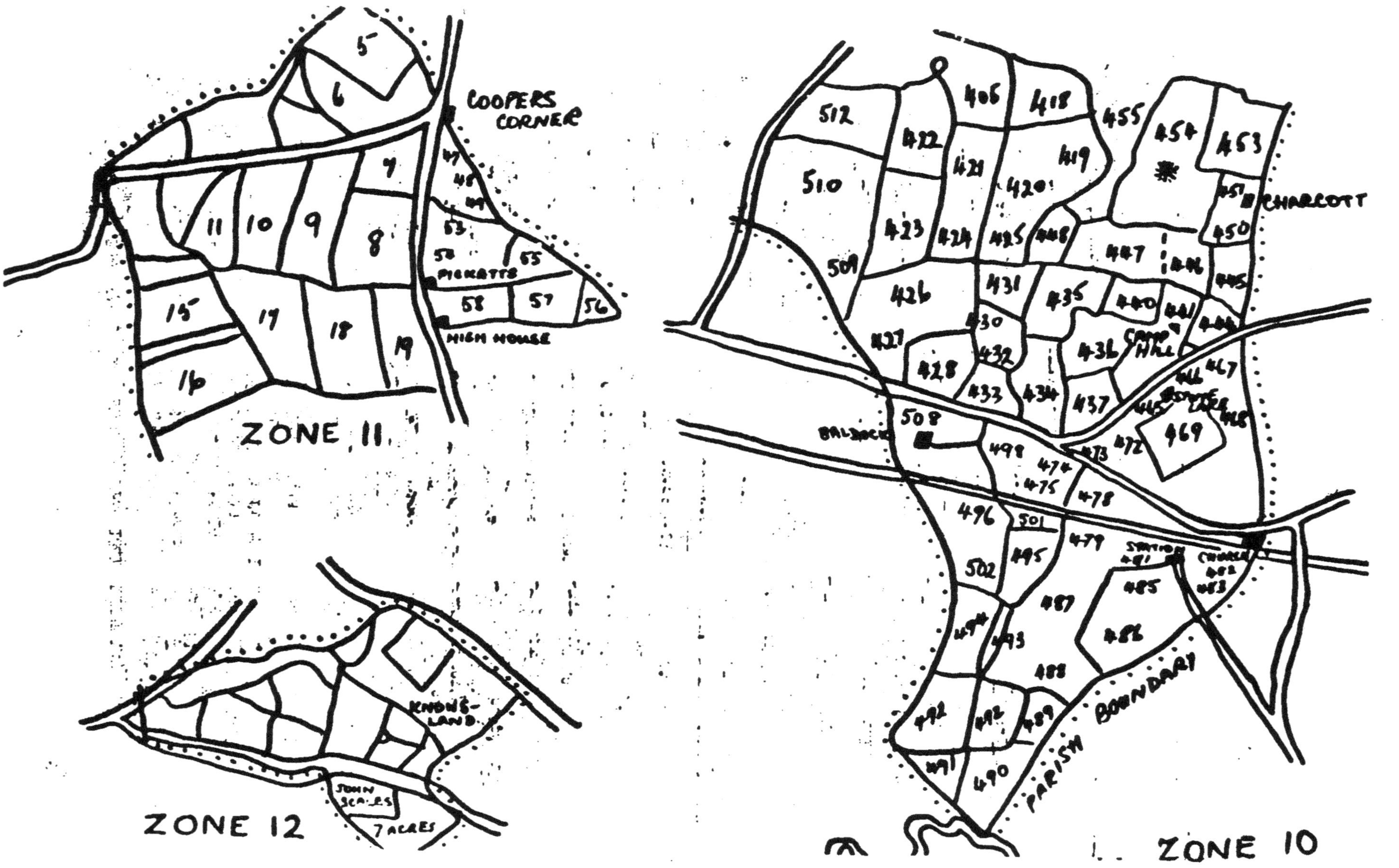
COOPERS CORNER
PICKETTS
HIGH HOUSE
ZONE 11
ZONE 12
JOHN SCALES
7 ACRES
CHARCOTT
CAMP HILL
BALDOCK
STATION
PARISH BOUNDARY
ZONE 10

FIELD NAMES ZONE 10 From 1841 TITHE MAP

No.	Name	No.	Name	No.	Name
405	Kiln Field	444	Road Enclosures	485	Upper Four acres
418	Upper Yewtree Field	445	Pot Reeds Field	486	Six acre Field
419	Lower Yewtree Field	446	Calves Croft Field	487	Lower four acres
420	Middle Field	447	Bramley Field	488	Little Broad Field
421	Hither Bridge Field	448	Row Mead	489	Pasture Field
422	Upper Bridge Field	450	Barn Field (pt)	490	Great Moorden Mead
423	Lower Bridge Field	451	Farms	491	Gunnels Mead
424	Five acre Field	453	House Mead	492	Lake Field
425	Lodge Field	454	Banky Field	493	Clapper Mead Shaw
426	Lower Breeches Field (pt)	455	Bushy Field	494	Clapper Mead
427	Upper Breeches Field (pt)	465	Homestead(Stonelake)	495	Slade Field
		466	Barnfield	496	Three acre field
428	Hither Breeches Field (pt)	467	Camp Hill Field	497	Near Causeway Field
		468	Hartfield	498	House
430	Shaw	469	Kitchen Croft	500	Further Causeway Field
431	Woody Field	470	Bramley Field	501	Little Field
432	Spring Pit Mead	471	Woody Field	502	Lower Mead
433	Avis Field	472	CrosswayField	508	Church Field
434	Lower Causeway Field	473	Cottage		
		474	Two Cottages		
435	Five Acre Field	475	House and Shop		
436	Orchard Field	476	Cottage		
437	Upper Causeway Field	477	Cottage		
		478	Cottage		
440	Barn Pasture	479	Four Acres		
441	Home Pasture	481	Shaw		
442	Camphill & Brownings	482	Three corner Plat		
		483	Limekiln Field		

FIELD NAMES - ZONES 11 & 12 From 1841 TITHE MAP

No.	Name	No.	Name
1.	Pond Wood	16	Spilletts Wood Field
2.	Pond Wood Field	17	Marls Mead
3.	Upper Pond Mead	18	Marls Croft
4.	Lower Pond Mead	19	Hornfield
5.	Coopers Corner Field	47	Hollow Field
6.	Russett	48	Great Mead
7.	Coopers Corner Field	49	Barnfield
8.	Coopers Corner Wood	50	Orchard
9.	Coopers Corner Mead	51/2	Cottages
10.	Seven acre field	53	Barnfield
11.	Five acre field	54	House (Picketts)
12.	Chiddingstone Shaw	55	Three corner Field
13.	Chiddingstone Field	56	Great Mead Pit Field
14.	Little Dames Field	57	Four acre Field
15.	Railey Field	58	House field (High House)

LOOKING BACK

When the 1987 October hurricane left scenes of devastation and destruction over the South Eastern countries, Chiddingstone did not escape.

Time, with summer's growth, has veiled much of the damage, but there are many scars and mutilations among the hundreds of surviving trees; but still, the village retains its picturesque setting.

Looking back over the thirty years since I came here, I sense change, rather than see it. To the eye, the cobbled street, the National Trust row of old houses, the ancient Church (which suffered storm damage, too,) the adjacent Village Hall and the little school; none of these have changed. There has been added but one house, the New Rectory, which lies just behind the road, at an angle, next to the school.

Inside the Village Stores and the Castle Inn, I see and feel a difference.

Until the mid-seventies, the shop retained its "Olde Worlde" appearance, as laid down by the National Trust. Refrigerators and freezers had to be unseen in the stock room, behind the shop. Now, the ice cream self-service freezer and the "cold counter" are conspicuous in the shop, while the Post Office has been moved from just inside the door, to a small back room with its service window only on view. For a few years, this small room housed the public library, before the mobile library served the Village.

The oldest counter and all the shelving are used still, though with different stocks. Gone are the wools, the haberdashery. Gone, too, the "loose" brown sugars and the dried fruits, which had to be weighed out of bins. Cheeses were delivered in 40 and 60 lb blocks, which had to be "skinned", and bacon sides arrived regularly, to be cut up and boned on the premises, and rashered to each customer's requirements. Now, we have reached the age of "Prepacks".

There were few car owners in and around the village, or the surrounding countryside and customers' orders were delivered from house to house, cottage to cottage and farm to farm, over a radius of approximately 4 miles. Gradually, the village acquired a new and more mobile population and with the coming of the supermarkets in easily accessible towns, deliveries dwindled and finally faded out. At the same time, with more and longer holidays and an ever increasing number of cars, the tourist trade greatly increased. Chiddingstone Village had always attracted visitors from all over the world and gradually, it became evident that they should be catered for, while local trade was falling. In 1981, a tea room was fashioned from the old stable at the end of the shop's yard, which passes under the old Tithe Room of long ago. The Tea Room won the "Egon Ronay Award" for two years in succession and was soon too small, so that in 1987, the whole of the old stable was converted into a modern, licensed restaurant.

The Castle Inn, too, has changed in character. Once just a country "pub", it began to cater for British customers with growing continental tastes, as well as for the many visitors from abroad. Now the Inn has an up-to-date "Reynard Restaurant" and also serves hot and cold meals from the bars, and in the well kept garden, there is a popular barbeque.

Traditional British foods, as well as exotic continental dishes are served to visitors from all over the globe.

The butcher's shop, which had been in the village for generations, closed at the end of 1966 and in February 1967, the shop premises became what is now a well known antique business. The slaughter house was turned into garages for the National Trust tenants in the old houses.

Change has spread mostly to the environment. There are fewer farms, and with added mechanisation too, far fewer farm workers and "tied cottages" are on their way out of date. Most of the old farm cottages have been transformed and now belong to town commuters, business, or retired people.

The changes in life style have brought about an influx of cars, which, parked on both sides of our unpaved High Street, hide the beauty of the old buildings. If you can catch a glimpse of the Village early on a quiet morning, you may again feel the old fascination that age has given to it, with its long and interesting history; and there are families living here to-day, whose names are there, in those old pages.

The "Chidding Stone" must ever be in its place behind the village, unchanged for many a generation to visit and debate its history.

E.D.H.

www.ingramcontent.com/pod-product-compliance
Ingram Content Group UK Ltd.
Pitfield, Milton Keynes, MK11 3LW, UK
UKHW050615260726
13967UKWH00008B/2871

9 780955 465789